The SIX
GREAT
THEMES
OF WESTERN
METAPHYSICS
and the
END OF THE
MIDDLE AGES

The SIX
GREAT
THEMES
OF WESTERN
METAPHYSICS
and the
END OF THE
MIDDLE AGES

HEINZ HEIMSOETH

Translated with a Critical Introduction by
Ramon J. Betanzos

Wayne State University Press

Detroit

Heinz Heimsoeth, Die sechs großen Themen der abendländischen
Metaphysik und der Ausgang des Mittelalters. 8. Aufl.
Unveränderter reprogr. Nachdruck d. 3. Auflage
Copyright © 1987 by Wissenschaftliche Buchgesellschaft,
Darmstadt, Germany.

English translation copyright © 1994 by Wayne State University Press,
Detroit, Michigan 48202.

Library of Congress Cataloging-in-Publication Data

Heimsoeth, Heinz, 1886–1975.
    [Die sechs grossen Themen der abendländischen Metaphysik und der
Ausgang des Mittelalters. English]
    The six great themes of western metaphysics and the end of the Middle
Ages. / translated and introduced by Ramon J. Betanzos
        p.   cm.
    ISBN 0-8143-2477-0 (alk. paper).—ISBN 0-8143-2478-9 (pbk. :
alk. paper)
    1. Metaphysics—History. 2. Philosophy, Medieval. I. Title.
B738.M47H4513   1994
    190—dc20   93-33894

Designer
Mary Krzewinski

Special Acknowledgment

Grateful acknowledgment is made to Wayne State University's Office of
Research and Graduate Programs, College of Liberal Arts, and Department
of Humanities for financial assistance in the publication of this
volume.

Contents

II. Infinity in the Finite 82

III. Soul and External World 110

IV. Reality and Life 152

Contents

V. The Individual   193

VI. Understanding and Will   224

Translator's Introduction

Standard biographical reference works list Professor Heinz Heimsoeth (1886–1975) as a German philosopher or, more frequently, as a historian of philosophy. It was in fact in the latter capacity that he philosophized and acquired his reputation. He was born in Cologne and held professorships in philosophy at Marburg (from 1921), Königsberg (from 1923), and Cologne (from 1931 until his death). Most of his eminent scholarly career focused on modern European philosophers, notably such figures as René Descartes and Gottfried Wilhelm Leibniz, but it concentrated especially on Immanuel Kant, Johann Gottlieb Fichte, German Idealists in general, and Friedrich Wilhelm Nietzsche.[1] In 1976 W. H. Walsh called Heinz Heimsoeth "the most distinguished German commentator on Kant of the last half century,"[2] and the editors of *Kant-Studien* have not only published many of his essays but also devoted an entire edition to the observance of the ninetieth year of his birth.[3] He wrote the biographical article on Fichte, first of the great transcendental Idealists, for *Die Großen Deutschen*[4] and was the continuator and reviser of Wilhelm Windelband's landmark *Lehrbuch der Geschichte der Philosophie*.[5]

I.

By and large, the method of historians of philosophy has been to review and analyze prominent philosophers' and their systems seriatim in more or less neutral fashion, or to engage in meticulous *explication de texte*, or sometimes even to examine philosophers and their systems as stepping-stones

9

toward some philosopher or system of their choice. Heimsoeth, however, does not view the history of philosophy primarily as a collection of biographies or of systems or of ultimate solutions; he sees it mainly as a history of problems. The wag who said, "philosophy is the disease of which it is supposed to be the cure" in fact has a point: Philosophy is, indeed, a dis-ease or un-ease in the face of one or more of the mysteries of existence, and it never really ultimately "solves" these mysteries. Philosophy is an attempt to grapple with "what's bugging someone" in the realm of philosophical inquiry. Thus at the very outset of *The Six Great Themes of Western Metaphysics and the End of the Middle Ages* Heimsoeth mentions "the proper subject matter" of the history of philosophy as "the philosophical problems themselves."[6] Heimsoeth's method in writing history of philosophy is explicitly committed to focusing on fundamental, hence perennial, philosophical *problems* (aporias, conceptual impasses, perplexities, questions, themes). As early as 1912, in a discussion of Heimsoeth's doctoral dissertation, Nicolai Hartmann wrote: "Heimsoeth proceeds from problem to problem, not from solution to solution. His historical work consists entirely in investigating, properly juxtaposing, weighing, clarifying, searching out and confronting difficulties."[7]

Of course Plato's *Dialogues*, especially those dealing with Socrates' views, are full of references to such problems, for example, when Socrates defended himself against Meno's charges of deliberate obfuscation concerning the nature of virtue: "I perplex others, not because I am clear, but because I am utterly perplexed myself" (*Meno*, 80). Similarly, near the start of Book 3 [995a, ll. 29–31] of his *Metaphysics* Aristotle notes the importance of addressing and solving difficulties in thought first, "for it is not possible to untie a knot of which one does not know. But difficulty in our thinking implies a 'knot' in the object." And of course the millennia-old philosophical tradition of skepticism is grounded precisely on this issue. Needless to say, grappling with philosophical problems as such is not an invention of Heimsoeth.

Nor is Heimsoeth the first historian of philosophy to focus on what Germans call *Problemgeschichte* as a formal subdivision of the field of history of philosophy. Its origins go back to the late eighteenth century, and there are a number of efforts throughout the nineteenth century and into the twentieth to realize its program.[8] In his history of philosophy, for example, Kuno Fischer wanted "one to see clearly from what problems [philosophical systems] issued forth, how [those systems] solved them, and what unsolved and still to be solved questions they have left behind for the world."[9] In the foreword to his *Geschichte der Philosophie* (1892)—a study that became a kind of standard work of the problem-centered historical genre and that later

10

bore the subtitle History of Problems and of Concepts Generated to Solve Them—Wilhelm Windelband stated, "I am emphasizing . . . the development of what is the most important thing from the philosophical point of view: the history of problems and of concepts."[10] It was only natural that Heimsoeth should be the one to continue and update Windelband's work after his death.

It was not merely these partly long-standing positions regarding aporias and partly modern developments in *Problemgeschichte* that influenced Heimsoeth to write his histories of philosophy with a focus on problems, however. He was also strongly influenced in this direction by his friend, the philosopher Nicolai Hartmann (1882–1950), who explicitly adopted aporetics as his philosophical method.[11] It is of course notorious that one of the most fundamental of all philosophical questions is the question of what philosophy itself is and exactly what its proper object is. One cannot neglect the history of philosophical speculation and simply put forth a would-be "definitive" philosophy as if there were and are no serious competitors in the field. As Hartmann once put it:

No one begins with his own thought. Everyone encounters an already present condition of knowledge and of questioning in his own time, into which he grows and out of which he begins his own search. He takes over the great problematic contents of the historical stage at which they have arrived. For problem-contents move forward through the centuries without changing substantially: these are the metaphysical problems concerning which Kant said that they are the destiny of reason, because reason can neither dismiss them nor solve them.[12]

It is essential to inspect carefully what philosophers have done or tried to do throughout the ages, especially the problems with which they have grappled, to find out what kind of "philosophical game" they have played and by what rules. Philosophy is and has been a struggle, not simply about a single issue but about a number of persistent and perhaps insoluble problems. The serious historian of philosophy—one who is something more than a mere chronicler—becomes a philosopher himself. In Hartmann's words, "Philosophy itself, however, does not consist in philosophizing personalities, but rather exclusively of philosophical assertions [*Philosophemen*] or problems. Hence its history must be nothing other than the history of problems."[13] In later writings Hartmann specified that it was especially *metaphysical* quan-

11

daries or even skepticism that were the basis of his concept of problem and of the history of problems:

> The contents of problems are present throughout the centuries without substantial change. . . . The boundary questions of all areas of knowledge are in this sense "metaphysical," that is, burdened with an irrational (unsolvable) residue that accordingly undergoes innumerable attempts to solve it, to be sure, but that remains fundamentally unsolved. . . . Systems or isms are made-up world pictures, thought constructs that then collapse under the slightest criticism. They dissolve one another without any one of them being able to survive. If the history of philosophy consisted only of them, it would be hardly anything more than the history of human errors. But it is something more besides: the history of problems and their solutions [*sic*!]. . . .[14]

Heimsoeth was thus one with Hartmann not only in adopting a method centered on philosophical problems but also in identifying these problems as typically metaphysical. He was also one of the principal Kant interpreters to identify specifically metaphysical concerns in the latter's philosophy and to argue that Kant smuggles considerable metaphysical content even into his *Critique of Pure Reason* as well as, more obviously, into his practical philosophy.[15]

II.

How does Heinz Heimsoeth's *The Six Great Themes* fit into this discussion? Why is it that this most wide-ranging of Heimsoeth's numerous publications is still available (in an eighth edition) nearly three-quarters of a century after its original publication and has been translated into Spanish, Dutch, and now into English as well?[16] In a 1976 article on Heimsoeth's work from 1911 through 1924 H. J. de Vleeschauer recalled the impact *The Six Great Themes* made on him when he first encountered it as a young student:

> This book made a profound impression on me, an instinctive impression of having discovered a "great" [*"grand"*] book, and this impression has stayed with me. It is great because it is brilliantly written and because it moves forward with enormous power of expression; great also because of the originality of its presentation. If one could believe with regard to his book on [Descartes's] method

12

that one found oneself in the presence of a kind of profession of faith, with how much more reason can we say the same thing with regard to the historical inquiry that we are going to review now.[17]

Despite many personal reservations about *The Six Great Themes* (even serious ones, to be discussed later), I experienced a reaction similar to de Vleeschauer's when I first read it. Here was something dramatically different from customary surveys of philosophers and systems of the past: here one genuinely and intensely encountered what is meant by *Problemgeschichte*, a longitudinal history of some of the most basic metaphysical issues—a sort of "Great Inquiries" exercise—in philosophy and life: God and the world (the one and the many), infinity in the finite, soul and external world, being and life, the individual, and understanding and will. With the focus on the "biographies" of these great, perennially living pivotal themes in philosophy, one feels the excitement of an elemental and fundamental confrontation with the heart of philosophy—the great issues themselves, clothed in their ever-changing historical garb, to be sure, yet preserving their basic identity. Whoever does not become excited about the odysseys of *these* ideas is not likely to become excited by philosophy at all.

In the introduction to *The Six Great Themes* Heimsoeth advanced a bold thesis about historical periodization, namely that the roots of modern philosophical thought lie not in the Renaissance, as commonly believed, but rather in the period of late Scholasticism—what is commonly called the "decline" of Scholasticism. Instead of adopting the usual tripartite schema of ancient, medieval, and modern philosophy, Heimsoeth adopted a two-part schema consisting of ancient and modern metaphysics: ancient metaphysics dominates philosophy right through the period of the High Middle Ages and Scholasticism. The roots of modern thought lie specifically in Christianity, especially the nominalism and German mysticism of the late Middle Ages. Heimsoeth's main thesis is that "the metaphysics of the Modern Period in its bold outlines grew out of the same soil and was nourished by the same sources of life as that of the Middle Ages and that modern metaphysics is more inwardly intertwined with medieval metaphysics and its basic direction and themes than it is with Antiquity" (p. 33). The great key to Christian thought, as Heimsoeth sees it, lies in the discovery of the soul, of genuine inwardness and spirituality, which stood in dramatic contrast with the ancient concept of soul as simply a kind of "engine" or source of motion for a living body. The six chapters that make up the body of his book set out to demonstrate Heimsoeth's double thesis that modern Western metaphysics is based essentially on the link between the Christian late Middle Ages and modern German philosophy and that both of them stand in opposition to Greek Antiquity.

Chapter 1[18] demonstrates how basic ancient Hellenic dualisms—especially that of matter versus form (content vs. idea)—give way in the Middle Ages to a God who created all things *ex nihilo* and found them all "good." The medieval antithesis between matter (or flesh) and spirit was really just a hangover from antiquity. But in the late Middle Ages the mystic Meister Eckehart [c. 1260–1327/28] stressed the goodness of all things created by God (and nothing else exists); natural scientists like Roger Bacon [1220–92] and Jean Buridan [1300–58] gave a positive evaluation of material nature; Nicholas of Cusa [1401–64] made an original synthesis between mysticism and mathematics—these in turn led to Renaissance enthusiasm for this world, to Leibniz's theodicy, and so on.

Chapter 2 shows how Hellenic preference for form and limit, the finite and the specific, gave way first to the strong Christian emphasis on the infinity of God, then to Nicholas of Cusa's and Giordano Bruno's enthusiasm over the concept of an infinite universe or macrocosm, and later to Leibniz's concept of an infinite microcosm.

Chapter 3 shows that, whereas ancient Greece viewed the human psyche merely as a part of the objective physical world, Christianity (especially since Augustine, "the first modern man") made the knowing, willing (this especially), subjective, personal, spontaneous soul the basis of philosophy. Hugh of St. Victor (ca. 1096–1141) and William of Occam (ca. 1285–1349) are links in the chain of this idea which leads first to Descartes's *cogito* and later to Leibniz's monads and Fichte's metaphysics of the ego.

Chapter 4 shows that, in contrast to the static view of nature entertained by Hellenism, the Christian-Germanic spirit stressed nature's dynamism, the soul's spontaneity, the historical process, and even an evolving God (Meister Eckehart).

Chapter 5 shows that Christianity puts a primary focus on the idea of the individual, whereas Greek tradition had always stressed the primacy of genus, type, and concept. The idea of the individual grows in force and definition at the hands of John Duns Scotus (*haecceitas*), Leibniz, the Earl of Shaftesbury, Johann Gottfried von Herder, and others, culminating in the great weight put on the value of the ethical person in Friedrich Schleiermacher and Fichte.

Chapter 6 shows how Antiquity's primary emphasis on intellect over will (contemplation over creative action) was reversed by Christianity, beginning especially with Augustine, carried forward in the late Middle Ages and beyond by Scotus, Occam, and Descartes, and culminating in Kant's and Fichte's emphasis on total human autonomy.

14

Not surprisingly in a book that puts forth such a bold thesis and that ranges so far and wide into difficult metaphysical issues, there is no lack of potential criticisms—including many serious ones—to make about Heimsoeth's *The Six Great Themes*.

One might complain that Heimsoeth is not the initiator of aporetics-based history of philosophy and that such famous scholar-philosophers as Wilhelm Windelband and Nicolai Hartmann had already done fundamental work in this area. Why, then, should one bother with Heimsoeth? One might regard Heimsoeth's book as an anomaly, in that it has none of the typical scholarly apparatus one expects in such a work. Although containing numerous quotations, it offers no specific references; it has no notes and no bibliography; its "index" is but a bare-bones listing of names mentioned in the book. Many a reader might find *The Six Great Themes* "too Germanic" in emphasis and "too Protestant" in tendency.[19] It seems quite a monstrous exaggeration to suggest, as Heimsoeth does, that the entire Middle Ages (in the traditional sense) have virtually no philosophical content that differs radically from ancient thought until the fourteenth and fifteenth centuries.[20] Heimsoeth himself admits that the treatment of his material in his book is quite one-sided in order to present a clearer broad picture (pp. 37). Some may wish to downplay Heimsoeth's importance on the grounds that he is not *really* a philosopher, nor has he erected any significant philosophical system; he is merely a "historian of philosophy."[21]

Reviewers of *The Six Great Themes* have accordingly expressed some major reservations about Heimsoeth's book, for example, about Heimsoeth's line of demarcation between ancient and modern philosophy. Dietrich Mahnke points out, "Is not Greek philosophy, like German, a microcosm that concentrates an entire philosophical development within itself?" Heimsoeth himself shows that Greek philosophy provides evidence of an opposite pole with regard to all six themes except the last.[22]

Siegfried Behn protests, "Heimsoeth's violent separation between ancient and modern thought pushes one into one-sidedness, indeed lack of clarity."[23] Behn goes on to enter a whole series of objections to Heimsoeth's thesis, such as the following:

—Heimsoeth's thesis would logically force one to consider the high tide of Scholasticism to have died with Antiquity.

15

—It would rob Christianity of much of its breadth and depth if one insisted on removing from it all vestiges of Greek thought and formulation, even if one identifies Greek thought closely with the thought of Athens in the fifth century B.C. (which Germans tend to do) and neglects the entire Hellenistic period.

—Augustinian thought is, in cultural terms, not only Christian but also ancient in character.

—Heimsoeth's own favorite modern thinkers—Leibniz and Georg Wilhelm Friedrich Hegel—were themselves in search of a restoration of ancient objectivity in thought.

—It is certainly going too far if one claims to derive modern subjectivistic priority in thought, which puts major emphasis on *how we know* and far less emphasis on *what we know*, from Christian metaphysics of being without further ado. [One of the most burning questions of Christian metaphysics, after all, has to do precisely with the origin and reality of the soul.] "This means ascribing too little Christianity to the Middle Ages and altogether too much to the moderns (p. 548)."

—There are very serious problems in trying to derive modern German philosophical development from late Scholasticism, unless one is identifying the latter with Cusa alone, for apart from him late Scholasticism is nominalistic. But neither Eckehart nor Leibniz nor Kant nor Hegel is a nominalist. Indeed one must look to such figures as David Hume for examples of modern nominalism.

—The intellectualism of classical Scholasticism, which Heimsoeth judges to be ancient and of little value, does not in fact prejudice the powers of will that he so values. For the great Scholastics regarded will as much more than mere instinct or conation: will calls for wise choice and ordering among competing motives; it calls for insight and conscientiousness; and it is sensitive to the vital task of reason in sorting out motives.

Heimsoeth clearly seems to view the development of modern philosophy in the manner he describes as overwhelmingly, if not exclusively, positive in character. But this would seem to be a very moot point to say the least, especially in the light of his apparent view that modern Christianity is essentially vested in people like Kant and Fichte, who believe in virtually Godlike autonomy for human beings, or in pantheists like Friedrich Wilhelm Joseph Schelling and Hegel, or even in some respects in the anti-Christian Nietzsche. Heimsoeth begins early in his book by noting the central importance of the Christian doctrine of creation—God creating all else *ex nihilo*—and ends with philosophers who have human beings create God. Historically,

16

people have summarized reality under some combination of three headings: God, man, nature. The ancient world, for all its emphasis on man, made nature its absolute; the medieval world made God its absolute; the modern world—at least the world of German Idealism—for all its emphasis on nature, has made man its absolute. In this new alignment, to the extent that it is true, God is dead. Hence it seems quite appropriate that Heimsoeth ends his discussions of the six great themes with Nietzsche.

Despite Siegfried Behn's serious criticisms of *The Six Great Themes,* he has much to say that is positive as well: "Heimsoeth's historical knowledge is rich, his eye for developments in specific problem areas is serendipitous [*glücklich*], his presentation often eloquent"; and "It does honor to Heimsoeth" that he pleads so strongly on behalf of German philosophy precisely in areas in which it is often misread. Behn finds it "painful that one must quarrel with this noble book on many counts despite how much one admires it."[24]

Josef Bernhardt notes and agrees with Heimsoeth's own confession of one-sidedness and its consequent tendency to mislead to some degree. But he then adds:

[*The Six Great Themes*] has long since acquired renown. It makes little difference whether it is correct in every particular; its great importance consists in the fact that it broadly and powerfully proclaims the fact of how wrong it is to say that the Middle Ages have been nothing but the great gap in the history of thought that ignorance and error (indeed, worse than that as well) have established as a convention of long standing.[25]

K. J. Grau observes that there has hitherto been no history of German philosophy except Eduard Zeller's in the nineteenth century, "but if there is anyone who seems called to the task of providing us with the missing history of German philosophy, then it seems that Heinz Heimsoeth of Marburg is the man. He has provided the proof for this with the book we have before us: *The Six Great Themes of Western Metaphysics.*"[26] Although Grau describes Heimsoeth's historical analyses as "superbly penetrating with respect to the inner continuity of development of problems," he is also at pains to point out that *The Six Great Themes* is not intended to provide an exhaustive treatment of these themes in any sense and he reminds the reader that Heimsoeth himself admits his "onesidedness of description for the sake of clarity of presentation of the themes to be pursued." Grau says that Heimsoeth is not so much offering us a completed work as stimulating hints for further work, that his work is a very promising and significant *program* that he hopes Heimsoeth will himself pursue.[27]

Artur Schneider believes Heimsoeth's book to be of interest not only to the historian of philosophy but also to the cultural historian, for "we are dealing here with a book that has very broad perspectives. The development of the most important and ultimate metaphysical problems with which Western thought has struggled since the beginning and corresponding attempts to solve them pass before our mind's eye." He notes that a series of monographs has shown far-reaching dependencies in the thought of Descartes, Baruch Spinoza, and many other modern thinkers on medieval influences, but that no one has undertaken such a project in such wide-ranging parameters as Heimsoeth has. Hence "this work deserves to a high degree the recognition of anyone interested in cultural history."[28]

In the last analysis, one must keep even the serious flaws that one might find in Heimsoeth's *The Six Great Themes* within the perspective of the grandeur of conception and the plethora of penetrating insights that he brought to this work. This is not a book free of errors, but, far more significantly, it is a book charged with most useful engagement for the philosophical mind. Here we find an ongoing dialectic of question and answer—though on a vast geographical and chronological scale—of the sort that Socrates and Plato might have found congenial; here we find that spirit of perpetual inquiry that makes each "answer" the springboard for another question; here is the spirit that makes the questionable the unique focus of inquisitive reason and views perpetual seeking as a kind of "piety of human intelligence."

Aristotle remarked that all philosophizing begins in wonder; Heimsoeth shows that wondering has never ceased in philosophy. His account is not a purely conceptual one; on the contrary, he enters boldly into the historical drama of Western philosophical thought at its deepest level and tells a story focused not so much on actors as on the plot itself: the great metaphysical questions about God and the world, the finite and the infinite, being and life, nature and spirit, understanding and will, the universal and the individual. These are questions that philosophy itself cannot seem to answer through its own resources, but only by embarking on some sort of leap of faith: man is the question, but he is not the answer. At the same time, within the very context of his underlying beliefs, man does not surrender rational inquiry. He continues to pose radical questions and to test attempted answers to them: that is, he continues to philosophize. The story Heimsoeth tells in *The Six Great Themes* is a wonderful and wondering one about Western man's journey along this selfsame path, ever old yet ever new. It is a story about man the perpetual brooder about the mysteries of life and existence.

Translator's Introduction

Notes

1. Heinz Heimsoeth's main writings include: *Die Methode der Erkenntnis bei Descartes und Leibniz,* 2 vols. (Gießen: Töpelmann Publishers, 1912–14); *Die sechs großen Themen der abendländischen Metaphysik und der Ausgang des Mittelalters* (Berlin: Stilke Publishers, 1922 etc., [8]1987); *Fichte,* (Munich: Reinhardt Publishers, 1923); *Metaphysik der Neuzeit* (Munich and Berlin: Oldenbourg, 1929, repr. 1967); *Studien zur Philosophie Immanuel Kants,* vol. 1, *Metaphysische Ursprünge und ontologische Grundlagen,* (Cologne: Cologne University Press, 1956, [2]1971), vol. 2, *Methodenbegriffe der Erfahrungswissenschaften und Gegensätzlichkeiten spekulativer Weltkonzeption,* (Cologne: Cologne University Press, 1970); *Studien zur Philosophiegeschichte* (Cologne: Cologne University Press, 1961); *Transzendentale Dialektik. Ein Kommentar zu Kants Kritik der reinen Vernunft,* 4 vols. (Berlin: Walter de Gruyter Publishers, 1966–71). For additional bibliography, see Friedhelm Nicolin's article "Bibliographie Heinz Heimsoeth," in *Kritik und Metaphysik. Studien: Heinz Heimsoeth zum achtzigsten Geburtstag,* (Berlin: Walter de Gruyter Publishers, 1966), pp. 383–395: 133 entries.
2. W. H. Walsh in *Kant-Studien,* vol. 67, no. 3 (1976), p. 374. Walsh is making a large claim for Heimsoeth, of course, given that commentary on Kant is virtually an industry in its own right in Germany.
3. Heinz Heimsoeth was born on December 8, 1886 and died on September 10, 1975, short of completing his eighty-ninth year. *Kant-Studien,* no. 3, in 1976 was thus dedicated to him posthumously. Apart from publishing many of Heimsoeth's individual articles, *Kant-Studien* also published supplementary numbers containing collections of Heimsoeth's articles in 1956 and in 1961. [See Friedhelm Nicolin, "Bibliographie Heinz Heimsoeth," nos. 60 and 75.]
4. Heimsoeth. "Johann Gottlieb Fichte" in *Die großen Deutschen: Deutsche Biographie,* ed. H. Heimpel, Th. Heuss, B. Reifenberg (Berlin: Ullstein Publishers, 1956), vol. 5, pp. 178–190.
5. Wilhelm Windelband. *Lehrbuch der Geschichte der Philosophie* (Tübingen: J. C. B. Mohr Publishers, 1892; 14th ed., rev. by Heinz Heimsoeth, Tübingen: J. C. B. Mohr Publishers, 1948).
6. Heimsoeth. *Die sechs großen Themen,* p. 3.
7. Cited by Nicolin, "Bibliographie Heinz Heimsoeth," p. 386.
8. "Problemgeschichte," in *Historisches Wörterbuch der Philosophie,* ed. Joachim Ritter and Karlfried Gründer (Darmstadt: Wissenschaftliche Buchgesellschaft Publishers, 1989), vol. 7, cols. 1410–1417.
9. *Ibid.,* col. 1411.
10. *Ibid.*
11. Nicolai Hartmann. "Zur Methode der Philosophiegeschichte," *Kant-Studien,* vol. 15 (1909), pp. 459–485. On relations between Hartmann and Heimsoeth, see B. Liebrucks, "Philosophische Freundschaft. Zum Briefwechsel zwischen N. Hartmann und H. Heimsoeth," *Kant-Studien,* vol. 73, no. 1 (1982), pp. 82–86.

12. H. J. de Vleeschauer, "L'Oeuvre de Monsieur Heinz Heimsoeth de 1911 à 1924," in *Kant-Studien*, vol. 67, no. 3, (1976), p. 320.
13. Hartmann, "Methode der Philosophiegeschichte," pp. 465f.
14. "Problemgeschichte," *Historisches Wörterbuch der Philosophie*, vol. 7, col. 1412.
15. See, for example, W. H. Walsh. "Kant and Metaphysics," *Kant-Studien*, vol. 67, no. 3 (1976), pp. 372–384; Ingeborg Heidemann, "Person und Welt. Zur Kantinterpretation von Heinz Heimsoeth," *Kant Studien*, vol. 48, no. 2 (1956–1957), pp. 344–360; *idem*, "Metaphysikgeschichte und Kantinterpretation im Werk Heinz Heimsoeths," *Kant-Studien*, vol. 67, no. 3 (1976), pp. 291–312; Hinrich Knittermeyer, "Zu Heinz Heimsoeth's Kantdeutung," *Kant-Studien*, vol. 49, no. 3, (1957/1958) pp. 293–311.
16. Heimsoeth's *Die sechs großen Themen* first appeared in 1922 in the *Schriftenreihe der Preußischen Jahrbücher* (Berlin: Stilke Publishers), no. 6. As of 1987 it is in its eighth edition (Darmstadt: Wissenschaftliche Buchgesellschaft Publishers). It was translated into Spanish by José Gaos as *Los seis grandes temas de metafísica occidental* (Madrid: Revista de Occidente Publishers, 1928; reissued 1946, 1960). The Dutch translation appeared as *De oorsprong van der westerse metafysica* (Utrecht, Amsterdam: Aula-boeken Publishers, 1965).
17. See n. 7 above.
18. The synopsis of the chapters of *The Six Great Themes* provided here follows the general précis made by Dietrich Mahnke in his book review in *Kant-Studien*, vol. 29, (1924), p. 548. Cf. Josef Bernhardt's book review summary in *Deutsche Vierteljahrschrift für Literaturwissenschaft und Geistesgeschichte*, ed. Paul Kluckhohn and Erich Rothacker (Halle/Saale: Max Niemeyer Publishers, 1927), vol. 5, pp. 208–209.
19. Heimsoeth concentrates so much on German philosophers that K. J. Grau says (*Preußische Jahrbücher*, vols. 193–194, 1923, pp. 91–92) that *The Six Great Themes* constitutes an argument for the view that Heimsoeth is the man best qualified to follow Eduard Zeller in writing the history of German philosophy (see p. 17). Heimsoeth views Copernicus and Suso (usually regarded as Poles) simply as other Germans, along with Paracelsus and Nicholas of Cusa (p. 26). One must not take Italians seriously as metaphysicians, certainly not in comparison with Germans (p. 26). He gives virtually no serious credit to any of the philosopher/theologians of the classic Scholastic period, such as Thomas Aquinas and Bonaventure, simply identifying the entire period prior to the fourteenth century—with the exception of Augustine and perhaps Hugh of St. Victor—with Antiquity. He deals with Augustine and with his Germanic heroes of the late medieval period as Protestants before their time, because evidently "Christian" means "Protestant," and Protestants are the ones who have discovered individuality, personality, and the power of the self.
20. Heimsoeth seems to disregard the fact that the great issue faced by the Scholastics of the High Middle Ages was the reconciliation of their religious faith with the claims of reason (especially after the large-scale importation of Aristotelian philosophy into the West in the thirteenth century) and that there were many abso-

Translator's Introduction

lutely fundamental disparities between the worldviews of the ancients and the medievals (as well as considerable variety among the views of the medievals themselves). Thus, for example:

1. Whereas the Greek concept of being meant intelligibility and metaphysical perfection (which led Plato, for instance, to ban some religious myths and poems because they conflicted with his metaphysics), the medievals used their religious beliefs to judge the validity of metaphysics. Hence, whereas the Greeks—even Plato and Aristotle—were polytheists, Christianity was absolutely monotheistic, with all the metaphysical implications that entails; and although being meant mere intelligibility and perfection for the Greeks, Being meant an existing, living, personal God for the medievals.

2. Whereas the Greeks regarded the physical universe as ultimate being (beyond the control even of the gods), Christianity espoused the doctrine of *creatio ex nihilo*.

3. Whereas the Greeks saw man as part of nature, the medievals viewed man—according to the same creation account—as made "in the image and likeness of God," but only according to an analogical mode of predication (*analogia entis*).

4. Whereas the Greeks had no proper notion of sin in the Christian sense of ethical responsibility to a personal God and his will, the medievals' idea of conscience and ultimate accountability was fundmentally related to God.

5. Whereas the Greeks lived essentially within a purely temporal, here-and-now horizon, the medievals believed in a much more important eternal and transcendent dimension which, combined with the "image of God" notion, made the worth of the human being infinite.

6. Whereas the basic Greek notion of history was a cyclical one (suggesting no ultimate meaning or direction to the historical process), the Christian view was unilinear, namely, that history began with creation, culminated in Christ, and will end with a Last Judgment.

Of course there was a generous admixture of religious beliefs here, but there is manifestly a great deal of metaphysical weight connected with these religious beliefs and with similar assertions. In their light it seems quite bizarre to divide the history of metaphysics simply into ancient (pagan) and modern (Christian), with the break coming in the fourteenth/fifteenth centuries. [On these points one may usefully consult, among others, Etienne Gilson's many studies of medieval philosophy, particularly *The Spirit of Medieval Philosophy* (London: Sheed and Ward, 1934; New York: Charles Scribner's Sons, 1934. Gifford Lectures, University of Aberdeen, for 1931 and 1932).]

21. This charge has already been addressed earlier (p. 11) in the observation that philosophy is largely the *history* of philosophy and that Heimsoeth's Kant interpretation has had a major impact on understanding the role of metaphysics in Kant's thought.

22. S. Mahnke, in *Kant-Studien*, vol. 29, p. 548. Siegfried Behn makes a similar point in *Hochland*, vol. 20, no. 2 (1923), p. 548.

23. Behn, *Hochland*, p. 548.

24. *Ibid.*, pp. 548–549.
25. Bernhardt, *Deutsche Vierteljahrschrift*, vol. 5, pp. 208–209.
26. K. J. Grau, *Preußische Jahrbücher*, vols. 193–194 (1923), p. 91.
27. *Ibid.*, p. 92.
28. Artur Schneider, *Historisches Jahrbuch im Auftrage der Görresgesellschaft*, ed. Erich König, (Munich: 1924), pp. 135–136.

Beginning of the Modern Period
in the History of Philosophy

Our historical knowledge and re-
search is still so recent, and yet how deeply mired it already is in its formulas.
How dependent its classifications are, not only on current prejudices but on
long-dead ones. How slowly change occurs in the concepts, value nuances,
and divisions in which we try to lay hold of the stream of life gone by.

The time to reconsider many of the best-received formulas has finally
arrived. Above all, schemata regarding the great periods in history are tottering. What really constitutes the essence of ''the Middle Ages,'' for example, has become no less questionable than where they began and when
they ended. But this means that every single branch of historical research
faces the task of drawing on its own special material to contribute to a solution of the problems that have surfaced. The more we have learned to
disregard the comfortable assumption that tells us that a single historical
force (economics, say, or political events) should explain all other movements, in other words, the more we are able to distinguish the plurality of
autonomous and largely independent currents, the more confident we can be
in expecting that the convergence of isolated inquiries will yield decisive
results for the larger issues. We march separately to strike together: this is
what we have to do until the grand synopsis is achieved and revision is
accomplished.

When one considers the enormous wealth of important historical research that has already been accumulated in this area, one is amazed at how
little the history of philosophy has thus far concerned itself with reviewing
traditional classifications. How much it has simply taken over from textbooks
of general intellectual and cultural history! How seldom are the great arteries

of development here really chiseled out from proper material, the philosophical problems themselves.

Thus the usual tripartite division of all history into Antiquity, Middle Ages, and the Modern Period is adopted without hesitation. And if one asks about the turning point when "modern philosophy" breaks off from the philosophy of the Middle Ages, one finds the complete, undisputed answer everywhere, an answer that even a person least affected by philosophy could answer from his general knowledge: the Renaissance.

This is a point that we would like to reconsider here. It seems to us that the question would have to be restated: In the evolution of the threads and fabric of thought, what has that great universal transformation contributed, that distinguishes systems and developments of modern philosophy from Scholastic metaphysics of the Middle Ages? Where does one find the decisive motifs of this change? And when do they occur?

Let no one say, now, that these are idle questions. Or that it makes little difference how one labels and demarcates historical periods, because in the last analysis, after all, every historical division remains arbitrary and artificially divides the ceaseless flux of living events. Or that such divisions can never amount to more than makeshift contrivances of abstract thought groping on crutches for living reality. . . . As if the stream itself did not meander, or life did not experience rise and fall in its own development, or as if the man were not inwardly and essentially different from the youth. What difference does it make that the transitions are in flux and that the decisive moments are hard to grasp? This only makes the task all the more important for us!

Then, too, in such matters the question is never ultimately about purely formal division, about historical dates or centuries. For this external aspect of division, after all, always expresses substantive convictions also. The terms "Middle Ages" and "Renaissance" contain an entire theory and valuation. If one raises anew the question about the beginning of the Modern Period in the history of philosophy, this also automatically means the same as to ask oneself: What is it that essentially defines modern thought and how do its ultimate contents and perspectives differ from those of other periods that preceded it? How do the great themes of this modern philosophy relate to the Middle Ages and to Antiquity? What is it that links them to the traditional, and, on the other hand, what is it that creates the new impetus, the new dimension?

The traditional schema is the following one. Philosophy is really worldly wisdom, free science about the essence of natural things. It was not that in the Middle Ages: as the handmaid of theology it elaborated given dogmatic truth. Authority was decisive, not reason. But the Renaissance emancipated

24

us from that. It ushered in the birth of a freer age, in which science knew nothing of coercion and obfuscation through church and religion. The philosophy of the ancients came to life again, mediated to us completely anew by Greek scholars who fled to Italy from Constantinople when it fell into the hands of the Turks. Just as the emancipated age had brought the ancient statue and the ancient state to full light again, so now it did the same for the ancient concept: in the "New Athens" of Florence free spirits founded a Platonic Academy. From it sprang the new, worldly thinking; Plato defeated an Aristotle who had been fused into the ecclesiastical system, and now the great ancient thinkers were alive again—Democritus, Epicurus, the Stoics, and even Aristotle himself. The friends of Antiquity and its free humanity— the Humanists—were the source for the renewal of philosophy.

The new development began, then, in Italy, and from there it carried its victorious campaign into all countries. From this Italian Renaissance—which contains all the seeds for what came later and which in Giordano Bruno's beauty-intoxicated world picture elevated itself in grand style before all other nations to the level of a universal view—sprang the English Renaissance whose spokesman [Francis] Bacon (Lord Verulam) pronounced the watchword for the following centuries; from it also sprang the French Renaissance, which led from Montaigne, the skeptical-worldly reverer of Antiquity, to the real "father of modern philosophy," Descartes. And from there issued everything decisive: Hobbes and Locke, Spinoza and—Leibniz.

In other words, Germany arrived altogether last on the scene. Torn by religious strife, it was unable for a long time to enjoy the freedom of the new ancient thinking. There were, to be sure, German Humanists, and Melancthon pried Aristotle loose from Catholic Scholasticism; but the eternal questions of faith stifled the wisdom of this world. So not very much came out of German Renaissance philosophy, and it was not until two hundred years later—after that immigration of Greek scholars, after confessional struggle had abated and the freedom of "natural reason" had finally awakened—that the ground was cleared for a German system, for Leibniz. In grand style he pulled together all the themes: the philosophy of the Renaissance and Bruno's world picture find their late fulfillment here, enriched by what other lands and their renaissance had garnered. And now Western philosophy had once again recovered its own proper ground and its own problems and marched on, in league with free science, into the eighteenth and nineteenth centuries toward its own proper objectives.

But there are extremely serious objections to this construction if one investigates the ultimate contents and themes of the systems themselves with respect to their tendency, origin, and importance! Indeed, if we begin by looking at the situation purely from the outside, is it not remarkable that

25

German thought should have contributed so little to the evolution of our modern philosophical period and Italian thought virtually everything? Are not the talents of nations otherwise remarkably similar throughout history? In those centuries where was the speculative power of the German mind that later on surpassed that of any other people? And whence did the Italian, whose greatest achievements came at a later time and in completely other spheres, suddenly at this time derive this capacity—even though fructified and nourished by Antiquity, nevertheless, with new self-assurance—to illuminate the path for others with the torch of metaphysical knowledge?

To begin with the last point, if one now examines the philosophy of the Italian Renaissance period with regard to its own indigenous accomplishments, one's reading-inspired enthusiasm is diminished very quickly. Speculative power and true metaphysical talent lag strikingly behind nimbleness of creative imagination, fiery impetus of expression, and dazzling abundance of material picked up from everywhere. Few periods in the history of philosophy are so fragmented, so inwardly insecure in simultaneous adherence to the most diverse traditions, so indiscriminate and without a proper estimation of magnitudes, even in comprehending the legacy of the ancients. In one breath one names Cicero and Plato, least autonomous rhetoric and deepest speculation. No, this period is not one of the truly productive periods in the history of philosophy. Everything that suggests something outstanding here points to something else as the true source of its merit.

This is true even in the case of the one great figure, Bruno. Nor did he hide the fact. And it is not compatriots he names above all, not Humanists and also not the ancients, but rather—three Germans: Copernicus, the astronomer [see p. 20, n. 19]; Paracelsus, the physician and mystic of nature; and Nicholas of Cusa, the great churchman and metaphysician, whom Bruno's compatriot Cardano also esteemed above all contemporaries, indeed above all men. How completely Bruno's entire new world picture rests on the accomplishment of the first of these is something everyone understands who knows about it. Copernicus is of course a man of science, not a philosopher. But the other two are German philosophers—who therefore existed at any rate in the centuries of transition from the Middle Ages to the Modern Period. . . . Little research has been done to this point about what Bruno derived from Paracelsus for his concept of the monad. But it has become entirely clear for several centuries now (since people in general have once again been made truly aware of one of the greatest philosophical minds in German history) that all other decisive themes of his speculation derive from Nicholas of Cusa and were virtually taken over from him in their profoundest formulations. We shall come back to this point later. But if Bruno points back in this way to this German of the age of waning Scholasticism, must not the picture of the origins of Leibniz's system also be completely transformed? People have always observed Leibniz's similarity with Bruno, but no one has been able properly to demonstrate his dependence on him. In that case would not Leibniz be not so much a capstone of the Renaissance but rather the carrier and shaper of an indigenous German tradition, a son of that stock of people around Nicholas and Paracelsus? . . . If one investigates the innermost tendencies of the monadology with this issue in mind, he will readily see Leibniz in a different light than the light in which traditional historical construction has seen him.

But to what origins do Nicholas and Paracelsus refer us? In order to save the old [historical] division even in the face of newly observed facts, people have introduced the concept—extremely questionable in so many respects—of the German Renaissance, here and in other contexts as well. Because Nicholas studied once in Padua, he must belong to the early Renaissance. But these kinds of schemata break down entirely when one goes from the externals of education to the inwardness of compelling motives. Both of these men point to another stream of intellectual life, one in which they stand with both feet and from which they derived their deepest thoughts: the broad stream of German mysticism. No one could mistake how completely the theosophist and mystic of nature, Paracelsus, drew from it. But that even Nicholas of Cusa was also rooted in this soil is something his theological as well as his more philosophical writings could have sufficed to point out; in one of them, in fact, he expressly defended Eckehart as well against the bitter opponent of his own doctrine. There would scarcely have been any need to allude explicitly to the fact that part of Meister Eckehart's long-lost Latin work was discovered in a transcript that Nicholas had had copied for his library and provided with his notes.

Mysticism, then, was German philosophy at that time. Jacob Böhme also, the great developer of this tradition in the century of the Reformation, compared to whom all contemporary philosophy of the Humanists sinks into nothingness, was called simply the *philosophus teutonicus*. Indeed this mysticism, from Eckehart on and from the author of the "German Theology," was speculative; it sought to speculate about the soul, God, the world, and philosophy, not just to express religious life verbally and conceptually! Take a look at this mysticism and you will see at once that those German centuries prior to Leibniz were not poor and constricted, dependent on foreign achievement, and without any native power; on the contrary, they were rich and free and great, perhaps more original in the directions of their thought than the high-sounding proclamations of the Renaissance and of Humanism. And it is not just the select company of leaders in this so significant movement who (from Meister Eckehart through Suso and Tauler to Paracelsus, Weigel, and

27

Böhme and beyond to the two Helmonts and to Angelus Silesius [Johannes Scheffler] in the period of Leibniz) must capture our interest; nor is it even just the breadth of the movement (from the Lower Rhine, the Netherlands of Ruysbroek, it extends to Suso's Lake Constance; from Strasbourg, Cologne, and Frankfort to the Silesia of Böhme and Scheffler); on the contrary, it is above all its popularity and profound influence on the feeling for life and for thought of the Germans of that time, even of such popular circles that must have remained fairly far removed from all the theological-professional and all the educational philosophy of the Humanists. History of philosophy is more than just a chain of finished systems and isolated peaks. What it is that cogently determines a period's or a people's attitude toward life—but at a level below the obvious tradition of books and of theories that have matured into systematic concepts—is something the importance of which one can subsequently easily underestimate when compared with the strident words of those who assume the role of loudspeaker for something that has grown up quietly.

In the influence of German mysticism one thing has been of decisive importance, something that is also not without significance for the inner development of ideas, and that is the language that served these religious thinkers. In the transformation from the Middle Ages to the Modern Period one of the most important phenomena that has always been remarked is that process of inner self-differentiation of the West that has led to the rise of our present-day nations with their special character and variety. In this connection people have also always stressed what an important role the penetration of vernacular languages into religious life, law, and learning played. Of course there is no need to explain what importance breaking away from medieval Latin must have had, particularly for the development of new philosophical thought. For coining a philosophical concept is after all related much more deeply and decisively to power of expression and to correspondence between outer form and inner intuition and unconscious groping than it is in the case of any other formation of knowledge or science. So long as people wrote in Latin and thought in Latin, they remained under the sway of traditional concepts; and that is so, even if what they had to say might contradict the formulas of a past that had become alien and often threatened to burst those formulas, even with regard to bare language form (as in the barbaric Latin of the late Middle Ages). Indeed, as a matter of fact, at the outset of modern philosophy the new thinking appeared everywhere in the guise of a new, special language form; and in many cases creators of concepts simultaneously played a decisive role in developing national cultural languages in their countries. This is what Galileo and Bruno did for Italy, Montaigne and Descartes for France. If one also looks at Germany in this regard, one finds the traditional picture still more murky than before. Leibniz, to be sure, with whom people begin to reckon modern German philosophy, knew what immense importance even for the content of thought is due to the language in which that thought becomes conscious of itself and expresses itself. And he expressly stressed the fact that as far as he was concerned German was the proper language of philosophy (as he, the German thinker, understood it), in comparison with all the awkward abstractness and speculativeness of the Latin Scholastic tradition. But if he wanted to be heard by the leading minds of his time, he had to accommodate himself to the old shackle himself or to express himself in the polished forms of French culture. For in Germany at that time there was a chasm between new life (the germinating ideas of popular consciousness) and a scholastically and humanistically petrified scholarly world sealed off from living development. If one looks at the connection between philosophical thought and the life and language of the people in whom that connection takes form, then modern German philosophy began even later than people usually think. It was not until the eighteenth century, with Wolff and his school, that philosophizing in German began to take place in German institutions of learning; and it was not until the *Critique of Pure Reason* that Latin was completely abandoned. In fact, not really completely, for conceptual language or philosophical "terminology" everywhere was shot through with derivatives of scholarly speech and its barbaric transformation of the language of the Romans. Even the mighty will and great expressiveness of Fichte, who fought against this old burden as an enemy, were unable to bring German philosophy to pure expression in German for the time being.

And yet this goal for which Leibniz and Fichte had striven and fought had once been reached in a way. At the same time that the language of Italy had been driven to new poetic flowering in Dante's work, Meister Eckehart in Germany formulated the intuitions of his mystical speculation in German words and forms of a purity, indigenous quality, and intuitive richness never again achieved. Is the importance of this accomplishment diminished by the fact that these new verbal constructs came about for the most part through translations of Scholastic terms? As if they had thereby failed to attain completely transformed life and to be emancipated for entirely new development! In Jacob Böhme's turbulent struggle with the German language, with the overt and covert meaning of familiar old words, one can still clearly sense what a wellspring was tapped with that leap from the Scholastic scholar's study and monk's cell into the broad, richly varied life of the people. Nor can one reduce the unique value of Eckehart's linguistic accomplishment by saying that "extrinsic" challenges provided the impetus for it (Sermon for Women and "the Uneducated" ["*Ungebildete*"]), for after all precisely these new challenges in the life of that time were also a moment that pointed to a new future. Has it ever happened again in later periods in German countries that anyone has spoken so profoundly to women and to ''the people'' [*dem ''volk''*] about ultimate and most difficult issues or that what they heard was felt and repeated and passed on more fully? Even in later centuries it was always those who developed Eckehart's mysticism who tried to clear a path for the German language in modern German thinking. Paraclesus was the first one who taught by lecturing in German, and in like manner Weigel, Böhme, and Scheffler wrote their German philosophy, while universities and scholarly and humanistic schools kept themselves sequestered for a long time in their exclusive cultural world—to the detriment of German philosophy and German language.

One of the moments that we seem to have insufficiently noted is the importance of Meister Eckehart and his successors for the emergence of ''modern philosophy'' in German lands and beyond. We believe, despite all the extrinsic residue from Renaissance Humanism and Reformation Neoscholasticism up to Leibniz, Wolff, and Kant, that that first effort and struggle for the modern mind still had a decisive impact on the inner growth of German philosophy. This is not always demonstrable through direct ''influences'' and immediate ''dependence'' (for which even historians of philosophy so desperately search), but instead as something that propagated itself in traditions of spiritual and religious life under cover of traditional ideas and books, from mouth to mouth, through poetry and sermon, custom and linguistic form. If one wants an external sign of this, let him read Leibniz's youthful treatise (in German!), ''On True Mystical Theology,'' or Hegel's youthful treatises, not to mention Schelling and his associates, who most expressly clung to Böhme.

Does one take exception to the fact that in this way the first germs of modern philosophy are being sought right in the midst of the Middle Ages? In history of philosophy textbooks the time from Meister Eckehart to Nicholas of Cusa and the ''Early Renaissance'' is called the period of the decadence of Scholasticism. Oddly enough this ''decadence'' (along with tendencies that really did work toward dissolving the rigidly closed system) also manifested itself in the fact that modes of thought and ideas cropped up which no one had previously attempted and that later development has never forgotten. . . . The single figure of Duns Scotus counterbalances the greatest figures of the classical period of Scholasticism. It seems to us that this entire period, not just Eckehart, is seriously underestimated with regard to its positive importance for the rise of modern philosophy. In those centuries new religious and mystical movements in all countries, in their struggle with the rigid forms of traditional philosophy, led to new formulations not only of

30

life in the world but even of the concept of the world—formulations which then found their full usefulness in a later period. If one is looking for the source of the modern in the metaphysical systems of the Modern Period, one must not be so taken up with the prophets of the fifteenth or sixteenth century as to forget the masters of the fourteenth and the transition from the thirteenth to the fourteenth centuries and their true successors.

Ultimately it is no different in all other areas. Research into the origins of the Modern Period has spilled over everywhere beyond the centuries of Renaissance and Reformation to the beginnings of the fourteenth century, whether one is talking about the beginnings of modern art or music or painting; or the rise of capitalism; or new concepts of the state, social theories, or the development of nations; or about natural science; or the onset of inventions and discoveries. Duhem's research into the beginnings of modern science and the view of nature—which otherwise began for us with Copernicus, Kepler, and Galileo—has produced perhaps the most surprising results in this regard. Beyond the early Renaissance of the natural scientist Leonardo da Vinci—whom people like to praise as a uniquely original precursor—there are threads that lead us back to Occam's fourteenth-century school in Paris, in which so many anticipations of new methods and new insights were elaborated.

Whatever stands in the way of truly unbiased examination of the determinant factors and decisive turning points in that still predominantly murky transition from the Middle Ages into the Modern Period, this is still the universally accepted, yet not intrinsically unambiguous thesis: It is the moment of secularity [*Weltlichkeit*], freedom from religious/ecclesiastical tutelage, that separates the Modern Period, especially its science and philosophy, from the Middle Ages. The great achievement of the Renaissance (and the liberating influence of Antiquity as an autonomous worldly culture that the Renaissance brought to life again) is supposed to consist in the fact that the Renaissance provided an independent footing for art, the state, life, and science—and secularized them. Thinkers of previous centuries—Scholastics as well as mystics, even up to Nicholas of Cusa—so the story goes, show themselves to be completely medieval precisely in this particular. Nicholas stands exactly at the turning point; not until after him did Humanists and freethinkers of the Renaissance clear the path for the pursuit of new goals that were more akin to those of ancient thought than to the Middle Ages.

Now, the question is precisely whether this view is tenable. There is no question about its origin: the assessment of the eighteenth century—the age of "Enlightenment" with its absolute orientation toward a purely "secular" ["*weltliche*"] culture and worldview completely transparent to man's ordering intelligence and accommodated to his immediate needs—lives on in it.

31

Religious powers are readily regarded as unenlightened constraints placed on not yet fully emancipated man, restraints to be overcome by exact science. Philosophy primarily—that is, secular wisdom and moral philosophy—is to occupy the leading place that more benighted times had assigned to religion. . . . But the first ones to tread this path were precisely the freethinkers of the Renaissance. They played off the conceptual clarity of Antiquity against the ignorant torpor of the Middle Ages, and thus led modern man to victory. . . .

There is no question that the emancipation of individual areas of culture (including above all philosophy and science) from theological legislation played a very important role in the process of that transition. But it is entirely erroneous to conclude from that—as if it were somehow the same thing—to a corresponding total transformation of the problems with which thought grapples or to wish to distinguish modern philosophy, as purely secular and directed toward nature and natural existence, from medieval philosophy, which always inquired about ultimate supernatural things, about God, immortality, and the soul. Separating philosophy as autonomous science and secular wisdom from theology is absolutely not the same thing as separating their contents from the sources and the great questions of religious life. It is not true that the metaphysics of the modern age, at least in its greatest representatives, became hostile to the religious element. The great life forces that profoundly determined the thousand-year development of the Middle Ages were also the sources that stimulated the great impulses of modern philosophy.

In the final period of the Middle Ages there already existed two streams in which the struggle for a restructuring of spheres was expressed. In classical Scholasticism roles were so distributed that above the realm of natural reason hovered articles of faith, untouched and untouchable; that rational wisdom—autonomous in a way within its restricted field at any rate—was accommodated and subordinated to the dominant theology, which was solely competent to deal with ultimate questions, so that no contradiction could arise between philosophical knowledge through "natural illumination" and knowledge from revelation. But in the last phase of the Middle Ages both modes and spheres of knowledge strove either to separate totally from each other (so that they became completely independent and not responsible for each other) or, on the contrary, to come completely together, with the goal of total identity. The famous doctrine of double truth (which held that something could be true in theology but false in philosophy, and vice versa), which emerged (following Arab precedent) from about the time of William of Occam, was the crassest expression of the will to separate them. In this period nominalism, at first on behalf of faith and with an expressly skeptical posture against all purely natural knowledge, tried to free faith from knowledge. In time, however, broad currents issued from it that preferred to cling to science as something that was independent in its own right and that represented reality on the basis of immediate and palpable experiential certitudes, compared with which the products of theology remained a mere matter of faith. At the same time, however, a contrary tendency set out to penetrate the totality of the mysteries of faith completely with the light of natural reason! And here belong not only the rationalism of Lully but also Gerson's or even Eckehart's mysticism; for even here the goal was to transpose totally the truths of faith contained in the dogmas of theological tradition into a system of immediately comprehensible ideas. Both tendencies, not just the first, have continued on into the Modern Period! To be sure, if one places in the foreground thinkers of the type of, say, Locke and Hume or of Germans since Hegel's death or naturalists and positivists of all countries, then it might seem as though modern philosophy has trodden the path of indifferentism and of complete separation of faith and reason and has cast off not only theology but also questions posed by religion as foreign baggage. But if one considers the great metaphysicians of this development—Leibniz, Malebranche, Berkeley, say, or Fichte, Schelling, Hegel—then one finds everywhere the same uninterruptedly pronounced tendency profoundly determining the entire problematic: to reconcile faith with reason, to build a Christian philosophy, to elevate the great truths of religion by way of metaphysical speculation to the clear form of the philosophical concept. Even Kant's critical posture (after his youthful work had gone completely in that direction without reservation) expressly had this in mind as its ultimate goal: to establish the limits of reason in order to make room for faith. For him that meant to restrict theoretical knowledge of nature and being in order to lay the foundation for a new metaphysics of practical reason whose contents are—God, freedom, and immortality.

Accordingly, one might surmise that the great themes of this modern metaphysics are not so totally far removed from speculation of the Middle Ages as people commonly believe, and that the Modern Period does not stand together with Antiquity over against the theologically and religiously constricted Middle Ages, as many a Humanist in the days of the Renaissance and later on would have us believe. On the contrary, it is important to recognize (and then also to bring to full fruition in the historical treatment of systems) that in its broad outlines the metaphysics of the Modern Period grew out of the same soil and was nourished by the same sources of life as that of the Middle Ages and that modern metaphysics is more inwardly intertwined with medieval metaphysics and its basic direction and themes than it is with Antiquity. It is important to recognize further that there is an incomparably sharper division between the philosophical development of the ancients and everything that subsequently constituted the great leading ideas in the Christian epoch—from Augustine virtually to the present—than there is between medieval and modern philosophy. This sounds so obvious if one only considers that philosophical systems are always, after all, only the expression of the innermost attitude of consciousness of their creators and disseminators and that in fact it was the same peoples who brooded and searched in the Middle Ages as in the Modern Period, the same peoples influenced by the same basic experience of the common religion of Christianity. In the type of people they were, as in their faith and education, they were different from the culture of the ancient Mediterranean; why should not all the phases of their history of philosophy in general be different from the history of philosophy of the ancients! Exact science might in large measure be independent of the nature of the mind of people that produced it, but philosophical knowledge and formation live (and this does not relativize them!) entirely from the forces, the perspectives, the faith, and the innermost need of their agents and discoverers. The riddles of existence are so deeply entangled, run off as it were in so many directions, that it is possible for everyone, even for the greatest of men as well as for every people and every historical movement, to have access and overview and prospect of the totality only from a particular, intrinsically limited perspective.

If it is true, therefore, as we thought it was, that the Renaissance, insofar as it signified and wished to be a rebirth of Antiquity, was not decisive in the transition from the philosophy of the Middle Ages to the Modern Period, this should not surprise anyone. If there is a division there (less important, to be sure, than the one marking the collapse of Antiquity, but nevertheless important enough in spite of the prevailing similarity between philosophizing nations), then other moments must affect it. It seems to us that one of these moments is insufficiently noted, one that certainly runs directly counter to the view of the Renaissance that traces its path back to ancient worldly wisdom.

Indeed, if one traces the basic outlines of worldview and philosophical thematic in the Middle Ages and in the Modern Period, one finds that they differ in their essential traits from those of the ancient world, in fact often run directly contrary to them. Now, it is a strange spectacle that from the earliest beginnings of Christian-European philosophizing onward this contradictory relationship led to strong inner tension in the systems themselves. For those Church Fathers and Scholastics, in whose hands philosophical speculation since the collapse of the ancient world was placed, were unable— for reasons we shall not pursue here—immediately to provide complete conceptual expression for the new goals. They took over what the legacy of Antiquity offered them in its incomparably rich treasury of systematization and conceptual definition. And if thus, on the one hand, modern philosophy in general first became possible and received stimulus, support, and instructive form for thousands of years, nevertheless, on the other hand, the disparity between its new tasks and traditional abstraction, which had rigidified in other directions, brought about serious conflicts in its development. It has been rightly said that the history of philosophy of the Middle Ages can be divided simply according to the new influxes of ancient tradition that cropped up from time to time. But in every case they provide not only new material, new stimulus, and new possibilities, but above all once again new tension and conflicts! It was only very slowly that philosophy's position become independent and self-constituted vis-à-vis the traditional; the weight of a complete conceptual world from another age bore down for a long time on thinking that was entirely in need of its own proper development.

Now, it seems to us that the period that immediately followed the high point of classical Scholasticism (with its new application of the ancient heritage recently transmitted by the Arabs and with the great mature systems of Albert the Great and Thomas Aquinas) led to a decisive turning point and to the start of modern philosophy itself precisely with respect to this point: here, for the first time since the struggle of the Church Fathers, especially Augustine, inner freedom won out against the ancient conceptualism that was completely woven into the Scholastic system; people now finally arrived at an expression of their own tendencies and learned to distinguish between what was being forced on resisting ideas as a foreign decree from tradition and what, alongside of that and in somewhat altered form, could perhaps serve one's own conviction after all. If the golden age of Scholasticism was oriented toward constructing ''*Summae*'' of philosophy and theology, which were really essentially attempts to interweave the whole of theological tradition with the conceptual framework of philosophical authorities into a system of doctrine (whereby the fundamental assumption was simply taken for granted that in their career these ancient philosophers had already attained the maximum attainable by merely natural knowledge), then the fourteenth century advanced with great strides in the direction of its own research and new organization. In a certain sense the influence of Antiquity still stood in the foreground up to that point (indeed all the more so with the growing influx of materials!), and one could conceive of a history of philosophy that would include the entire Middle Ages to that point in the framework of ancient philosophical development and its lengthy terminal period. It was not until this point—when, because of the superabundance of ancient material, tension increased to the utmost and the possibility of reconciling the many traditions all at once became ever slighter—that individual will began energetically to transform itself into concepts, terms, and systematic new

35

constructions. (Just as earlier in architecture the Gothic did with respect to Romanesque forms, in which also individual will contradicted traditional forms. It still learned from ancient beauty, to be sure, but no longer walked in its paths.) The sixteenth and seventeenth centuries, and with them all of modern philosophy, first became possible through this preliminary labor in the "period of decadence of Scholasticism." Here is the source also of the battle that the awakening modern age, especially the Renaissance, relentlessly waged against Aristotle. For the Thomistic system, which was the highest achievement of Scholasticism, the philosophy of Antiquity was embodied above all in Aristotle. Now the opposition that people identify as that of Augustinianism versus Aristotelianism permeated the entire Middle Ages. The former always expressed the new original element of the Christian world with less restraint: Augustine produced the first really great turning point in philosophical thought. Ancient tradition also lived on in "Augustinianism" and always profoundly influenced it: Plato, but above all Neoplatonism, which, with the oriental tinge in its thought and experience, had developed and redirected the ancient classical system in a direction that was at any rate much more suited to the inclinations of the Christian world than Plato was. Thus it was now possible—as it already was in the Middle Ages, but most especially at the beginning of the Modern Period—to combat the now dominant influence of the ancient thinker Aristotle through Plato, as people understood him and wanted to understand him. The "Platonism" of the Renaissance means this above all. Pico della Mirandola and Marsilio Ficino did not fall outside the lines of development of Christian metaphysics at all, as people love to imagine. Thanks to the work of that earlier age, the Renaissance had attained that inner emancipation from tradition that allowed it to play off the traditions of Antiquity against one another freely and to set aside the dangerous exclusive validity and authority of "the" philosopher Aristotle especially. That in the process people also learned new things from Antiquity once again and sought to corroborate their own new ideas by referring to hitherto overlooked or forgotten initiatives of Antiquity should not be disputed at all, so long as one does not exaggerate such agreement to the point of the false thesis that we are fighting. Just as Bruno could appeal to Democritus for his conception of infinite worlds, so could Hegel still appeal to the ancient Heraclitus for his logic of becoming. But one must also not forget in this matter how Descartes (with whom, after all, the series of systems always begins)—as well as Telesio, say, in the Renaissance itself—sought to free himself entirely from Antiquity, often more sharply (despite the battle against theological-Scholastic constraint that preoccupied him at the moment) than from medieval teaching! And even if Leibniz, with broader vision and greater justice, set out once again to adopt values and truths of ancient wis-

36

dom, he extended this very same tendency of his to make full use of all previous material in exactly the same way to medieval speculation. But that his system as well as that of the others was really more closely connected with the themes of the period just before his own than with what Antiquity sought for and saw is something we believe is demonstrable.

We must now test the view we have sketched here about the course of medieval and modern history of philosophy by discussing a few themes that traverse the entire period but do not reach their full resolution until the close of the Middle Ages. We do not claim to offer something exhaustive here, and for the sake of clarity about the themes we will pursue we have not shied away from one-sidedness of treatment. We confess at the outset that one can fully harness neither the totality of Antiquity nor the conceptual world of the Christian West within clearly defined concepts. Much of what we consider to belong to the special nature of the later period emerged already in Antiquity—but not as essentially defining its image; above all the image that subsequently passed on to the later period through the mediation of later Antiquity and continued to work further! Again, a large part of what we include in our ''great themes'' first appeared in the Hellenistic-orientalizing period. Here, too, for the sake of clarity of outline and in order not to venture all too far at this point into extremely cloudy issues, we content ourselves not only with a general reference to the close relationship of some oriental motifs with the religion of Christianity that arose in the Orient but also, most obviously, with the special character of the peoples who are the agents of modern Western development. We also do not wish to try to decide what is attributable in this evolution to religious doctrine itself and what, on the contrary, to the inner endowments and powers of those peoples in whom, after all indeed, the ideas and dogmas and mental tendencies of Christianity were first fully developed. If we speak so simply about the themes of Christianity and their philosophical consequences and contrast them with basic tendencies of the ancient world, we are aware, for all that, that we are using a single word here to describe an enormously complicated interworking of the most varied historical forces. But our purpose here is merely to point out something new, not to master all questions.

37

I.
God and World—the Unity of Opposites

Among all the philosophical questions that loom early before the human mind, never again to be silenced, the one closest to hand and most primordial is the question about the hidden unity of the totality of being which, however, always shows itself to us only in multiplicity and division, in the manifold-motley character of experiences. This most primitive problem of all metaphysics first acquires its full weight through the perception of *oppositions* in reality and through the exceptional force with which these oppositions obtrude themselves on us as the ultimate determinations of intellectual existence.

Even the most unpretentious view of nature has identified its polarity of warm and cold, light and dark, from the manifold mass of what we perceive, whereas more mature thought pursues the same law of opposition into deeper levels. Thus at the very beginnings of Greek philosophy of nature Anaximander asked about the single origin and principle not only of the multiple manifold but of oppositions. But all thought regarding oppositions does not reach its limit or its most extreme point until one poses the question of life and coordinates it with a worldview. Life is fragmented into beautiful and ugly, holy and sinful, good and bad. Here we seem to encounter an ultimate duality that is insuperably harsh and simply tears all unity of existence to pieces. If one were to juxtapose fire and water in the same space, they would unite more readily than these forces do, for one of them always signifies and intends to signify the destruction of the other; one of them is an object of enthusiastic affirmation and the other of passionate denial. Though both of them are equally real and function alongside one another in the world, this should not be so. . . . Thus this absolute division and tension between worth and worthlessness is added to contrariety of content in the world.

In any assessment of the world that includes values, therefore, there is an inescapable tendency toward *dualism*, toward discharge into an ultimately irreconcilable split. Whatever one might otherwise call dualism—where, for example, someone teaches an irremovable difference between two opposite and independent kinds of being (as with Descartes's bodily existence vs. existence of conscious beings) or the polarity of all ultimate forces of nature—this is just a pale reflection of the truly unfathomable split that is posited in the hostility between worth and worthlessness, a split that proceeds above all from experiences of moral and religious life! When those oppositions one perceives or discovers in nature lead to a strict dualism, this usually happens because, either openly or hiddenly, one has somehow related those oppositions to that primordial duality that manifests itself only in the life of the mind, because one connects, say, the dark and the cold with evil, that is, the negative poles with worthlessness. Thus the more deeply philosophy takes its direction from the experiences of such life values, the more powerfully the seed of, and inclination toward, dualism exist in it.

But at the same time reason demands unity or system in everything that exists. Ultimate duality leaves the ultimate question open. The inquiring mind never comes to rest if it does not find the unity of opposites. And not simply reason but the soul too presses toward reconciliation and ultimate resolution: for that evil is invincible in itself and is just as fully primordial a law of being as its opposite pole, good, is something that morally and religiously determined thought in particular always strives to escape. Hence it happens extremely rarely that anyone conceives of absolute dualism that decisively renounces any comprehensive, reconciling unity, or of triumph of opposition over unity undiluted by any final transformation; and in principle it has never really happened that absolute dualism has matured into a philosophical system. In their time religious doctrines of Zoroaster and mythological speculations of the Manichaeans and other Gnostics amounted to such radical dualism of good and evil, God and the devil; but this always remained an isolated experience and idea, and no one ever erected a metaphysical edifice on such a disunited basis. Always and everywhere we find dualistic motives intertwined with threads that the will to unity has developed. But metaphysical systems, ideas about the world, and concepts of existence part company with regard to what ultimately determines the structure and coloring of the fabric as a whole, what holds the upper hand: unity or opposition. And historical periods part company in this fashion just as individual systems do.

Greek philosophy, which was uniquely oriented toward unity from the start, never again surrendered its dualism from that moment on, when the

Pythagoreans made opposition in life the focal point of metaphysical thought and in their table of opposites made the first effort to grasp the world's principles in fundamental duality and value-fragmentation. To be sure, Heraclitus wanted things differently. The "Obscure One" from Ephesus conceived the great idea of a unity that did not hover over oppositions, smoothing them out and obliterating the struggle, but rather lived and functioned in the very tension of those opposites itself. Just as in the case of a bow or a lyre, an alliance of opposing forces is the law of things, the unity of the world. This is not a unity above or below the opposites, but a unity of the opposites themselves. But for a long time this was not understood, and it remained without effect; this was not the initiative that determined the worldview of the classical systems. But when, on the other hand, Parmenides wished to do away with all opposites and even with variety and multiplicity through an authoritative edict of reason—proclaiming the absolutely unruffled, serene unity of perfectly integral and unfragmented being—just then duality sprang forth again with renewed acuteness. For if the multiplicity of things is only appearance, then we still have these two things after all: reality and appearance, the one denying what the other affirms. To convince men living in multiplicity and separation that this appearance did not exist—was an *ouk on*, a nonentity—is something that could not succeed.

Thus from the basic motif that first sounded with Anaximander and the Pythagoreans, never to be silenced thereafter, and from the demand of the Eleatics, the dualism of the great Greek systems emerged, and it never let itself be driven into the background through the idea of unity, for which everyone was nonetheless striving. Plato did justice to appearances by turning them into phenomena. There was a midpoint between two opposite poles: what shines through in appearances and echoes as true being is the idea, but that in which the idea appears and which draws the idea into the realm of the apparent is space, the content for all material, sensible-contingent being. Disjunctions of religious origin nourished the growth of a deep division in the concept of the world. The eternal ideas [*Gestalten*] shine into our existence, but always only in a muddied, distorted way, girt about with the sensible, caught up in transformation and in death. The Good is the sun of all existence, the father of the ideas. But in reality as we know it, the light of this sun struggles against the dark force of spatial matter as the *hupenantion ti to agatho* [opposite of the good] that is the source, for us and for all beings, of everything unsettled and indeterminate, everything senselessly mechanistic and unformed, all decadence and attraction to evil. Life longs for purification, that is, for freedom from matter that perpetually drags it down and never fully adapts itself to form. Escape from the world of the senses, from life in time, and transition to what is eternal and lasting: all the great dialectical effort of the late Plato never set aside the dualism that reaches its apex in this sort of philosophy of life. And Plato's influence on later times always remained overwhelmingly determined by this doctrine of the contrariety of the world right to the end of the Middle Ages and on into the Modern Period.

Plato's denial that one can impute being in the proper sense to that primordial principle of the unformed-material does not undermine the dualism. For even if it is supposed to be a *me on* [nonexistent thing], nevertheless this nonexistent thing is still not nothing (*ouk on*). And when the ideas, in contrast to the reality we know, are called existing being [*das seiende Sein*], this intensification shows that one is only looking for a way to intertwine the good and the perfect more profoundly and inwardly with being than one does with the evil and the impure. Even the fact that, at the end, the idea of the Good becomes transcendent beyond all existence and is in the beyond does not lead Plato to conclude that the source of the power of spatial matter, which though negative nevertheless is effective in creating resistance, resides in it also. The evil sensual element derives from the *me on*; this gives renewed hope of victory in moral struggle and in religious longing. But this world and this life would not be mixed and impure, dominated by death and by the pressure of the sensual—which they certainly are—if nonexistence were nothing and only the good existed.

Although Aristotle is much less harshly oriented toward contrariety in ethical matters and is much more inclined toward the this-worldly, nevertheless he expresses metaphysical duality just as sharply as Plato does. There is nothing actually existing that is not a mixture of the two elements of matter and form. Their opposition is absolute. Neither can be reduced to the other: form does not create matter, nor does matter, of itself, give birth to form. A real object comes to be only when the two come together.

Here, too, the priority of the good is manifest. In its highest expression in the divine nous (comparable to Parmenides' **one** being or to the idea of the Good) only form already possesses in itself total, self-sufficient being. Under ordinary conditions of existence, to be sure, only a mixture of the two principles can exist; in itself pure matter and pure form are figments of abstraction. And so actually even pure matter has no proper being or concrete actuality of its own; it is bare indeterminate possibility, without purpose or power, shy of any actuality whatever, a *me on*. But matters are different in the case of form: it exists at the upper boundary of existence, as it were (whose lower boundary is matter); it is entirely absolute being, free from any admixture with matter, the form of itself, the One God, free from everything worldly. Toward him, the nous—who thinks only himself but not the world; who abides in himself, has nothing to do with and needs nothing of matter—everything strives as toward the summit of being.

SIX GREAT THEMES OF WESTERN METAPHYSICS

Once again contrariety is supposed to be the final word, and yet one member takes priority and preponderance in "being." The one nous is being in a fuller sense than anything else is; matter, on the other hand, is not being, is not yet actuality, hovers before it only as an indeterminate possibility, enters into substance organized by form. And yet that divine nous is not total being for itself and the unique source of all objects; on the contrary, matter always exists alongside form in them. Form impresses itself on matter as upon something passively resistant that ultimately escapes being shaped. Everything that comes to be and lives bears the brand of this twofold origin.

But the way that Aristotle wanted to demonstrate the great organization of world structure in the duality of basic principles was through his hierarchical ordering, the idea of ascending development. Plato did not go on to ask how the idea and the sensual-spatial fit together. His great student now established the connection by viewing form at the same time as purpose. The lower does not merely participate in the higher but itself strives toward it; in that consists its life and all activity in the world. Striving toward the higher permeates all reality. But that was an old, yet perennially new, motif dating back to the first days of Greek natural philosophy: to combine world unity with multiplicity and contradictions through the concept of development. That philosophy conceived this in temporal fashion: it wanted to teach how the world arose from its beginning. Just as all the mythical poems told how the ordered world of objects and beings, adorned in all its rich diversity, emerged from chaos. But such unitary becoming always implies the principle of antithesis: the process of being, the system of being, ascends from the dark-unformed upwards into the higher and purer, toward form and eternal order. For the question at issue it does not make much difference whether one regards this ascending development as a process in time or as an everlasting stratification; whether it happens spontaneously, from the powers and offspring of chaos itself or, as it were, is enticed and drawn upward through a supreme teleological principle that hovers over all reality as the prototype of all perfection (as in Aristotle's nous); whether therefore the effect, as it were, is supposed to contain more than the cause from which it arose or whether all value and all perfection of form were grounded from the outset in an ultimate "final cause" ["*Zweckursache*"] toward which the "effects" strive to attain. Dualism lurks in this conception as it did in the other.

Despite all the counterinfluence of, say, Epicurus and the Stoics, this dualism remained a dominant theme in the philosophy of the ancient world. However, at its close, another motif of unitary explanation now aligned itself with that explanatory concept of *evolution*; this one, too, was profoundly linked with dualism and not suited to obliterate it: *emanation*. This motif was extremely ancient also and rooted in myth and every sort of oriental world speculation. If cosmos was supposed to emerge from the unfragmented-unordered, must it not be then that everything was somehow posited in primordial being [*in dem Ursein*] and that, accordingly, undifferentiated unity contains more power and value than the image of chaos conveys? Even at the outset of ancient Greek development Anaximander had already spoken about the "separation" [*"Ausscheiden"*] of opposites out of the boundless-indeterminate: Do they therefore exist in the latter, only in a hidden way? And when he goes so far as to say that separated beings must atone for their crime by having to perish: Does that not conceal the idea that that undivided being is the higher after all, despite all its indeterminacy and lack of order, and that, on the contrary, the individual-opposite is refuse and the dissolution of primordial being into impudent [*kecke*] nothingness? The path of the world goes downward then, not upward!

This was the doctrine of Plotinus and his disciples. The original motif of the Orient and classical concepts of the Greek systems coalesced for him. Undifferentiated unity is the first and profoundest thing in all of being, highest perfection, deity itself. It is removed from all multiplicity. It is only mystical ecstasy, in which everything fuses into one (as Xenophanes said, of whom people thought that he led Parmenides to his One Being), that uniquely touches that unity, grasps it, and penetrates it. But from that unity the richly varied world shines forth, as light and colors do from the sun: first the nous, the manifold of ideas and forms, and then souls and all objects. This is discharge out of superabundance that does not diminish Supreme Being, which abides within itself and is pure light. The primordial brightness of the One illumines every existing thing, which after all derives from it alone. Whatever lives in this world of the many is prefigured in nonmultiple unity, emerges from that unity as ideal being first, and proceeds from there to actuality. With that we seem to have taken a major stride toward a conception of the unity of all being, and indeed broad features actually point in this direction. But contrariety still permeates this entire world of emanation. The dualism of the Orient—with its profound dread of contamination by matter, sensuality, and the body, and its vigorous tendency toward escape from the world and asceticism—links up with the opposites in the classical world concept of the Greeks. The image of radiation itself shows this: the further one goes away from the source of light, the fainter become the rays and the duller the colors, whereas darkness waxes ever more menacingly. It is not just varied richness of colors that emerges from eternal process; no, eternal struggle with darkness is posited at the same time. The dark element exists— even though it can never exist by itself, and radiated light is weakened in it. Thus for these Alexandrians and Neoplatonists, being is graduated downward to the point of matter and with it to everything sensual and evil. Degree by degree it plunges downward from primitive unity, degenerates from that pure power that abides unchanged and has as little to do with what has decayed and emanated as Aristotle's nous had to do with a world composed of matter and form. The greater the distance from the light, the more light-poor, even light-hostile reality becomes, even to the point of total opposition! Consequently, if he does not wish to be totally ruined, sinful man needs an absolute turnabout or "conversion," a flight from matter, and a boundless, world-emancipated commitment to the One that is withdrawn from the world! Everything that is in Pythagoras and Plato by way of world-escaping motifs returns in heightened measure here in the world of emanation—which is in fact a fallen world [*Welt des Abfalls*]. Here, too, in the final analysis no positive characteristic remains for matter and for this entire principle of opposite poles; it has no true existence. And yet it does exist and function; it brings destiny with it; this *me on* is not nothing. In defiance of all of mysticism's beginning and ending with a drive toward unity, dualism breaks through triumphantly; opposition has never been reconciled with integral being in this world. Only the isolated soul in holy ecstasy soars upward and beyond this existence, which is only a mixture of evil/sensual matter and pure forms—exactly as it was for Aristotle and Plato. There as well as here, earthly destinies and the world's course unfold between the levels of the absolutely perfect and of total darkness; the path goes upward or downward between worth and worthlessness, matter and form, unity and division.

With the coming of Christianity the doctrine of **creation**—that is, of *creatio ex nihilo*—now confronts evolution and emanation. In it there is a significant tendency toward eliminating dualism; unity seeks to conquer contrariety. Usually one particularly stresses this point with the concept of creation: that the world did not come into being here out of unity or chaos spontaneously and through inner necessity, but that it was created through the deliberate activity of a spiritually conscious God. This is certainly an important motif. Thus Plato looked for a mediator between eternal ideas and changing world in the demiurge who made the world in space according to the models of those ideas. From the time of the Church Fathers on, philosophers and theologians of Christianity have always readily appealed to this precedent in Plato's system. But the question before us now is rather that other moment, which sharply distinguishes Plato's demiurge from the creator of all things: creation out of nothing! Craftsman of the world and creator of the world—these are two fundamentally different concepts (as Kant, e.g., explains in his early work as well as in his critique of the proofs for God's existence). For what creation from nothing wants to say is this: that here form is not impressed on preexisting matter (whether one calls this non-being or makes it as dependent as one likes), but rather that there is nothing, in the absolute sense, existing apart from God out of which God might create! Here matter in the world has its origin exclusively in God, just as all form does. If one still asks about the matter out of which the will of the creator makes the world, the answer must point to God's own essence; there are contents of the divine spirit that are immediately transformed into reality in creation. Thus matter is simultaneously posited with idea; both of them derive from the same ground. For the concept of world creation one may no longer use the model of a human artist who shapes external material nor a demiurge who uses eternal givens in his work. God creates from nothing; he posits all of reality from his own bare power alone; he achieves his purposes without any struggle with obstinate material or inert indeterminacy. The power of his light no longer loses itself in darkness "below." There is no more below; there are no longer two levels between which reality fluctuates in ascent or descent. The world is simply the work and revelation of One God: it has come into being just exactly as God wills it, for outside his absolute power nothing exists, not even darkness. Then whence were duality and insuperable tension supposed to come, whence downward-pulling force in opposition to the sublime? The value of the world is one, in full agreement with the principle of good from which it arose. The world admits even what is perfect (which was unthinkable from the Greek point of view)! No matter how much we men experience and suffer contrariety in the world, no matter how much sin banishes us from closeness to God and seeks to tear our lives to pieces— as God's creation the world must be a perfect unity, beyond any separation into good and evil, spirit and flesh. As paradoxical as it sounds—given that the lower level, that of matter, has after all ceased to exist—the concept of the world must be totally raised up to the level of the perfect. What moves God toward the world and the world toward God must now play itself out on one level. A final *Yes* encompasses all of being in all its parts and levels (insofar as these still exist) in single undivided love.

At this point let us set aside the question regarding what inner difficulties must arise from the side of religious life itself if one posits the absolute carrying out of such world affirmation. Our thesis is not, say, that Christian doctrine logically demands complete annihilation of opposites through unity. But we should now investigate this one motif that was sounded with the idea of creation with regard to its historical consequences. Doctrines regarding sin and man's fall—insofar as they are not inherent in the essence of creation itself, but rather arose from the act of his free will, and this free will in turn is integrated into the plan of creation—may all be set aside for the time being. The paths of the spirit are not so direct as one simplistically imagines them to be; only one who first traces the individual threads along their separate paths can hope to understand the incomparably rich fabric of its work.

It has long since been recognized how much the mood and style of life of senescent Antiquity (especially through the oriental element in it) influenced the evolution of the Christian church and its doctrines in the direction of flight from the world, asceticism, and fear of contamination by matter and sensuality. Thus the battle between that world-affirming principle that proclaimed the integral value of everything real and ancient doctrines of opposites continues not only through the early history of Christianity but through the entire Middle Ages and beyond. The existential split of ancient dualism was transmitted to the doctrines of the Fathers of the Church and the edifice of Scholastic philosophy, constantly drawing sustenance from the oppositions within religious experiences as well. And yet the strong, deep tone of the modern concept of the world always sounded forth and would not be suppressed. The fact that as early as the first centuries the Gnostics sought with such energy to interweave their dualism even into the Christian idea of the world and had the temerity to attain the extreme form of the Manichaeans, for example, is something that helped the motif of unity more than it harmed it. For it forced the Church Fathers to protest and battle, and perhaps led them to become more conscious of that world-affirming tendency in the idea of creation than they would have been without this. In this struggle Clement of Alexandria, Origen, Gregory of Nyssa, and Augustine arrived at formulas of the idea of unity that elevated them far above the dualistic straitjacket one finds otherwise in this period. Discussions about the eternity of evil and punishments of hell also went on in this direction. Dealing with such questions clarified the concept of the world implied by the doctrine of creation and safeguarded the creator's freedom from bondage to any previously existing matter and freedom of his work from any forced emanational descent. The religion of reconciliation sought to conjoin to that beginning of a *creatio ex nihilo* the eschatological idea of *apokatastasis*, the doctrine about the final return and restoration of all things, even the devil, to God in the redemption of the universe [*der Allerlösung*].

Nevertheless, dualism always continued to press onward. Conviction about the necessary descent of everything that is not the primordially One [*das Ursprungs-Eine*] itself was part of the controversies about the dogma of the Trinity. For it seemed to the ancient way of thinking that the Son himself, insofar as he is the radiation of the first light—even though eternally begotten by the Father and independent of temporal reality—must be less perfect (''subordinationism''). This was the conclusion of Clement and Origen, of the Greeks who grew up in the intellectual atmosphere of the idea of emanation, and of Tertullian the Latin. It was not until Athanasius had

46

fought his battle against the Arians that this residue from alien conceptual paths was eliminated from the doctrine of the Trinity.

But the concept of the world remained ridden with dualistic motives! With Augustine even the doctrine of redemption of the world was surrendered again; his profound grappling with the problem of evil made a pact with ancient dualism. Two realms gape at one another across the abyss; the kingdom of the devil is as eternal as the city of God. The evolution of the world ends in an insoluble-irretrievable separation of the two realms from one another. The "nothing" from which the creator made his world was secretly related after all to the ancient nonexistence of matter. As for the question about the matter of which the world was formed, Augustine expressly refused to look for a positive answer by referring to the essence of God himself. God did not generate the world from his own substance—that would make it like him after all! It must be simply that the world carries its own non-being within it since it bears within itself for all eternity what is evil and turned away from God. The matter of how seriously the Middle Ages, in its form of life and in its doctrines, was continuously shot through with dualism has been stressed too often to make it necessary for us to refer to it in any special way. Regardless of whether Augustine or Aristotle had the strongest influence on the Scholastic systems in every case, contrariety stands in the foreground with either of them. Even where (as in mysticism particularly) Plotinus has the preponderant influence, it is the dualistic aspect of doctrine that is decisive. And corroboration for this was always ready at hand from moral experience, from the religious tension between evil deed and purification, sin and grace.

The mysticism of Meister Eckehart took the first step toward a complete shift in the direction of the world-affirming aspect of the idea of creation. He, too, lived in the tradition of ancient ideas, in that of Plotinism and its Christian successors. But from the idea of the unity of the world radiated from God he now separated the contrary motive of light and debilitating darkness and thereby paved the way for a new development that leads into the Modern Period. The doctrine about the One Being in the Latin writings of the Meister already sounds completely different than the statements of classical Scholasticism. As Albert the Great and Thomas taught, God and his creatures have nothing in common; there is complete incommensurability between them. Difference and opposition are absolute. But Duns Scotus then declared (something Scotus Erigena in the early Middle Ages and several heretical sects in the thirteenth century itself dared to express as well): the concept of being is valid for God and the world, and this overcomes their opposition. This single predicate of existence is attributable to both of them in the same sense. Hence Duns also fights against the conviction of classical

47

Scholasticism, deeply rooted in the idea of emanation, that divine activity in making the world could occur only in a descending way because, after all, it is a universal rule that every effect must be less than its cause! Duns says, on the contrary, that this old axiom applies only for worldly objects; but God can create what is perfect. It is along these lines that the writings (developed systematically by the Scholastic Eckehart in academic format) taught—in contrast with everything that the chief Scholastics had said about the merely participated being [*esse participatum*] of creatures—that the existence God imparts to objects in creation is absolutely none other than that which he himself is. God and being are identical. Therefore, whatever God creates, he creates *within himself*; it is his own Being that extends itself into objects. Being and existence [*ens und esse*], existing object and existence of God are not separated from one another by opposition; on the contrary, "nothing is so one and undivided as God and everything created." Created beings stand in the same relationship to God "as the formed (*constitutum*) to the principle from which and through which and in which it has been made (constituted)."

The German mystic's sermons and writings then developed the idea further and gave it graphic significance. His fundamental experience (like that of all mysticism) is ultimate unity and identity, the surrender of all separation. In the "soul's depths" [*Im "Seelengrund"*] it feels united with God; nothing more remains of separation, of the "alien and distant" of the world in space and time. Here is the death not only of all dissimilarity but even of all similarity, because similarity is not precisely identity but only harmony between things otherwise dissimilar. In fact, then, all being must ultimately mean undifferentiatedness or divine unity absolutely removed from any distinction whatsoever. This is the One of Plotinus; but clearer than in Plotinus, who in so many respects remained attached to the Orient and its flight into nothingness, is its expression by Eckehart: that this single Godhead is not only removed from all opposition but that all division in the Godhead is "sublated" [*"aufgehoben"*], preserved, and made one in the Godhead's power and undivided fullness. Distress and unrest of our many-faceted existence do not drive this mystic in flight from the many into a bottomless abyss, the quiet desert of the Godhead; on the contrary, his longing and his love for everything that exists remains unmitigated so long as multiplicity and opposition reign. "Where two things exist, there is deficiency. Why? Because one is not the other; the Not that makes the difference is bitterness." Thus "not" must perish, but not fullness and abundance in all its variety. The world of broad, vast space is abandoned for the sake of what is "constriction" [*"Enge"*] in it and confining seclusion; in the unity of God and its "innermost inwardness" [*"innersten Inwendigkeit"*] there is expanse

I. God and World

without expanse; it is "broader than breadth, a shadow of breadth beyond comprehension" ["unbegriffener Weite ein Umbering"]. The eternal Now of this unity likewise comprises the "fullness of time," an everlasting greening and flowering, where nothing ever becomes "tired and old," or ever becomes the past. "Take away the 'not' from all creatures, and all creatures become one." "In God there is no 'not'"; in him "all things are in all and all are one." The One is thus not abstract emptiness of nothing but precisely concrete fullness that exists in annihilation of all differences. God is not the opposite of the world but is rather the unity of its opposites; in him are all creatures and especially all objects, without separation. The "contradictions, attractive and hostile [leit], white and black" penetrate each other and lose their alienation; they fuse together in one fullness of being. Prior to any multiplicity in being this all-inclusive unity exists as the absolute.

But how does the world come to be from all this? Is the manifold a fall [Abfall], a division that leads to darkness and that forces battle on light? Does the separated element, does the creature, by its very essence strive away from the divine stream that is and remains undividedness? So that now once again opposition arises that remains irremovable: God and a world alienated from God? Eckehart links up with ancient doctrines of the Trinity that had first overcome the idea of fall. There, in a certain sense, multiplicity already exists—prior to the world and to all creation; the community of persons who are nevertheless one. Here it is clear that such "outflow" from primordial unity is not alienation from God or descent to another level. On the contrary (and many thinkers from the time of the Church Fathers had referred to this): in this separation—which is really not a separation—the One Godhead first comes to itself, recognizes the Father in the Son, reveals itself! Thus for Eckehart this is now a process existing within God himself, an eternal flux that flows back into itself. "God's becoming is his essence." That the one Godhead, which in its quiet desert is still "unknown to itself," comes to itself, knows itself and "shines forth in revelation" in the Son who is the image of the Father—all this is the profound meaning of this eternal process of the Trinity, this triplicity that does not signify loss, fall, or diminishment, but rather that first completely brings the essence of God to fulfillment. Evolution and emanation coincide here, as it were: becoming, yet no ascent from a lower level; shining forth from the fullness of unity, yet no descent.

And now this is the great turning point in the framework of the concept of the world: that the idea passes over in uncurtailed form to "creatures" as well, to the world. Evolution and emanation now join hands with creation. At no point was Eckehart's struggle for concept and expression so difficult

49

or his controversy with tradition, from which he preferred not to feel separated, so arduous and consequently his expressions so equivocal, as here in this most fateful transformation. The pantheistic danger, that the difference between God and the world completely vanishes, threatened the new path. And yet it comes out clearly and sharply from time to time: "The Father expressed himself and all creatures in the Son"; "The Son and the Holy Spirit and all creatures are but one word in God." Consequently, the existence of objects is meaningful for the life of God, too, and is implied in his self-revelation: "The Father looks at himself, and there he sees all creatures represented." "God could never know himself without also knowing all creatures." The world and every creature belongs to the self-revelation of God himself! The dictum of Angelus Silesius (the last great offshoot of this mystical speculation in the seventeenth century) is well known: "I know that God would not live a moment without me; if I were annihilated, he must necessarily give up his spirit." The same meaning is clear in Eckehart: "God does not will to become without the soul"; God cannot understand himself without the soul"; and with complete bluntness: "I am the reason for God's existence." Without the creature or the world, which are one with the Son, the "*Godhead*" would be unexpressed [*ungewortet*] in the quiet desert; "God" would not be the revealed one, illuminating himself in himself!

Hence not only does God's power exist in all creatures—Plotinus taught that much, and even Aristotle did. But it exists entirely and exclusively in them, for their illuminating indeed creates and is existence. The image that Plotinus also uses—of the One who in his *superabundance* overflows—is exploited here fully for the first time with respect to its world-glorifying aspect, inasmuch as it says that the world that has issued forth from this superfluity must in fact be the same in its essence as its origin; it must consist of perfect matter. With that the creation loses its aspect of arbitrariness and becomes like a necessary happening and production—which introduces emanation. But descent or ascent are no longer involved; instead there is only unfolding of hidden fullness towards self-knowledge of the One. The unitary valuation inherent in the concept of creation is totally caught up here in a new concept of the world. As the eternally necessary image of the divine the world flows out of unity—for how could it participate in hostility to God or striving against God; whence could such a thing occur! The mirror that issues from the One Being cannot be a murky one. It also does not require a great deal of reflection to see the profound difficulties that such a concept of the world must result in. When that other element of the concept of creation, the moment of free activity, is eliminated, what then still distinguishes this inner connection of the existence of God and the world from pantheism? The world

50

I. God and World

as eternal as God is, souls as moments of the Godhead itself: where then do oppositions in life remain and where is sin? What permits men then simply to forget that they are not separate and independent beings, but rather images of God? How is it then that they are slaves to selfishness, and what makes them feel like the center of things? If this division, seen metaphysically, is merely their blindness or just an illusion, does this deception nevertheless produce real effects in life and influence moral-religious life profoundly? And is it also the source of every ultimate misery? Does God's glory really shine forth just as fully in everything evil as it does in the holiest being? And again, because the deity itself is beyond all opposites, is one no more allowed to call it "good" and goodness itself, than one is to call it white or black?

Eckehart struggled with all these questions, all the more so as the church called them to his attention in a roster of complaints against him. (In addition, flirtation with pantheism spelled misfortune for many of those who sought to carry forward this new affirmation of the universe. Those thinkers in the philosophy of the Modern Period who felt most urgently driven by religious knowledge of the greatness of the divine to proclaim God's world had to suffer grievously from accusations of religious zealots—like Eckehart as well as Bruno, Spinoza, and Fichte.) Indeed, it will never be possible to establish a sharply defined system for what is taught in these sermons and writings. There is no doubt that in order to avoid harsh consequences Eckehart tried to steer clear of the contradiction between a transfigured world and moral-religious tension in life (which he felt so strongly, as only a great religious figure does). There are plenty of declarations in which he set out to delimit that concept of the world, indeed even to recant it. But this great nature never achieved harmony, any more than did the age to which he belonged—a decadent Scholasticism that at the same time was turning toward something completely new.

Although the effect of this new doctrine has not been noted even in the history of the Scholastic systems and has received no praise from later spokesmen of the Modern Period, nevertheless—in many underground ways, as it were—it has been of extraordinary importance for the history of meta-physics. The energy of its idea has carried forward as far as Fichte, Schelling, and Hegel and the "developmental-historical pantheism" of their systems; it found its final crowning point here at the threshhold of the nineteenth century. To this point far too little has been done to bring to light the often deeply hidden systematic framework (which Dilthey saw with full clarity), that is, the unity of this great tradition (which is above all a tradition of German intellectual life).

In that age the world-exalting tendency fell on well-prepared ground. A new attitude toward nature had arisen and began to predominate in all countries. The new existential inwardness of Saint Francis of Assisi, who called the earth his mother and sister and the wind his brother, had not been lost again. Interest in external nature, which was newly awakened in the thirteenth century through the influx of Aristotelian–Arabic natural philosophy and science, began to lead to a revival of true scientific research, especially at the hands of the Franciscans. The saying about the "book of nature," in which the creator revealed himself no less than in the books of sacred Scripture, now attained renewed acceptance. Everyone spoke of it, from the time that [Saint] Paul had interwoven the ancient motif into the doctrines of Christianity; Fathers of the Church, such as Irenaeus or Tertullian and especially Gregory of Nyssa, emphasized it. And yet matters remained completely dominated by interest in the soul and God as well as by aversion from external nature—a condition that was characteristic of the entire Middle Ages up to the thirteenth century. Even though people frequently spoke of nature and the marvels of its beauty and constantly looked for proofs for God based on the wisdom of its organization; nevertheless knowledge of nature never became the expression and means of religious inquiry in the grand style. When one does find a program of this sort (as in Gregory of Nyssa, e.g.), what one demands primarily is an allegorical interpretation of phenomena with regard to their symbolic value for good and evil or the purposes and paths of moral experience rather than dispassionate dedication to natural processes themselves as events that mirror the creator in a special way. Augustine's ambivalence in this matter is peculiar. Just as he urgently stressed that the worldly does not separate us from God if we rightly understand and use it, that God reveals himself in this world, that the world in its orderly arrangement according to "measure, number, and weight" (as the old dictum has it) reflects his greatness and perfection; nevertheless it is also true, especially in Augustine's later life, that special research into external nature is idle curiosity and is not merely useless but actually harmful to the salvation of our souls. We should look for God within ourselves, not in physics. The Middle Ages then proceeded to follow this advice.

The Franciscan, Roger Bacon (who is so much more important for the developmental history of modern natural science than his namesake [Francis]

I. God and World

Bacon of Verulam, who later became so famous at the time of the "English Renaissance" and who knew how to assume airs so well), also spoke then of the book of nature in a new and fuller sense. The newly awakened dedication of researchers to the external world of experience, a dedication that did not probe that world merely for signs and symbols of totally different kinds of things but rather for its own proper structure and laws, expanded with Roger into a great scientific program. As its decisive thrust, it demanded a new method (which was still unknown to Chancellor Bacon three hundred years later!), the same method that Galileo later expressed in the formula that the book of nature is written in *mathematical* letters. The independence of the science of nature, in which people have always recognized a distinctive moment of the Modern Period, had its beginning here with Roger Bacon; and yet behind the impulse to know there was still always a religious quest. Roger's goal was reform of theology; new insight into the all-too-little-observed and -utilized book of nature was supposed to serve that purpose. And this was then the deepest motive force in all those after him who turned to natural research: to follow God's footprints in the external world and its order, to grasp the divine idea in hidden laws of events and in the abundance of forms, and to read the word of the eternal one in this great book. This was the desire not only of those mystical natural scientists of the transition period but just as truly of the great leaders of modern science up to Leibniz, Newton, and Kant. A religiously indifferent later age was all too ready to regard the countless and unmistakable assertions of those scientists merely as manners of speaking, accommodations to the fashion of the time, echoes of unenlightened transition and theological bondage. This later period has regarded Bacon of Verulam, whom the really substantive development of modern science bypassed, as more of a prophet and a pioneer than the thirteenth-century monk—from whom, however, as we know today, the threads of the new type of research always run further, through the Parisian Occamists to Leonardo and Galileo. One simply states the issue falsely when one makes freedom of science from theological tutelage the same thing as separation of interest in nature from religious impulses. On the contrary, it is exactly this that led natural science at that time to become an end in itself: conviction about the special revelatory value of everything in nature—in accordance with the idea of creation! What Aristotle had to say about the world could no longer suffice. One who sought for God's essence in the depths of the soul alone or in the scriptural books had no need of any special investigation and experience in external being; but the task at hand now was to open up a new source of revelation.

Eckehart himself, the mystic of souls, shunned such a novel twist in the way one searches for God although he, more than anyone else of his time,

53

discovered the speculative expression for the new significance of the world. On this point his teacher Dietrich von Freiberg (who also certainly had a significant influence on Eckehart in joining the concept of emanation with that of creation) anticipated him. But when Henry Suso, the poet among Eckehart's students, sang about how all creatures around him "that God ever created in heaven, on earth, and in all the elements . . . birds of the air, animals in the woods, fish in the water, leaves and grass on earth, and numberless sands of the sea, together with all the tiny dust particles that appear in the brightness of the sun, and all the little droplets of water that ever fell or continually fall from the dew or snow or rain . . ."—how all these things, the immense multitude of all creatures, each strikes up its stringed music and sounds forth praise of God, every one of them in its own way . . . : then one senses in advance how this mysticism of the soul also will transmit its feeling to all life in nature and to every creature, down to the very dust of matter, into the most minute and most insignificant particle. One could almost believe that he foresees how Paracelsus and the whole rich wave of natural philosophy of the sixteenth century gushes out from the stream of mysticism that sprang up in Eckehart. And that poetry already contains a complete precedent for Leibniz's view of nature and teaching about the monads—where in fact every smallest particle of the minute and all creatures down to infinitely tiny elements in matter really mirror the richness of God and manifest that richness from themselves!

It is from religious sources that the new love of nature and zeal for investigation derive that lead us to the natural philosophy of the transition period and toward the natural science of the Modern Period. Even the esthetic enthusiasm over nature in the Renaissance, which people so like to place at the focal point of the question about the origin of modern science and the modern world picture, is only a special phase in that great development. Nowhere is this easier to trace than in the case of Kepler, in whom new mathematical knowledge of nature grew with palpable clarity out of mystic-esthetic natural philosophy of the German tradition.

The dictum about the book of nature continued to be varied in new ways, from Roger Bacon on to Raymond Sebond's natural theology (which analyzes the idea so thoroughly), then to Campanella, and to Galileo—whose famous letter to the Grand Duchess-Mother Christine knew how to use precisely this symbol to defend his own freedom of inquiry so marvelously against ecclesiastical-theological narrowness! And further also by those German natural philosophers from Agrippa [of Nettesheim] and Paracelsus on to the younger van Helmont: what they all find lacking among the God-seekers and God-experts of the previous age is that they did not know much about God's revelation in works of nature; and this is something for which

I. God and World

not even the holiest books could compensate. Also well known is the beautiful passage from the *Table Talks* of Luther (who was otherwise more hostile and unsympathetic to worldly science than any scholastic): "We are now at the dawn of future life, for we are beginning once again to acquire the knowledge of creatures that we have lost . . . now we see creation properly, better than we did under the papacy, for example. With God's grace we are beginning to recognize his marvelous works and miracles even in little flowers . . . in his creatures we recognize the power of his word, how mighty it is." Suso's voice echoes in such words.

The nominalism of the fourteenth century assumes an odd double posture in this development. Deep skepticism regarding the sufficiency of all worldly knowledge is a basic feature of William of Occam's makeup—hence so much the more dazzlingly does the glory of faith and of supernatural grace and revelation radiate. Luther could invoke nominalism to strengthen his hostility toward the "beast of reason." And yet, on the other hand, the connection of modern science with the nominalistic–empiricist strain of the waning Middle Ages has been rightly emphasized. It was here that the ancient-Scholastic schema, the system of "substantial forms," was broken for the first time and the claim to reality of rigidly assumed concepts was denied in favor of the immediate symbolic value of sense experience. Thus in the battle cry of experience against outmoded conceptual science leaders of modern science always felt themselves akin to the nominalists. And, indeed, it was the circle of William of Occam's students that laid the foundation for what essentially determined the image of nature in the modern period from Galileo and Descartes on.

The philosopher who really carried forward Meister Eckehart's speculative concept of the world and took up anew the question of the essential and axiological connection between God and the world was Nicholas of Cusa. Both fundamental pillars of his doctrine grow with new systematic definition out of those mystical intuitions: the *coincidentia oppositorum* [coincidence of opposites] in God, and the world as *explicatio Dei* [unfolding of God].

Unity of opposites, their total coincidence in the primordial One, was in itself certainly not a new philosophical theme. Fundamental experience in mysticism of every age pushes in that direction. Plotinus above all seized on the theme in a major way, and it goes forth from him to such Neoplatonically educated Church Fathers as Synesius and especially Pseudo-Dionysius, to Augustine as well, and on into the Middle Ages where, before all others, the great Scotus Erigena modeled his doctrine about God on it. Eckehart and Nicholas stand in this tradition. But with Nicholas a new phase in the history of the problem begins.

In the life of man, as Eckehart sees it, two experiences occupy parallel positions alongside one another with absolutely no mediation between them; there is no bridge from one to the other. These are daily experience of the reality in which we stand and work, with its variety, multiplicity, and opposition, and the so rare, always ephemeral illumination of the God-seeker, in which he enters into a unity where there is no place whatsoever for opposition. All the capacities of the soul, its "powers," are incapable of carrying it beyond this apparent division; they remain essentially relegated to inadequacy. Not only the lower powers, the sensual ones, whose activity virtually consists in dissipating us totally among a scattering of things; no, even the higher and the highest powers remain stuck in contrariety. For even purest unifying reason nevertheless remains stuck in duality, in the contrast between knower and known; and even noblest will or highest love—regardless of how inwardly one feels its touch or how ardently one longs for union—remain in this irremovable tension between I and thou, man and God, subject and being. The soul's "powers" never take it into the truly One. It is not until a man puts all this away from himself, not only desire, perception, and sensuality, but even all spiritual willing, loving, and knowing; not until he contracts himself into the innermost foundation of his soul and is in a state in which he is utterly separated from the world and dead to his own powers; not until he allows the "little spark" to kindle and to consume his ego: not until then does mystical union with God occur and he attains unity without opposition: he and God are then one and undivided. Whatever his powers grasped in mulitiple form and whatever he had to surrender and despise, is suddenly all back again in fullness of unity: fused together, totally and utterly united with this "departed" soul who is consumed in the Godhead. To lose the world in order to gain it: it is impossible to contrast more glaringly the two paths indicated here, whose unrecognized unity one at the same time assumes, than Eckehart did.

A difficult unsolved issue opens up here, in life as well as in thought. Even with respect to what is noblest and deepest, man is chained to multiplicity; he must turn away from it no less than from everything sensual and divisive if he wants to come to unity. Thus it seems that a death sentence is levied on thinking as well: if all science essentially lays hold only of the apparent/divided (just as sense perception and daily experience do in the last analysis) and if even philosophy, or rational knowledge based on ultimate causes, remains stuck in duality and can never sense anything of true unity, then all investigation is really worthless. Concept and term, justification and proof, are empty and must remain silent and make room for mystical ecstasy alone.

This is where Nicholas of Cusa, the philosopher among the successors of Eckehart, builds a bridge with his doctrine of *docta ignorantia* or learned

I. God and World

ignorance. Understanding (*ratio*) at any rate—insofar as it combines experienced realities, compares them, conceptualizes them, and evaluates the patchwork of objects [*die Dinge durcheinander mißt*]—always stays tied to what is given by the senses and is consequently inextricably entangled in multiplicity and opposition. In itself the science of intelligence is thus at any rate not knowledge of true being, which is one; it is therefore ignorance. But this in no way means that all knowledge is ultimately worthless and to be given up or that a person must "lose" the world by turning his back on it and closing his senses and his mind, despising their vision and quest. For between this mind and the ineffability of union with God a higher power of the spirit is at work that *mediates* between them and brings it about that even knowledge of the manifold has meaning and value for every last quest for one being, for God! Reason (for Nicholas: *intellectus*) knows that specialized knowledge is ignorance. To be sure, reason itself never possesses totality; and in that Eckehart correctly recognized that "greatest identity"—which does not differ from anything, namely, absolute identity—also transcends every concept. Nevertheless reason rises above its knowledge of the many through knowledge of its ignorance and sets its sights on what exists without plurality! Now, this is not just an isolated warning, so to speak, not to take the mind and its utterances as the ultimate, or just a solitary reference to mystical union with God, which is otherwise ineffable; on the contrary, it is on the basis of all the contents of specialized knowledge that rational necessities—demonstrable with full conceptual rigor in and about those contents—lead us beyond plurality to unity, from opposites to their convergence or coincidence. Straight line and crooked line come together as one if a person merely thinks of the radius of that one as infinitely large. It is the same with rest and movement and with all opposites that permeate reality. It is only in the finite that members exclude each other; in perfect infinity everything falls together into one. And all investigation necessarily strives toward the infinite, for after all it always relates the unknown to the known, compares what is sought for with what is given and what is questionable with what is certain; and in this process the mind never attains simply absolute or perfect harmonization, but rather the search goes on forever. Now, even though reason for its part cannot grasp the absolute or pure total truth conceptually, nevertheless it knows that it cannot and therefore knows also that all conditioned knowledge is inadequate in principle and is accordingly really ignorance. Reason can think the unconditioned and can draw the consequences that ensue if one conceptualizes the finite into what is absolutely infinite.

Thus a continual path and connection ascends from the senses through science of mind and insight of reason up to the frontier of the incomprehensible-One. Human knowledge sketches its lines on the basis of all the indi-

57

vidual contents of reality, all its divisions and oppositions (which, accordingly, the God-seeker now no longer skips over!); these lines all converge and make it clear how they link up at a single point beyond all visiblility—in the coincidence of opposites, concrete totally filled unity of the infinite where there is no opposition left to create separation or hostility. Through its knowledge of ignorance and its insight into the law of infinity, reason guides all our knowledge, which in itself must always remain finite and fragmented, and yet is on the path to the absolute One, on the way to God. The entire book of nature remains mute only for one who remains fixed at the finite level of letters and propositions. But for one who expands his thoughts and draws lines based on experience out into the infinite, God speaks to him from every particular being in reality and from all creation. Thus in the final analysis every effort of science and philosophy truly serves the highest goal. Knowledge of nature is not making oneself dependent on the fragmentary that only leads one away from the true goal of the soul; speculation is always more than moving about within the purely finite and fragmented! The path to God lies in all knowledge of the world (so long as it is properly guided by reason and rightly understood).

In this new positive orientation the theme of the coincidence of opposites then wends its way through the history of modern metaphysics; affirmation of contrariety and preoccupation with it in life and research did not die out again. The view of nature and the natural philosophy of the following centuries live on in this attitude and under its banner struggle against dualistic tendencies. The Renaissance (like Plotinus and Augustine earlier) readily used the image of harmony: beauty is the unity of things different, accord among opposites. The eternally rich book of nature—even in its contradictions, in fact precisely in them—afforded a glimpse of the meaning of the oneness of the creator. Everyone varied the motif—Humanists as well as theosophists, Italians and Germans, from Pico della Mirandola and Reuchlin on. And not only Giordano Bruno's hymn to nature, which clothed Nicholas's concept most magnificently in the garb of esthetic enthusiasm, but in equal measure Kepler's world picture, were defined by it. Kepler himself emphasized that his discovery of the elliptical form of planetary paths (in place of the old circles) sprang for him from this conviction: that the great harmony of the astral world attained the richness of its unison not in what is uniform-identical but rather in what is manifold-opposite. Then with renewed energy thought asserted itself once again in opposition to the division that Luther's religious experience of contrariety threatened to introduce into the world picture. Heirs of the old mysticism here too turned contrariety into something positive and universally affirmative. Paracelsus stressed the point anew that there must be differentiation precisely so that we might have a notion of God;

that no one can know good who has not also experienced evil; and that in fact all the different objects in the world that split off from each other as opposites sound together in a single great harmony and manifest their full meaning in their mutual relationships and interpenetration. And so German mystics of nature as late as the younger van Helmont demanded the same thing that Hegel was to teach so impressively later on: not to be afraid of the "pain of separation" and not to skip over work on what is negative, because the path to concretely filled unity of the absolute, as the unity of opposites, is revealed only by contradiction in reality. All of them teach that we must probe deeply into this world, including all that is evil and otherwise contra- dictory in it, to arrive at the true richness of divine unity. The profoundest struggle with the theme of dualistic tendency occurs in Jacob Böhme who, though he was deeply moved by Luther's fear of sin and belief in the devil, nevertheless tried to win the victory for Eckehart's notion of the irreplaceable importance of the world for God's self-knowledge; the primitive contradic- tion between good and evil too, and even the preponderance of evil in the world, was in his view necessary for the self-revelation of God that creation serves.

At this point we are not going to pursue the question any further as to how all this reverberates later on in Leibniz's theodicy and in general in the evolution of the theodicy question about the axiological significance even of wickedness and evil in God's world [*Gotteswelt*] in the eighteenth century. And even the great new phase in the history of the coincidence-theme—a phase that Johann Georg Hamann's aphoristic intuitions introduced and that culminated in Hegel's doctrine of the "concrete universal"—is something we will barely touch on in passing. It is well known how Schelling looked for the solution to the riddle by linking up with Böhme; how divided being could issue from indifference of opposites; how his entire later philosophy struggled with the concept of creation in our sense, now transferring the origin of negation and of opposition entirely back into the absolute itself, into God's "primordial being" [*"Ungrund"*]. But nobody worked out all of this so profoundly in the form of conceptual speculation as Hegel did, who made "contradiction" the basic principle of the world and of all life and whose dialectic (fully in the spirit of Nicholas of Cusa's doctrine about how reason points to the coincidence) tried to demonstrate that it is precisely in opposites that every finite being strives to transcend itself and inevitably leads to the infinite-One. "To show the finiteness in everything finite and to de- mand its completion through reason": Is this challenge of Hegelian dialectic not laid down in the same spirit that once motivated Nicholas of Cusa? Each one of the "infinitely numerous drops" of reality (Does this not sound like Suso and Leibniz?) leads reason by necessity to the absolute. Therefore anyone who wishes to approach God must live and act in this world of opposites, and come to recognize and understand it in its fragmented state; worldly wisdom in search of God must always press toward the conclusion that "difference is not left aside but proceeds eternally from substance, without becoming petrified in dualism."

Nicholas of Cusa carries forward his doctrine of the *coincidentia oppositorum* and of the paths of reason toward it in his concept of the world as *explicatio Dei*. Whatever else might give rise to conceiving of the world in opposition to God, there is the fact that precisely within the world itself there are oppositions at work: good and evil, light and dark, elements of being and non-being. But if the superabundance of God comprises all oppositions within it, and if, as Nicholas explains, God as the greatest is at the same time the smallest, both center and periphery, past and future, indeed even coincidence of being and non-being, of everything and nothing, light and darkness—then one must no longer understand the world in which opposites split off from one another as foreign to God; on the contrary, one can understand it as a resolution of what God in his abundance already contains within himself. One absolutely cannot any longer understand the world with its oppositions as something opposite to God, who is the unity of all opposites. Thus, as Nicholas sees it, the world is unfolding and explicating what God contains "complicitly" in his primoridal unity. In God the many exists, but without multiplicity; in him there is opposition, but as identity. *Deus ergo est omnia complicans in hoc quod omnia in eo, est omnia* **explicans** *in hoc quia ipse in omnibus.* [Therefore God implicates all things because all things exist in him, and explicates all things because he exists in all things.] Just as God is unity of origin for the many, so does he also live in each individual thing in the world; what exists only as unity in the fullness of God, that is, what is "unfolded as creature-world," spreads itself out in space and time, differentness and opposition. In this sense the world is the image, the full revelation of God.

At this point the world-affirming, dualism-negating moment of the doctrine of creation comes fully to light. When God fashions the world, he does not function as "form" that stands opposite matter that is to be informed, but rather as "cause and ground." God is the "*unique* ground" of the uni-

I. God and World

verse. If it is right to call creatures images of God, Nicholas insists never-theless that in using this metaphor we must remember that in this case we are not dealing (as in ordinary mirroring) with an external, independent entity in which an image is first formed and in which it is captured; on the contrary, the creature's existence is nothing else than mirroring, it is manifold reflec-tion of the One. There is no medium present in which the likeness hovers, no darkness from which it emerges. The world is nothing other than the visible manifestation of God, a multiplication, as it were, of the One Being, just as indeed in Paul's epistle to the Romans God is called the invisibility of what is visible. Lessing's expression that "God thought of his perfection as divided up, that is, he created beings" echoes distinctly here; the path also leads from Nicholas through Leibniz directly to him.

Hence nothing exists in the world that is not an expression of God. Composite and simple, matter and form, perishable and indestructible—all of it belongs in equal measure to the unfolding of God. What we consider imperfection or contradictory-negative in all this can have no cause outside of God; we cannot impute it to resistance and darkness of matter, for it is the mere consequence of finiteness as the manner of the unfolding! The world "is like a completed work of art that depends totally on the artist's idea and has no other existence than that of dependence on the one from whom it derives its being and through whose influence it is preserved." This artwork-creation is in fact not the deed of a world master builder who depends on matter, but of the creator of the world. Hence Nicholas does not shy away from this bold formulation: The world is "like a finite infinity or a created God (*deus creatus*)."

The upshot of this is ultimate exaltation of the world. This universe is the best of all possible worlds. It is common knowledge how Leibniz made this expression of highest affirmation of reality (an expression at which Chris-tian metaphysics from Augustine to Thomas had also aimed) the fundamental principle of his system and of the doctrine of creation contained in it. The "sufficient reason" for the fact that all the infinite possibilities for forming a world converged precisely into our own world can only be the "reason for the best," which aims at the maximum of reality and perfection. Leibniz sometimes describes creation in a manner that suggests an image of personal, deliberate activity, sometimes as more like emanation (fulguration, efflu-ence), or as striving of countless essences for existence. But what always remains the same in his doctrine and makes up its core is this: that our world is constituted precisely by those ideas and essences that produce the greatest universal perfection that can coexist simultaneously (compossibility), an ul-timate harmony. This basic principle of optimism, that played such a great role from Leibniz (and Shaftesbury) on in the metaphysics and worldview of the eighteenth century is the product of that doctrine of the unfolding of God. The bridge between Nicholas and Leibniz consisted of philosophers of the Renaissance, Ficino's doctrine of creation, and especially Bruno, and at the same time German philosophy of nature, most effectively indeed Valentin Weigel's theory of universal perfection of reality. It became perfectly clear as early as [Cusa], the German cardinal of the fifteenth century—and not for the first time with Leibniz—how such talk about the best of *all possible* worlds differed from ideas like Plato's idea that sounded like the same thing. For Plato this world is the best possible one under the conditions of spatial matter [*Raummaterie*], with its indeterminacy that will never be totally overcome, its unstable mix of more and less, and its contingent-mechanistic component! This formulation of the idea is not far removed from world-denial and even from pessimism. But Nicholas's (and Leibniz's) meaning is this: the world as the unfolding of God cannot be precisely divine unity itself— that which is not unfolded; and only to that extent is there limitation in the words "all possible"! "As if the creator had said: Let it come to be! and since God, who is eternity itself, could not come to be, the thing that did come to be is whatever could be most like God." The world cleaves to "the source and ground through which it is what is with all possible closeness and likeness"; it is "the greatest possible imitation of the absolute."

Hence if one speaks here, too, of inadequacies, imperfections, and evils in the world of "contingency," or of perishability and decline, darkness and non-being—it is nevertheless always the case that even all this derives from one God as the expression and unfolding of his essence. Non-being, which every created being carries within itself (otherness, separation, perishability), exists together with being, precisely in coincidence! Even the world as a whole is a unity, not a coincidence, to be sure, but a harmony of opposites. It is in this that the meaning of its unfolding is fulfilled. "All beings cry out with one voice and proclaim the One and the Same, and this unanimous cry . . . is the fuller and richer presentation of the One and the Same." "Inasmuch as the One manifests itself in the greatest opposition of forces, a battle of forces . . . ensues and from it new generation and destruction." The world is not the same thing as God; and insofar as it is supposed to be an unfolding, it must assume separation, destruction, opposition, and everything else that we experience as imperfection! In this sense it always takes second place to God; "the universe never attains the highest point of the absolutely greatest." Nature cannot really unite opposites. To this extent the world is only the best of all possible worlds, but not absolutely the best thing. But this limitation is necessary, and not because some alien fate or inert matter unavoidably and blindly forces it; on the contrary, it is meaningfully necessary: imposed by the great task it fulfills, that of revealing the richness of God. "Thus the

I. God and World

universe has a reasonable and necessary cause for its concreteness'' (i.e., its separation into multiplicity and contrariety). ''All jealousy is far removed from the one who is the highest good and whose activity cannot be imperfect; but because he is the highest good, his work will also approximate as nearly as possible to the greatest.'' Every creature is therefore created in such a way ''that it exists in the best possible way''; hence, despite all differences in worth among existing things, ''every creature as such is perfect.'' There is, to be sure, a hierarchy even in this thoroughly perfect world, but what is greater or lesser in degree is not a gradual ascent from matter alien to God and indeterminacy with respect to pure form; instead, each level is necessary in its own place to the general meaning of the unfolding, hence is also perfect in itself. It is impossible for each thing to be the whole, otherwise it would be God himself. If God's fullness is to be extended forth, everything cannot be one and the same thing; ''that is why God created everything on varying levels.'' It is true here too that God ''communicates his being without partiality or jealousy,'' thus ''every created being reposes in its own perfection that it has generously received from divine being and does not desire to be another creature, as though that would make it somehow more perfect.'' No level could be what it is and fulfill its purpose in the great evolutionary ordering without the other levels; all things support each other reciprocally. Thus, says Nicholas, it was not as though intelligence came to exist first, then souls, and only then nature (as in a gradual descent), but there issued forth all at once from God everything without which a universe—indeed a perfect universe—could not exist. Whether we go down or up the infinite hierarchical ladder of all objects, we shall arrive in one way or another at the source of all things. God unfolds himself in all levels, differences, and oppositions. The greatest as well as the smallest, the noblest as well as the insignificant, spirit as well as matter, mirror him in whom oppositions are united.

A complete revolution in the *concept of matter* is connected with this resolution of the opposites, insofar as they tend to ''fossilize into dualism'' (as Hegel put it). Creation out of nothing recognizes no previously existing and continually resisting matter which would have to be set in motion, as it were, from the outside and would have to receive the divine-spiritual element from above. Nor does it recognize, in the case of divine illumination, an ultimate boundary of light where reality would essentially fall off into darkness. On the contrary, matter and space, just as truly as the form-animated and living element, issue from the perfect world-plan and the hand of the creator. And this means that all the pejorative value-predicates that have dogged matter since Antiquity must now give way! In principle, the Christian doctrine of the resurrection of the body should also have pointed that way, for it assumes that the corporeal is also capable of glorification and is to be incorporated into the highest kingdom! Accordingly, sin cannot be situated in material nature, the body, or in material forces themselves; it too comes to be defined in terms of its own spiritual attitude—as turning away from God on the part of freely created will. The body itself is not evil nor is the brute animal called bad either, as Augustine in particular (after Origen and Methodius) pointed out; in the natural order of things they are necessary and good. As long as the sensual obeys the spirit, as the lower obeys the higher, it has its own value in its place. What introduces the danger of "the flesh" into the world, however—or of desire as a vice or sensuality as seducer and enemy of the spirit—is man's pride, his arrogance against God. The soul prefers its own ego to love of God, and this primordial sinful act is an act of will, spiritual in nature, not a natural and world-necessary "fall" of ["*Abfall*"] emanated being from its origin.

Thus all the Church Fathers—Theophilus of Antioch and Irenaeus as well as Tertullian, Origen as well as Augustine—try to incorporate the existence and special function of matter completely into the meaning of creation. This step was most difficult for the Greeks among them, for they were the ones most solidly rooted in ancient tradition. Origen stubbornly resisted the resurrection of the body. It was only after bitter struggle against Plato and the Platonists around him that Methodius was able to repel the view that the soul, originally preexisting immaterially, entered through fall and descent into the body as into its prison, from which body the soul must accordingly strive to free itself, as well as to repel the view that held that sin and evil made their appearance with the body as such.

Nevertheless, throughout the entire Middle Ages matter carried the negative stigma of something insufficient and flawed stamped upon it, which the Aristotelian concept of its non-being in particular (as mere unspecified potentiality to become anything actual) gave to it. Augustine, to be sure, attached great importance to the idea that something capable of receiving form is also necessary in making God's world, and that possibility is also a necessary prerequisite for a world that, according to the meaning of creation, is supposed to come into being, that is, after all to proceed from possibility to actuality; in other words, that matter, too, is a significant good. And yet the stigma remained. For Thomas Aquinas, completely in the spirit of Aristotle, matter always remains merely the principle of suffering and of deprivation, of mere toleration of form, something incapable of existence on its own account.

But the turning point is proclaimed as early as Thomas's great teacher Albert. The influence of Arab naturalism on the philosophy of the period contributed also, as in the new direction of attention to external nature. But even on this issue it was not so much a question of taking over Arab ideas as it was of a ready willingness to take up whatever could be useful to the specific, gradually maturing tendency to elevate the concept of the world and of matter. Everyone up to Bruno appealed to Averroës's doctrine that forms already exist in matter and had only to be drawn out of it; but it was no naturalistic tendency that led Christian thinkers in that direction! Thus Albert the Great taught, in opposition to Aristotle, that matter was at any rate the "beginning" of forms and carries within it the initial phase of becoming, so that form represents only the amplification or the complement of what was already on hand at the start. He connects this directly with the doctrine of creation: God, who needs no previously existing matter in creating the world, also created the lower, out of which the higher comes to be; hence he is not only present to the soul but is also in every material object.

In the "period of decadence," Henry of Ghent in particular (and Duns Scotus, arguing against Thomas, follows him) tried to remove from matter the stigma of being merely possible and nonexistent-in-its-own-right. For him matter is an actually existing substratum for forming, a *tamquam per se creabile* [something creatable in its own right, as it were]; the creator could have produced it even separated from all form. Matter does not achieve existence through its mixture with form; on the contrary, it has its "first being" directly from its participating in God as something made by him. Thus the mind of the creator includes matter's own specific idea. Capacity to receive forms is matter's "second being," and in the formative process itself still a third thing sprouts up in matter—Aristotle's reality. Roger Bacon and natural scientists following him remove the other imperfection from matter as well: its inertia and passivity. Forms are not impressed on matter externally, they now taught, but activity already exists in matter itself; external influences merely spur it on to transform itself by its own inner powers and to strive upward toward the forms. This transformation then attains clear expression in Nicholas of Cusa's concept of the world. For him, too, following Aristotle, the distinctive note of matter was its moment of potentiality for being. But—as he expressly argues against "the ancients" and their "perverse thinking," their "ignorance" in this area—one must not understand possibility as the imperfect, flawed, and purely passive. If there is an absolute possibility, this is God himself, from whom after all everything real derives and attains its existence. The ground of all matter and of all actuality based on it exists in God; he is both possibility and existence for everything. In him who is potency-existence ["*Possest*"], possibility-as-capacity and actuality-of-form-as-being coincide. Here God is no longer merely form as in Aristotelian dualism, excluding matter and having nothing to do with it! As absolute power [*Können*], possibility is in fact the fundamental moment in God's being, one designated through God the Father; from him, therefore, derives the "matter" in reality. Unlike a human artist, God does not require preexisting material; matter and form, which exist separately in the finite world, coincide in God. Body and soul likewise, "possibility" and "life-giving principle"—even if they separate from one another totally in death, body sinking back into its center and soul rising to the periphery—coincide in the infinite, like triangle and circle.

The Renaissance proceeds further in this direction. Telesio, who also expressly appeals to production of matter from the hand of the creator, sees something positive and powerful in the moment of inertia itself: it is the *conatus* toward self-preservation. Indeed, it explains how bodies influence each other, how they touch and limit each other in space. Therefore, no matter exists without its own power! It is its own inner powers, not its being attracted by form, that initially set it in motion. Hence cooperation of God (as the form of forms) in nature is no longer necessary; instead, once he has created matter, he leaves it to its own *conatus* toward self-preservation in which the parts fighting for their existence come together as structures of the corporeal world. In like manner, Campanella, coming from Nicholas's direction of thought, defended the aspect of power in matter as the capacity for existence or the ability to be and to function. And ever more distinctly people were now attempting to conceive of these forces as purely physical instead of as spiritual and immaterial ones dragged in from the outside. A causal picture of nature of a purely immanent-material kind began to shake itself loose from ancient dualistic teleology.

In line with this it was Giordano Bruno who developed the theme most extensively. Like Nicholas he traced matter as possibility back to power or capacity in God. But he goes further than Nicholas. For him matter and form do not coincide only in God; they are one in origin even in the universe. Matter is never dead and simply inert, for in it there also always exists a positive disposition toward form. Matter and form designate merely different facets of the same unitary being and becoming; neither of them has absolute priority over the other. Matter cannot be the *prope nihil* [nearly nothing] that it was for the ancients! For Bruno it is not only ultimately derived from God but is also accordingly itself essentially Godlike; he does not shrink from

66

appealing to pantheists like David of Dinant, against whose identification of matter and deity Albert and Thomas had fought so hard. Matter is divine power, and therefore source of all becoming, of inexhaustible generative power and all richness of nature.

There is no need to make special reference to how this transformation in the concept of matter must have favored the emergence of a new view of, and research into, nature. In place of the old doctrine of "substantial forms" (which, based on Aristotelian physics, established the medieval concept of nature and severely hampered all impulses toward new initiatives in research), the new view strove to test nature on the basis of forces and laws actually immanent in it and demonstrable through experiment. The mechanical view of nature in the modern period did not, like its forerunner in ancient atomism, arise on the basis of and with the thrust of materialistic philosophy! It did lead to materialism in many ways, to be sure, especially in the case of Hobbes and in eighteenth-century France and nineteenth-century Germany. But the great leaders of modern science have always been averse to materialism. They did not regard independence of matter as separation from a divine ground for the world but only as elimination of dualism in the concept of nature, hence aversion from any activity in nature that does not stem from self-contained and self-sufficient being of the created world. Forces [*Kräfte*] do not come from the outside and do not express longing for world-transcending highest form, nor do they stand as a system of substantial forms in opposition to matter; instead their efficacy and therefore the entire order of nature derive from matter itself.

Thus the mechanistic concept of nature held by Galileo and Descartes came about. Galileo's discoveries broke through the ban imposed on research by the principle of substantial forms. Now science searched not for immaterial forms—grounds of explanation for both corporeal bodies and the spiritual, impressed from above, as it were, into the being of nature—but for observable forces and laws of matter itself; not for formal principles of qualitative value and ideality, but for structural laws of the spatiotemporal and quantitative. The book of nature is written in mathematical letters, and it is precisely mechanism's independence and the homogeneous uniformity of this mathematical-material order that reveal the unique power of God, from

67

which after all matter derives as well as its form, which is mathematical law. Whereas spatial matter was for Plato the realm of the merely mechanical, hence of the merely contingent in opposition to the rational necessity of forms, here it is precisely mechanical occurrence that becomes the expression for inner lawfulness.

Descartes then goes on to expand this into an entire world picture. He separates matter and the entire being of external nature from everything spiritual-immaterial. The world organizes itself in space all the way up to organisms on the basis of its own laws. In fact, now—just to pursue the tendency in its pure form—everything relating to soul is totally separated from the spatial-material. It is clear, however, that this famous "dualism" of Descartes is not dualism in the sense of our opposites problem and that it expresses no axiological separation. Both of these things proceed alongside one another from divine substance: both *res cogitantes* [thinking things] and *res extensae* [extended things]. In combination the two make up the entire world of nature and man, not in a relationship of dominance like that of substantial forms over potentiality in matter, but rather in complete coordination, which expresses itself above all in the fact that both of them are equally called substances and that therefore matter is no more in need of soul or the material is no more in need of the immaterial for existence, movement, and formation than, conversely, the soul needs the corporeal. The ever more obviously emerging tendency of the preceding centuries to conceive of matter as an independent entity, with its own existence and its own powers, and to distinguish it conceptually as spatial-corporeal from the soul-like–immaterial (a tendency that crossed paths in a peculiar way with the fantastic need for universal animation and natural magic) came to full fruition in Descartes. If the transition to the theme of creation began once upon a time among the Greeks with Anaxagoras's doctrine of the nous, which, given simultaneously with matter, introduced movement and order into it, and if, with that, doctrines about a self-moving, inwardly animated matter were then dissolved by a new world concept, the reverse occurs now in the Modern Period—that is, it is the concept of creation, in its new sense of *creatio ex nihilo*, that returns to matter its autonomy and specific power! But this does not mean that we have therefore surrendered the rational meaning, the "intelligible" (i.e., cognizable in concepts alone) order of the world in favor of blind-fortuitous occurrence. For matter itself—with its forces and mathematically knowable laws and effects that lead to building up the entire external world—has after all issued forth from the mind of the creator! Ordering-activating nous does not lie alongside matter now nor above it, encroaching on it, forcing it to this or attracting it to that which is supposed to happen; on the contrary, matter itself with its own ordering forces is its own special, self-contained, and

I. God and World

complete expression of the nous of the creator, *explicatio Dei* [unfolding of God], creation according to eternal (mathematical) ideas without any opposing givenness.

Thus Descartes then also conceives the thought of world-evolution in accordance with its own purely mechanical laws. It is well known that the young Kant, in his *Universal Natural History and Theory of the Heavens*, was the first to make a scientific theory of permanent importance out of it (the later so-called Kant–Laplace hypothesis about the origin of the world). And now it is particularly fascinating to see in Kant's works how his conviction of the feasibility of such a mechanical theory of evolution grew out of metaphysical discussion of the theme of creation, in controversy with Newton, who did not completely grasp its consequences. Augustine and Albert the Great had stressed the fact that the ordered world, as God's image and creation, tolerates no miracles of a sort that contradict the order of nature. Action of God against the nature that he himself has implanted in objects would mean a self-contradictory initiative. In a bold development of this thought Kant now says: It would be to mistake the essence of creation if we were to think it necessary to assume any sort of supermaterial interventions in order to explain the great system of the material cosmos. Newton, the great systematizer of the universe, who was the first to trace the entire world process back to a single material fundamental system—the mechanical law of attraction—nevertheless erred against his own tendency insofar as he thought it necessary to explain the magnificent order of the structure of the heavens through immediate intervention by God, hence no longer through the operation of material natural forces. The same Newton, therefore, who stood so strongly in the tradition of the new motif of creation that he called space (the same space that Plato and others regarded as something essentially far removed from God and precisely as merely material-mechanical) the sensorium of God, believed nevertheless that the ordering of stars in space came about in extraordinary fashion, through external intervention and encroachment by a teleological principle of operation. Thus even here, in their highest triumph since Galileo and Descartes, mechanical principles and matter still preserved something of their ancient depreciation—it seems that alone by themselves they were unable to point the way to beauty and order.

It was precisely this that Kant fought. He demonstrated that such a concept of matter does not correspond to the true concept of world creator but only to that of world builder, who has to keep to given material and to impose order on refractory matter. This is the very point that is "an almost universal prejudice among most of the worldly wise against the capacity of nature to produce something orderly through its own universal laws ... just as if one disputed God's governance of the universe by looking for spontaneous for-

69

mation [*ursprüngliche Bildung*] among forces of nature and as if these forces were a principle independent of God and were an eternally blind fate.'' But one must not confuse the tendency to deduce the totality of the world's structure on the basis of purely mechanical principles with the view of ancient atomists from Leucippus to Lucretius: where the cosmic order was supposed to emerge from blind chance and the rationally ordered from unreason! The question is whether it makes good sense and is compatible with God's greatness to assume regarding the creator of matter and its fundamental mechanical forces and laws, that God is able to educe the form of the world structure from itself only if he intervenes further in it. All one is doing is to perpetuate the controversy with the naturalists and needlessly to expose a weak side to them if one insists on understanding the relation of nature to God (the physico-theological proof) only in this way. ''If through the eternal laws of their being the natures of things produce nothing but disorder and absurdity, they would by that very fact prove the character of their independence from God; and what sort of notion could one have of a deity whom the universal laws of nature obey only through a kind of compulsion and which, as far as they themselves are concerned, fight against the deity's wisest plans?'' Insofar as, on the basis of the prejudice that material forces ''of themselves can produce nothing but disorder . . . one is forced to twist all of nature into miracles,'' then one has lost the concept of nature altogether; in that case it becomes ''only a *deus ex machina* that produces changes in the world!'' Hence one misses the meaning of the concept of creation. Only he possesses a true concept of nature (which, as created world, ''bears a universal harmonious relationship to the will of the deity'') as well as a true concept of its creator, who thinks that all the splendor and order of the world system has arisen out of matter in accordance with laws that were invested in it from the beginning and that constitute its very essence. How could the mechanics of nature's movements ''have erratic strivings and untrammeled dispersion at their very origin, since all the characteristics of mechanics from which these effects develop are themselves determined by the eternal thought in God's understanding, in which everything must necessarily relate to and harmonize with everything else?'' The fact that everything in nature that develops purely mechanically comes together in a unique system is in fact the clearest sign of the unity of its origin, a sign that cannot be surpassed by any sort of reference to a special teleological event and intervention. The true physico-theological proof is not one that finds it necessary to expand the divine act that produced matter through a second act in which—just as if matter itself were inclined toward deformity and were imperfect from the very outset— order and form first had to be forced on it. ''If universal laws of operation of matter are likewise a consequence of the highest plan, then presumably they can have no other destiny than to strive to fulfill the very plan that highest wisdom has devised for itself.'' Only in this way will one really grasp the work of creation in its complete simplicity, wisdom, and greatness, and understand the creator not simply as ''great and mighty'' but as ''infinite and totally self-sufficient.''

Thus if we must regard the formation of the world as an evolution of cosmos from chaos, then the concept of creation demands that already ''in the essential properties of elements that comprise chaos we can trace the mark of that perfection that those properties possess from their very beginning. . . . The simplest, the most universal properties that seem to have been designed unintentionally, matter that appears to be merely passive and in need of form and measures [*Anstalten*], in its simple state strives to build itself up through natural development to a more perfect constitution.'' ''Matter, which is the original stuff of all things, is thus tied to certain laws; and if matter is freely left to those laws, it must necessarily produce beautiful combinations. It is not free to deviate from this plan of perfection . . . and there is a God precisely because even if nature itself is in chaos, it cannot proceed otherwise than according to rule and order.'' Thus for Kant autonomy of nature and of material evolution and with it the necessity of purely mechanistic explanation of nature, without any help from teleological interventions, follows immediately from the doctrine of creation, from the concept of the world as expression of God, not as opposition to him. A world constitution such as Newton's, with its assumption of divine intervention and maintenance of order, which consequently ''cannot maintain itself without a miracle, does not possess the mark of stability that is the hallmark of divine choice.''

All of these are complexes that have been evaluated far too little with regard to their historic importance, and one ought not to pass them by as if they were just currently fashionable turns of phrase; they are complexes that are very obviously also much more than subsequent mutual accommodation of orders of spiritual life that have grown up independently of one another. By contrast, people have always paid more attention to the influence that the turn to nature and the this-worldly, which set in with the beginning of the modern period, contributed to the revolution in the astronomical world picture. As far as the problem at hand is concerned, there is just one major point at issue: axiological unity against dualism, even in the conception of the astronomical world system as such. The entire Middle Ages also maintained this position, indeed precisely so, sticking to the teachings of ancient tradition. At the same time as the first hegemony of the motif of opposition (in the metaphysics of the Pythagoreans), that motif's application in astronomy also became the leading idea in research. Duality and axiological opposition dominated the world picture of Greek science from that point on, just as it became determinative for the medieval image of the cosmos, especially as represented by Aristotelian physics. The visible world was split in two: the starry heavens with their heavenly bodies eternally orbiting in orderly paths (as the realm of ether and harmony of the spheres) pointed toward the gods and the good; in the "world beneath the moon" (the realm of the four elements), on the other hand, disorder, the purely mechanical, chance, and transitoriness prevailed. We can pass over at this point how this fused together in the medieval world picture with that graduated ordering that Neoplatonism described as gradual descent from the divine-One to material objects and how hierarchy of beings was then coordinated with cosmic ordering, the spheres of the stars themselves were arranged according to gradations of spiritual beings, angels were credited with moving the stars, and so on. For our purpose a general reference to the intertwining of metaphysical-spiritual dualism and astronomic-cosmic dualism suffices. This metaphysical-physical opposition then stubbornly and bitterly resisted all attempts at new research into, or reordering of, the world structure that asserted itself with increasing importance from the late Middle Ages. Even Kepler, to whom modern astronomy owes so decisive a debt, could not interpret the origin of movements of planets and their mathematical regularity, which he himself had discovered, as a mechanical cause (as in the case of movements on earth), but only as purposeful activity of intelligent beings! Unity of the law of nature in Galileo's law of falling bodies and in paths of planets was something he simply could not conceive; for him gravity was valid only on earth and was a specifically different power than orderly regulated forces of "world harmony"—just as "earth" and "heaven" differed from each other.

Not until Huygens and Newton did the idea of *celestial mechanics* achieve total victory in science, although Parisian Occamists of the fourteenth century had already clearly conceived it. Newton was the first to think of gravitation now as universal reciprocal attraction among all parts of matter, which enabled him to erect a world system on the foundation of a single all-pervasive lawfulness. Now, for the first time (in its totality, actually, as we saw, first in the case of the young Kant), the "mechanical" lost the last vestiges of alienation from "heaven"; now for the first time the

I. God and World

paths of Kepler and Galileo converged into one. Henceforth one may not identify mechanical with merely fortuitous; mathematical order determines mechanical lawfulness in a falling stone exactly as it does the harmony of paths of heavenly bodies that has been a source of wonder since earliest times. Everywhere—"above or below," in the vast heavens as well as on the earth beneath the moon—the book of nature is written in mathematical letters!

To bring this scientific development to maturity one had to be convinced of homogeneity and similarity of the universe in all its parts, a view that was in sharp opposition to dualism. God "has created everything according to measure, number, and weight," as the old dictum of creation put it; hence Leibniz and the young Kant, in their battle against materialists and naturalists and in conformity with the views of Galileo and Descartes, taught that one should understand mechanics itself as the instrument and complete expression of the spiritual-teleological cause of the world. "*Tout comme ici* [everything as it is here]: this formula of Leibniz for homogeneity of the entire infinite universe does not mean that one has degraded harmony of the spheres of heaven to something mechanical-earthly, but that one has elevated this earthly level to a full expression of God, and that even in the tangle of molecular processes and of daily events one can find the entire miracle of absolute order and lawfulness once again! In a speck of dust and in the tiniest particle of matter one can still find a world of perfect lawfulness and regulated order of the sort that the ancients acknowledged only for the heavenly spheres: this is the profoundly blissful perspective that Leibniz saw in the new science.

Hence it is no wonder that Nicholas of Cusa, metaphysician of the world as *Dei explicatio*, was decisively important also for revolution in the astronomical worldview. It was not from Copernicus that Giordano Bruno received the ultimately decisive impulse for his world picture; no, he took his fundamental idea from Nicholas, merely linking it in a new way, however, with that astronomical discovery! This German had already completely overcome depreciation of the earth. He saw it no longer as unmoved middlepoint "below," toward which all else falls, in contrast with periphery and "above" in the heavenly spheres. The universe has no periphery and center, below and above; God is both periphery and center for earth, and one can reach him just as easily on the path that leads downward as on the one that leads upward! It must therefore be false "that this earth is the least and lowest part of the universe," and one can refute all supposed arguments in that direction. The earth is one "noble star" among others and interacts with them—just as in general the good God "has so created all things that every being, insofar as it strives to preserve its being and its divine calling, achieves this in com-

73

munity with others.'' From that it also follows that this earth is *not at rest,* as opposed to, and distinct from, orbiting heavenly bodies; in actuality it cannot exist without every kind of motion! It also follows that the planets contain life and rational inhabitants, just as our earth does. Thus the new attitude toward the visible world that speaks to us with such captivating pathos from the works of Bruno or Leibniz or the young Kant rests entirely on completely carrying through the theme struck by the doctrine of creation and on dissolving ancient dualism.

It is obvious that an entirely new assessment of the body and of sensuality in general asserted itself with this new conception of the world. One can now no longer regard sensuality merely as the opposite of sprituality; one must reevaluate it as a special function in our life that is not to be despised. It cannot be evil in itself or a shelter for error; on the contrary, in its own way it too cooperates with the true and the good. As Kepler says, the sensual as well as the spiritual come from the creator of all things. It is for that very reason that "natural instinct" and sense experience are able to lead us to grasp laws of reality and spiritual "reasons" behind events. What understanding penetrates with clarity, sensuality has already grasped, although initially in a still confused way. It is well known how the Leibnizian system's epistemological theory developed this idea, expanded it, and impressed it on the entire eighteenth century right up to Kant. The sensual feeling of pleasure and pain, just like sense perception and representation, is not something fortuitous and without content, but rather, in a confused manner, produces knowledge of being and therefore also ultimately embraces spiritual dimensions of the intelligible. Therefore it is just as true that elements of sense experience are representations that one merely has to elevate to the level of clarity and apperception in order for them to become intellect or spirit as that "the elements of sensual pleasures are *spiritual* pleasures, but we recognize them only in a confused manner." A similar view holds true for the life of passion [*Begehrensleben*]. Whereas the ancients considered sensuality as muddling of ideas by matter, now, on a new basis sensuality is the first, unalloyed expression of the spiritual.

Even in the case of the Kant of the critical system—who fought this theory and drew a new line of separation between sense appearance and the

I. God and World

purely intelligible, between sensibility and thought—sensibility nevertheless attained new dignity through the value of the "pure" that applied to it as well. There is an a priori, that is, rational lawfulness, inherent even in principles of sensibility. If space and time are merely forms of appearance, nevertheless mathematics demonstrates that here too true intellectual knowledge is possible. And even phenomena in space and time, though they can never deliver and signify something ultimate and can never lay claim to reality in an absolute sense, are nevertheless the ground of experience on which our life, including its supersensible element, can develop and must prove itself! The phenomenal world, the world of "sensibility," is the decisive locus of our knowledge and activity that is oriented toward the intellectual: this conviction is common to the Kantian system and to Leibniz; indeed the entire epoch of Kant, including Hamann, Herder, and the others (some of them at war with Kant's separation between reason and sensibility), fought for this kind of immanence in life. In Antiquity contrariety had to culminate in an ascetic, world-fleeing doctrine of life; in the world of creation the path of spiritual salvation went through the stages of a sensibly extended world.

With a new, great religious impetus Fichte then pushed this goal of " 'blending' [*"verflößen"*] the supersensual into everyday work on earth" entirely into the foreground as dominant motif of the new worldview and religious theory of life. With that, despite all his sharp intensity of ethical-religious will, he also attained an assessment of sensible life and especially of material labor that differs from antiquity (with its depreciation of manual labor), from ethics of ancient idealism, and from world-aversive tendencies of the Middle Ages. At the same time he struggled with renewed energy with the concept of the purely ideal meaning of the *body*. He provides the first philosophical mastery of this problem thrown up by the turn toward the this-worldly in modern religiosity since Leibniz's first systematic organization. Just as Leibniz regarded the body as a corporeal-sensible phenomenon that was above all the external expression of the unique posture of the individual soul reflected in that phenomenon toward the totality of other souls and monads, expressing value of a spiritual-intelligible order in a spatial appearance, so did Fichte, who now turned the idea entirely in an ethical direction, regard the body as expressing the unique task that is allotted to this individual self in the ethical world order, at once means and instrument of its progressive fulfillment. In this case also, as in the problem of sensibility and of sensual-material operation, Fichte's significance consists more in his basic grasp of the new problematic rather than in execution. There was, and still is, much to do in this area. One cannot sufficiently regret that the many initiatives made in this direction by the nineteenth century, from the Romantics or Feuerbach on to Nietzsche's sermon on "creative body" and on "meaning

75

of the earth," have skidded off so easily into naturalism and have lost their original direction.

The abundance of motifs that have been broached by the theme of creation as we understand it here has not been exhausted by these considerations. But this is as far as we are going to pursue the matter. There is just one final result about which we must speak yet, and it is a paradox. We have always referred to the inner problematic that ultimately must always bring world optimism of metaphysics of creation into conflict with simultaneous opposition in life (deepened by Christianity) between sin and redemption, good and evil. Antiquity—in the case of all its thinkers, from Plato on into its final period—had tried to force unity on the world, to be sure, insofar as it conceived of evil merely as "privation" of good, as mere lack and relative non-being instead of as positive being and action. Stoic and Plotinian theodicy expanded this idea, and all subsequent theodicies have adopted their arguments. The Christian era, precisely on account of the idea of creation, must have felt the challenge weighing on it with renewed urgency; hence the Church Fathers, especially Augustine, immediately grappled with this difficulty—which one could not remove merely by shifting sin from matter into an act of will, for precisely this act of will was clearly something eminently positive. . . . How could one reconcile it with God's creation and foreknowledge, with the idea of the best world? We have already seen how people sought to eliminate evil at least from the end of all things and, accordingly, conceded it a merely limited existence in the temporal process. But despite all such attempts this core problem remained unresolved and unreconciled with that idea of the world. Things persisted in this way in the waning phase of the Middle Ages also, when people continually made new attempts to understand evil as something that God somehow approved and willed. Such attempts emerged as a result of theological determinism and the doctrine of creation, but also directly out of the new feeling for life itself. If Eckehart in his wonderful *Talks on Distinctions* [*Reden der Unterscheidungen*] says that a man in proper conformity with God's will should not wish that a sin into which he has fallen and which has now been forgiven had never happened at all [insofar as, namely, the love of God would flourish more inwardly for such a person in repentance and grace], then this is something entirely in the

I. God and World

same spirit. From this perspective sin is like a transitory phase in the process of God's self-revelation. Thus Valentin Weigel also taught that even the devil is good in his own essence and that all sins had altered him only with respect to worldly incidentals but not in his eternal substance. But the mystics in particular experienced religious tension here most keenly and that tension pressed forward in opposition to the metaphysical construction toward fully acknowledging evil as something real, as a positive force.

Such reactions were also bound to arise from the optimism regarding creation in Leibniz's system. It is a matter of special interest how this inner problematic ultimately pushed the young Kant beyond the metaphysics in which he grew up, and in which he had complete confidence, into the later system. In that hierarchical system of the best of all worlds, as his first works written in the wake of Leibnizian–Wolffian metaphysics described it, evil was fundamentally nothing but a failure to assume a proper place in this order, from which point then all the steps were perfect in their own way. "The perfections of God are clearly manifest at all levels and are no less marvelous in their lowest classes than in their nobler ones." Thus one could no longer distinguish here between worthwhile and worthless or lower and higher among things in the sense that Antiquity spoke of ascent and descent in hierarchical ordering. If one now defined sin by saying that man, who was created as a rational-sentient being, failed (as previously prescribed in that hierarchy) to allow insight to govern desire (hence the higher over the subordinate) but instead, in exactly reverse sequence, placed reason in the service of passion and degraded the clear and enlightening element below the confused one—then with that the idea of sin had to fade away entirely.

Kant could not have been as deeply permeated by pietistic devotion as he in fact was, if this conception was supposed to satisfy him. And it seems that it was exactly this that was a serious motivation, if not the ultimately decisive one, behind his turning toward a critique of rational metaphysics and the primacy of practical reason. The basic idea of his work on "negative magnitudes," which was so important to Kant's development, is not aimed ultimately at "real repugnance" ["*Realrepugnanz*"] of plus and minus in mathematics or attraction and repulsion in nature, but rather at that between good and evil in moral life. In his view vice is not merely lack of virtue, but acting in opposition to law. "Love and non-love are each the contradictory of the other. Non-love is genuine denial, but in view of what one feels an obligation to love this denial is possible . . . only through real opposition. And in such a case *not-to-love* and *to hate* differ only in degree." If even in this context sin is still called a "deprivation" (privation), nevertheless this means something altogether different now. Opposition or real repugnance is the law of spiritual-moral life! In God, to be sure, there can be no such

77

opposition; but it is constitutive for finite being. With that Kant finally backed away from the metaphysics of reconciliation of his time, from mere degrees of difference according to the principle of continuity, and from the description of the best of all worlds as expanding in infinite gradations and as demanding shadow itself along with light; instead, he turned with new energy to opposition in life, which is then the basis on which all the dualisms in his system take shape: appearance and intelligible being, reason and sensibility, nature and freedom.

But others did not merely persist with that accommodating tendency of the idea of perfection of the world; they even dared to draw the final paradoxical consequence from it, one that ultimately denied the existence of moral-religious opposition! Two great thinkers (who otherwise seem to have little in common) traveled this path, both of them characteristically far removed from purely religious Christian tradition, hostile to the harshness of its view of opposites in life, and yet on the other hand sufficiently interwoven into the great metaphysical development of the Modern Period to be totally caught up by its world-affirmative direction (the consequence of the doctrine of creation): Spinoza and Nietzsche. The idea of the oneness of universal perfection seeks here to win so total a victory over the controversy about oppositions in life that the latter are annihilated.

Spinoza's famous pronouncement—that human emotions and behavior are nothing to laugh at nor to bewail nor to detest, but rather simply to contemplate as if they were just a matter of lines, surfaces, and bodies, and that one must regard passions such as love, hate, anger, and sympathy not as mistakes but as attributes of human nature that belong to it in the same way as hot air, coldness, and other phenomena belong to nature, for though these things are uncomfortable, they are nonetheless necessary and each of them has its own certain cause—is something that people are too readily inclined to understand as the expression of a coldly theoretical view of the world, a full-blown naturalism that ignores the world of values because that world does not appeal to it. In fact Spinoza himself goes on in that passage: "and true contemplation of these objects brings the same joy to the mind as knowledge of the most pleasant things does."

But here too, one could already sense that an entirely special *joy* was expected from knowledge of natures [*Naturen*] and their essential properties. For joy always refers to something of value, and when one contrasts this joy with other joys of the "pleasant," then does this perhaps indicate a value-moment in the beholder, except that anything subjective-accidental in the individual is excluded from that moment? It also seems significant that valuation of those passions and emotions is quite obviously excluded to the extent that it is a *de*preciation; this does not seem to have yet predecided the question whether somehow—in the midst of things worthy of derision and complaint as well as of "mistakes"—something positive, indeed simply and completely positive, might surface in the human soul and in the object of its experience!

And if Spinoza then always stresses that value-opposites—good and bad, merit and sin, order and confusion, beauty and ugliness—are mere prejudices that have arisen from a false teleological notion that wants to tailor everything to man and his subjective-arbitrary interest and that is merely a product of desire and of the illusion of freedom of will; and if he adds that people would never have grown out of such superstition if mathematics had not shown them another norm of truth—mathematics that is concerned not with purposes but only with the essence and properties of figures—one soon senses that this enthusiasm over pure knowledge, in its battle against value-relations of the human-all-too-human concept of purpose, is not at all indifferent to value or hostile to it. To be sure, Spinoza says only that if people had once really known such mathematical entities, those entities, if they had not attracted them, at any rate would have convinced them; but in this "convinced" there is obviously more than mere theoretical evidence. If one were to think of God as acting purposefully, that is, ordering nature in accordance with human purpose, that would be to introduce *imperfection* into the concept of God, the infinite substance. The world of finite objects is, on the contrary, the direct expression and the immediate consequence of the nature of substance. And, indeed, all objects in equal measure: no mode stands closer to infinite being than any other does! Nothing exists as mere means for something else. One must understand and treasure things according to their nature and their own powers, not according to their usefulness for human desire. One must understand all of them in this respect, however, as necessary consequences and modes of one, infinite, divine substance—which for Spinoza means precisely universal perfection! The "ethics" of this pantheistic mystic culminates in his praise of "intellectual love" for the infinite above all things, finding in it victory over all emotions that are mired in the finite and the subjective, and with that the discovery of the source of all profoundest and truest happiness. Thus he denies opposites in order to be able to pay homage to total, undivided being as the emanation of the most perfect Being. Joy of the knower in the grounds for mathematical relationships and in relationships of knowledge of the world *sub specie aeternitatis* [from the perspective of eternity] is the highest experience of value and as such it generates intellectual—love! He derides love and hate in the all-too-human sense; one should recognize them as part of the systematic order of necessary events. But in this eternal-objective, all-uniting sense that abides no opposition to it, love is the truest core of life, and is itself knowledge and truth.

There is thus a dimension of this that also belongs entirely in the context of efforts in theodicy. To the counterquestions that ask why such deception through imagination and teleological notions exists at all when everything is after all supposed to be perfect or why God did not create the world in such a way that all men, like mathematicians, would be guided exclusively by rational considerations based on objective knowledge of being, Spinoza replies: "Because he had sufficient material to create *everything* from the highest degree of perfection to the lowest. Or, to express myself more properly, because the laws of his nature are laid out so broadly that they would extend far enough to produce everything that infinite intelligence can conceive." Here, too, as in the case of so many world-extollers of the modern age, fullness of infinite being, demand for greatest richness in the harmony of the world, must justify the existence of defectiveness and unreason by elevating them into the all-perfect One. For Spinoza God is not "merely" nature beyond good and evil; on the contrary, his emphasis is exactly opposite: Nature is completely divine, is God, the infinite highest fullness without division or opposite. Just as there is nothing at all in the actual world that stands in opposition to the perfection of God-nature, so is there nothing actual in opposition to the *amor dei intellectualis* [intellectual love of God] (as is indeed stated toward the end of the *Ethics*). So Spinoza's apparent immoralism ends in a doctrine of highest virtue, that is, love with which the all-perfect One loves himself and permeates the individual.

Nietzsche's fundamental direction is very similar. One fails to understand this self-contradictory man in his essence if one understands the immoralism that he demanded merely as a protest against the morality of Christianity and all the "old tablets." Still less does one understand his real purpose when one seizes on occasional expressions of "freethinking"-positivist naturalism (Nietzsche likes to use the word "Réealism," because he once followed P. Rée in that view). Ultimate metaphysical world optimism, glorification of the universe and theodicy were, indeed, goals of the young Nietzsche, in spite of the fact that he otherwise stood under Schopenhauer's influence! The author of *The Birth of Tragedy* made it his project to "justify the world as an esthetic phenomenon." It is thence that his hatred of Christianity derived as well as his turning away from Schopenhauer shortly thereafter and his war against all metaphysicians as world-slanderers and "otherworlders" [*"Hinterwelter"*]. Everywhere he saw the same tendencies to hate life and disbelieve in this world. They link up with the opposites of sin and salvation, good and evil; they split existence into the here and the beyond, this world and another world, and in the process a shadow of negation always falls on our reality. Everywhere people lack the courage to say an ultimate total Yes and lack the full rich meaning of the holiness of the earth. Hence

80

I. God and World

the later Nietzsche counterposes to Christian-Schopenhauerian world pessimism based on weakness his own pessimism based on strength, one that is able to find ecstasy even in the bad and in evil. "Even this pessimism of strength ends with theodicy, that is, with an absolute Yes-statement to the world . . . and in that way to the conception of this world as the actually achieved highest possible ideal." "To gain an eminence and a bird's-eye view where one comprehends how everything is actually happening the way it is *supposed to happen*: how every kind of "imperfection" and the suffering it causes belongs to *highest desirability*." "It is part of this view to conceive hitherto denied aspects of existence not only as *necessary*" (Spinoza comes to mind!) "but also as desirable, and not just desirable with reference to those aspects previously affirmed (say, as their complements or preconditions) but for their own sake as mightier, more terrible, *truer* aspects of being, in which its will speaks more distinctly." "This is the type of mind that accepts and redeems contradictions and questionable aspects of existence . . . religious affirmation of life, total life, not denied and bisected life. . . . Dionysus against 'the crucified one': here you have your opposition."

"My intention is to show the absolute homogeneity in all events and to use moral distinction only as *perspectivally* determined." "The concept 'reprehensible behavior' causes me difficulty. Of all the things that ever happen, not a single one can be reprehensible in itself; hence no one should wish to be rid of anything; for everything is so bound up with everything else that to want to exclude anything is the same as to want to exclude everything. A reprehensible action means a reprehensible world in general. . . . If becoming is a great circle, then everything is of equal value, eternal, and necessary. In all correlations of yes and no, of reference and rejection, and of love and hate, it is only a perspective or an interest of certain types of life that expresses itself; in itself everything that exists pronounces its Yes." "This insight brings about great liberation: it removes opposition from objects and preserves the uniqueness of every event."

Thus in Nietzsche there courses a final consequence of the modern tendency toward glorification of the world that was set in motion by the doctrine of creation, a religiously felt and intensified longing (even in the case of this "atheist") for reality's freedom from everything negative and from all division, even to the point of—"immoralism." And as so often before, so here once again, the fullness and power of the world are the moment of theodicy which draws even the most questionable and the worst elements into universal blessedness and affirmation; on the basis of the experience of this overwhelming richness that makes it possible to regard even the most frightful and suffering-filled elements of this life as happy, Nietzsche comes to the highest expression that he could find for his Yes to the world: to the mystery of the "eternal return."

II.
Infinity in the Finite

Hand in hand with the transformation we have described in the metaphysical and scientific concept of the world goes an important development in defining the relationship between finite and infinite. Here, too, the decisive change comes in separating modern conceptual tendencies that had already become influential in the patristic and Scholastic eras from conceptual forms that those eras had permitted systems of Antiquity to impress upon them. The history of the problem of infinity, as a particularly interesting and relatively easy to define chapter in the developmental history of concepts, has been treated often. Nonetheless, the point here, too, is to take a new look at decisive motifs from the standpoint of modern historical perspective.

People have always stressed the priority of valuation that the finite enjoyed over the infinite in ancient thought and feeling about the world. And regardless of how much criticism we must levy against all-too-simplistic reconstructions of Hellenism, the core of that perception remains valid. Even though the great minds of Antiquity sought after and even opened up paths leading to a grasp of the infinite, nevertheless the clearly defined and formally evident in religion and art, worldview and philosophy, was predominant even into the final stages. And the most decisive thing from our point of view is this: It is precisely these characteristic features of finiteness in classical science and metaphysics of the Greeks that later ages, indeed starting with Aristotle, emphasized and transmitted to the inquiry of modern peoples! In fact, the incipient Modern Period first became really aware of the motif of infinity in the ancient picture of world as a result of its own modern investigation.

II. Infinity in the Finite

The alienation that the architecture, ornamental art, and polytheistic sculpture of the Greeks expressed against anything formless-immense or confusedly one is formulated by philosophy in this fashion: The perfect is the formal-complete, it is always bounded. The unbounded is undetermined, uncertain; it is like chaos, which lacks all form and measure. The metaphysical will to knowledge, as such, has the same attitude. It seems that only something that we can grasp and define in some way is accessible to thought and to concept. Hence, absolute faith in thought's capacity to deal with being concludes that something incomprehensible, something that essentially transcends any measure or limit, simply cannot exist; or it concludes that in any case such a thing is only demibeing, poor and wretched being, *me on* [nonbeing]. The contrary notion that concept as merely finite and delimiting thought is inferior to being as infinite is a totally foreign idea.

Hence, too, in the Pythagorean table of opposites the infinite—as the unbounded—belongs with what is inferior. And from that point on, concepts of finite and infinite were solidly rooted in the dualism that we described earlier. The unbounded is always the flawed-indeterminate, out of which objects in reality are first shaped according to the model of eternally clear forms; those objects, however, never entirely escape from the instability of the unbounded and always remain inferior to the true being of the formal-ideal. Cosmos—as something defined and solidly complete and as limit-positing order—arises out of chaos, that is, out of chance and indeterminate instability of the unbounded. The *apeiron* [the unbounded] lacks not only outer completeness but inner rule and order as well.

Closed circular motion serves as the primordial type for all events, just as the sphere does for all being. "Strong necessity [in Parmenides' classical formulation] holds being fast in the bonds of the barrier that girds being. Hence the existing thing may not exist without having a terminus. For it exists without blemish. If being lacked that terminus, it would be deficient throughout. . . . But since it does have a final boundary in fact, it is self-contained in every direction, like the mass of a well-rounded sphere." People have very properly raised the question whether Parmenides also thought of his One Being in spatial terms (which the *comparison* with a perfect sphere does not necessarily imply at all), and it was perhaps entirely in the master's spirit when Zeno [the Eleatic] argued from the difficulty of conceiving the infinite that space (which, after all, one can think of only as surrounded by more space *ad infinitum*) does not exist. But that Parmenides argued in favor of finiteness or boundary and contrasted what is strictly hemmed in (as the only perfect and complete thing) with anything that does not permit the mind to come to a resting point because it pushes beyond form and boundary—this is evident not only from his own clear statements but also from Zeno's further development of his ideas. For all the arguments Zeno introduced in defense of his teaching lead ultimately to the inconceivability and therefore the nonexistence of the infinite, most of all of any infinity in a given finite object, that is, infinity of division. Any time one stumbles into numeration that cannot terminate, one is not dealing with being and truth but only with appearance and error.

But here, too, things turned out the same way as we saw they did earlier: Unresolved problems in Parmenides' theory of being drove the classical systems in the direction of Pythagorean dualism. One had to acknowledge that the unbounded, too, is somehow connected with reality; the spatial, for example, also exists, even if merely as appearance and not as ''true'' being! Thus for Plato and Aristotle the infinite falls on the side of what barely exists, that is, matter; but what truly exists—contributing being, order, and stability to all reality—is the determinate and determining idea or form that sets a limit. So according to Plato (and this agrees entirely with what we know of the academic metaphysics of the Pythagoreans) all objects are made up of two things: the unbounded and the limiting or boundary; to the extent that the latter defines the former, cosmos or ordered reality comes into existence. Extended matter [*Raummaterie*] is the principle of greater and lesser in extension and division and even in the opposites of sensible qualities (warmer and colder); hence it always remains essentially an indefinite and unknowable entity, a *me on*. Only the idea—what intelligent insight can delimit—has lasting being in itself! To the extent, therefore, that the world of appearance possesses being and beauty, it is bounded; only the moment of non-being in it is unbounded, without terminus, hence utterly deficient.

But one must also not fail to recognize that alongside such indisputable preference for limit that is so extremely characteristic of the Greeks' general feeling about the world, the idea of infinity in a positive sense also permeates Greek philosophy from the beginning. Before the Pythagoreans with their theme of opposites spun the thread of what we are now tracing, Anaximander placed the beginning and principle of objects in the *apeiron*. To be sure, it is still uncertain whether he really saw in this unbounded-indeterminate origin a higher principle than reality or whether he intended to designate merely chaos and dark matter by it. The fact that informed individual beings regarded it as *punishment* or as consequence of their crime to be submerged once again into an undifferentiated state is something that could indeed point to the latter interpretation. But when it is also said of the *apeiron* that it encompasses and guides all things, is immortal, and is indestructible; when it is further expressly said that the reason why this principle is infinite in character is so that becoming should not come to an end—this makes it totally obvious that there is another avenue whose significance for the world image of the Greeks

84

II. Infinity in the Finite

we must not underestimate. From Anaximander, Heraclitus, and Empedocles all the way to the late Stoics the theory of periodization in world history surfaces over and over again—that is the idea of an unlimited succession of worlds in unbroken time sequence, such that every time a world perishes a new cosmic beginning comes immediately on its heels. Of course, the feature of finiteness is not lacking here either: for this endless process is made up of a chain of successive orbital paths that aimlessly move forward, expand, and increase. There is an enormously great distance between this and, say, Fichte's pathos of infinity, of cosmic evolution of worlds! And yet Greeks viewed this very boundlessness in the temporal process as something more than mere indeterminacy; the fact that the process is endless in no way stigmatizes it as flawed! As early as Anaximander and Heraclitus the idea of inner order, form, and lawfulness in something was present in those doctrines.

Thus in the case of Anaxagoras and even more of the atomists, infinity of the world asserted itself in a positive sense. To be sure, Anaxagoras still viewed the cosmos itself as limited; but when he came to explain its formation (which takes place through formative nous), he assumed given infinity in surrounding matter, an infinite number of kinds of matter, and even endless division. And though Leucippus and Democritus once again set hard and fast boundaries for the atom and conceived elements of existing reality in geometrically clear, circumscribed forms, nevertheless they not only demanded an infinite number of such atoms to explain the manifold of the world but also assumed infinitely numerous worlds juxtaposed to one another in the infinity of empty space, not merely succeeding one another in the flux of time.

Still, this turn toward complete and present infinity was not decisive for the Greek concept of the world as it was transmitted to later periods. With Aristotle the longing for finiteness completely gained the upper hand once again. Just as Zeno did, Aristotle regarded anything that led thinking to lapse into infinite regress as refuted from the outset. It is impossible for the *apeiron* or the boundless to *exist*. In Aristotle's view, actual, existing, completed infinity, as it were, was nonsense and essentially self-contradictory. As he saw it, even Plato conceded too much being to the infinite. The endless itself never *is*; it merely designates a moment in becoming. One can talk sensibly about something unbounded only with respect to potency or possibility. One can rightly call infinite the bare indeterminate possibility of existing. When one talks about the *apeiron*, what one means is the unbounded possibility all becoming has of progressing toward being (and correspondingly in our thinking about it); one does not mean the complete sum total of infinitely numerous objects or parts. One can always go further on in time; ever smaller parts arise in the process of spatial division. Thus infinity falls exclusively on the

85

side of matter—the *me on*, the indeterminate-formless—which also remains literally unknowable in its own right and in fact absolutely never *exists* in itself! Pythagorean-Platonic depreciation of the infinite is continued and even intensified.

The actually existing cosmos is therefore necessarily limited. To be sure, Aristotle recognizes neither beginning nor end in time. The world is eternal; it has never come to be and can never be destroyed, and the same is true of the movement in which objects are formed. Aristotle's theory of the periods themselves is disputed in any case, and in the question about the first cause that cuts off regression into infinity for the "whence" of becoming, [Aristotle] is seeking for a solid limit from this side as well. Aristotle believes that he has not introduced complete infinity with eternity of the world *a parte ante*. But the future is by definition the incomplete; its infinity is merely possibility of going further. Yet the cosmos is clearly and solidly bounded as to its spatial formation. In fact one should also no longer talk about the unlimited possibility of going beyond or of potential infinity: given the world, space itself is limited; space is the boundary of bodies! As attribute of a formally bounded cosmos, space can only be finite. There is no body without limits; nothing real is without limits, neither the four elements nor the heavenly firmament beyond them: in which, indeed, elevated above the incompleteness of rectilinear movements, spherical motion that is complete and perfect in itself reigns, bounded by its own completeness of form. All space and everything real is contained in this orbital course of the heavens; the world is cosmos only as limitation.

It is well known how this conception of the world's structure determined theory of nature and astronomy for two thousand years. The aspect of Greek philosophy and science that pressed toward the infinite, on the other hand, receded completely. As far as the world was concerned, infinity remained an expression for chaotic indeterminacy, dearth of being, and incompleteness of becoming.

But now in later Antiquity a different sort of infinite came into the picture. In its basic thrust, indeed, it stemmed from the Orient, but as a conceptual principle it had already been anticipated by the highest idea of being developed in the classical systems. For the more people attempted to use Parmenides' Universal One as a basis for explaining the manifold of existence, the inexhaustible multiplicity of forms [*Bildungen*], and the incessant flux of events, and the more the tendency to overcome contrariety through this single primordial principle also gathered strength during this process, so much the more urgently did ancient thought face the challenge of now trying to grasp the idea of a completed-infinite entity and to affirm the infinite in it as its highest and most comprehensive aspect. In the Eleatic school itself, it

86

II. Infinity in the Finite

is true, Melissus demanded spatial infinity for the One Being (over against which no limiting being can stand since it is the only thing that exists). But on this point Zeno proceeded more consistently in the path of his master when he denied spatiality altogether for the One. Thus development proceeded in the direction of conceiving a superspatial-supertemporal One as the highest principle of being. Plato's idea of the Good took the first great stride. Located beyond existence this idea is "the father of the ideas" and the sun whose illuminating power gives life to all that exists. The ideas however are infinite in number (just as the form-figures of the atomists were), and among them there is even an idea of the infinite itself (according to the efforts Plato made in his later dialectic to overcome division in the concept of the world)! Hence, is it not so, that the primordial principle that is source of everything is itself infinite, perhaps not in that old sense of spatial unlimitedless but in a higher sense that is removed from material existence?

This question (found in the *Parmenides*) remained an open one for Plato, and even Aristotle did not settle it. The old attitude toward the infinite as something lacking in form was simply too deeply rooted in Greek philosophy's concepts and feeling of existence. Aristotle's nous, successor to Anaxagoras's ordering principle and to Plato's ideas-sun, had no magnitude or parts and did not exist in space or live in time. To that extent one should call it neither finite nor infinite. As highest form and self-enclosed being this one God of Aristotle might more likely have led a person to argue for the predicate of "boundary," even though the one God does not limit anything or form any matter, but rather reposes in himself and is related exclusively to himself alone. Yet there is something of infinity here, because this nous is supposed to be the moving force behind the endless becoming of the world from eternity and on into all the future. And although, as Aristotle still rigorously stresses, infinite magnitude is an absurdity in itself, still the idea suggests itself that here we see something superfinite in power, in other words an infinite something of a higher sort and order! Anaximander's *apeiron* could have taught us that endless progression in time points back to a principle that stands above anything formally enclosed. But even Aristotle's theology does not dare go that far; that the infinite exists only as possibility and never as actuality remained a self-evident axiom for him.

It was not until late Antiquity that we arrive at complete transformation in the concept of infinity through the influx of oriental mysticism and religion. The connection is made in Alexandria from about the time of Philo on. Here infinity means divine perfection. And this means not just a vague transcendence beyond anything we can grasp and comprehend; nor does it signify merely an ultimate maximization of moral-spiritual predicates (whereby this

87

qualitatively infinite dimension, as it were, must have absolutely nothing to do in principle with quantitative limitlessness of the world's existence); on the contrary, insofar as God is related in knowledge and activity to all existence and becoming in all times and places, he sums up all these dimensions within himself. Thus the one primordial principle is infinite, but in a completely different way than one may call matter infinite. What began in Plato's *Philebus* becomes clear here: a double concept of infinity. This double sense then became extensively developed in Neoplatonism and passed on from there to all of subsequent history.

All of existence lies between two infinities. One of them signifies immense power that transcends all number and magnitude, and, accordingly, is not deficiency in limit and form nor failure of the given in comparison with its concept, but the other way around: it is something that surpasses all knowledge (as well as all usual "being"), something about which the words "indeterminacy" and "incomprehensibility" are precisely the expression of ultimate primordial power and fullness. The other infinity is that of matter, which, as the boundaryless, remains the principle of the bad, of non-being, of the not-yet-defined that still longs for form, order, and number in order to attain existence. The first (infinity of perfection) is located above the actual, as it were, whereas the second is below it. Plotinus expressly struggled for the unadulterated success of that new concept of infinity that does not take anything away from the One nor deny anything to it (limit and form)—in fact he characterized infinity in this regard precisely as "absence of all deficiency"—; on the contrary, in the case of the One that is without qualities, everything that might be endlessly extended was originally comprised in a center. Perfect infinity is thus the idea here, a whole (though not a whole in magnitude) that is infinite!

It is only because the One is infinite in itself that the total fullness of the world in its immense series of descending gradations can emanate from it and the inexhaustible power of countless forms for matter that is ever indeterminate and ever-to-be-determined as well as for matter itself flows forth from it. The most perfect and infinitely valuable being, as the source of all existence, is also related to infinity in space and time, to infinity of quantity, although the One itself, as such, remains within itself (like Aristotle's nous), has nothing to do with the many, and is removed from any order of magnitudes. As the perfect and infinite good this Divine-One also possesses infinite power (which is never used up in emanation); and through the power of its emanation this light—even though it remains within itself and is not fragmented in itself—maintains an original relationship to the extended manifold even down to matter.

II. Infinity in the Finite

It is hardly necessary to mention how much the philosophy emerging in the Christian community was led from the start to lay hold of this new conception of the infinite. The idea of its One God not only includes, as its most essential element, an absolute intensification of spiritual powers to perfection that elevates it—as the absolutely ineffable—beyond all conceiving and conceptual definition, beyond intuition and form; no, through its ideas of creation, conservation, and governance of the world, that idea is also always related to space and time and what is real in them, to every creature in other words. Just as the new demand for inexhaustible and absolutely undiminishable love differs from the ancient ethics of Aristotle (which was an ethics of *moderation* in all the soul's impulses), so also does the Christian God differ from a nous that was alien to the world and sealed up within itself. Attributes of eternity (so long as one does not mean by it mere timelessness and elevation above the time-bound but also permeating presence through all ages) and ubiquity also relate infinity of value everywhere to the world of magnitudes and the limitless.

But a further struggle was required before Church Fathers simply accepted this kind of perfect infinity in God. It was the Greeks among them who put up the stiffest resistance to the concept! Origen issued a totally explicit warning: One should not, "just for the sake of elegant talk," deny the boundaries [*Umgrenztheit*] of God's power! Where there is no limit, there is also no comprehensive concept. Hence if God were infinite, he would be unable to know himself. . . . And so the tenacious tradition of ancient finitism continues to operate even here: it is the finite-complete(d), not the infinite-unlimitable, that is perfect and intellectually meaningful. As the all-perfect One, God has measure and limit; he encompasses himself and grasps himself in a defining concept! Likewise, his activity in creation and conservation consists in self-limiting his power through his goodness. Just as all true being must have its measure, so also must God's power be *measured* by his wisdom and justice.

But there are others, most of all Augustine, who oppose this view. He says that it would be measuring God by human yardsticks to deny God's intelligence the power to encompass the boundless. The multitude of all numbers, say, transcends all finiteness; should God therefore be unable to survey their totality? In reality, God's omniscience defines every infinity,

89

too, and enumerates the innumerable, but without any change in thought and without any before and after! Thus God can also know his own perfect infinity and recognize himself as the infinite being that he is.

From this point on there was no further successful agitation against the perfect infinity of divine being (even though the battle over the new concept of infinity and the defense or refutation of ancient identification of perfection with limitation persisted on into Renaissance philosophy, to Campanella and others). Toward the end of the Middle Ages, as Duns Scotus once again questioned human capacity to grasp dogmas of faith through reason, it was precisely this predicate of simple infinity that he recognized as still demonstrable by human reason. This was entirely in conformity with the dictum from the end of the patristic period: "The divine is infinite and incomprehensible; and the only thing one can grasp about it is its infinity and incomprehensibility" (John Damascene). And at the beginning of the Modern Period Nicholas of Cusa—in carrying forward ancient "negative theology" that wishes to speak of God only through denials—regarded this as the only positive predicate of God: his absolute infinity that is complete in itself and to that extent seems to have an "end" in itself but that in actuality is without limit, an "end without end," the "unending end," whereas "every other end is finite." Positive evaluation of complete infinity, so to speak, which is real and not merely possible, actually and not merely potentially infinite, underlies all thought about the absolute everywhere since the end of Antiquity, in the Middle Ages, and in the Modern Period.

But as for the world itself, people continued to view it for a long time as simply finite, just as Aristotle and even Plotinus did. (In spite of all theories about infinite gradations, Plotinus regarded the cosmos itself, as a limited entity, as situated in the middle between the infinite-One and the endless chaos of matter.) And even the infinity motif, which the earlier age applied to passage of time, was something the patristic age and Scholasticism now regarded as incompatible with the idea of creation. In this respect they now conceived creation on the model of the Platonic theory of creation of the world: namely, that the world had its beginning in time and that time itself began at creation. Hence it will also end in finite duration of time. Everyone assumed the tendency toward finiteness in ancient theories of the world, especially their astronomical conception of the world. Only the value-symbol changed: What was once praised as an expression of perfection and order now serves rather to emphasize the enormous distance separating creature from creator. Thus it happened that ancient dualism (which for the time being, as we saw, survived everywhere in the metaphysics of the Christian era) won control over the opposition between limited and limitless in an entirely reversed sense: finiteness of the world in space and time is imperfection and insignificance in comparison with divine primordial being and is the clearest of all signs for its absolute dependence on God, the simply superfinite being. The other infinity—the merely potential infinity of matter—is kept, but now (at least for as long as matter is still subject to its old depreciation) it recedes completely in comparison with this contrast between the real (actually infinite) God and the real finite world.

Thus the world of creatures is finite not only for the case of Origen's fundamental finitism. Here, too, Origen establishes finiteness on the grounds that otherwise God could not even conceive of the world and grasp it with his spiritual vision. Unlimited duration in time would contradict the demand for God's foreknowledge, just as an unlimited number of created souls would contradict the idea of his universal providence and ubiquity. But even Augustine (and the entire Middle Ages after him) held fast to a finite cosmos! One may not even conceive of unlimited ages before the emergence of the world and unlimited spaces outside the cosmos; space and time exist only in a world bounded on all sides. Thus Plato's idea of creation of time simultaneously with the world linked up with Aristotle's conception of space (he wished to conceive of the spatial only as an attribute of bodies) in absolute conviction regarding the finiteness of the world. Ancient theory about an endless series of worlds (a view once again widely disseminated by Stoicism) was also rejected for another reason: human activity and effort, if placed in such an infinite process, will seem useless and hopeless to thought, which can make sense only out of processes that always strive toward finite and attainable goals.

At the height of the Middle Ages—the time of Albert and Thomas—it was still taken for granted that anything created is defined solely by its finitude. In spite of their doctrine concerning God, Aristotle's basic principle was still decisive: It is impossible for an actually existing infinite being to exist. Even conceptual motifs that attempt to soften opposition between God and the world, those that emphasize the reflection of divine perfection in the world as God's act of creation and so point to the infinite manifold of existing things, and especially of intelligences—even they do not really take us beyond this position. People viewed the edifice of the world as a rigidly enclosed sphere, at the middle of which rested the earth (on which man, the spiritual center of all creation, lived); the sphere of the fixed stars is the boundary of the universe. Created infinity is nonsense, says Thomas; the ''natural'' as such cannot be infinite! For in the material world there always exist only objects, each of which can exist only in a spatial area that is coherent and circumscribed; indeed, the particularity of bodies is precisely their external boundedness. Nor can unending multitudes actually exist; even in the continuum of the expanse of space there are only potentially, not actually, infinitely many points. Thomas, too, can conceive of this sphere as infinite only in the sense of something incomplete. For the world, after all, was called into existence by a being for whom it was impossible to create such multitudes of material objects that they could absolutely not be counted. The creator acts with totally specific purpose, not toward an indeterminate void (*vanum*)! It is even assumed as a matter of course that infinitely numerous souls cannot actually exist. But the most important assumption—true to Aristotle—is that it is impossible for actual infinity to exist in the realm of magnitudes and of space. The two concepts of infinity continue to exist in diametrical opposition to each other. God (even though the power of human intellect must remain inadequate regarding him) is, in himself, knowable to the highest degree, for he is pure form, undisturbed by matter, pure act, without any unfulfilled possibility; but a thing is knowable only insofar as it exists *actu* [in act]. But formless-indeterminate matter is, on the contrary, the most unknown, the unknowable, the irrational in the old pejorative sense. Here "privative" infinity rules: infinity in the sense of defect, as in the case of a thing that "by nature should have a boundary, but does not have one," and has not yet developed to perfection and complete existence. But God is "negatively infinite": he exists beyond all limits! The infinite in the realm of matter, of the spatially extended, and of quantity, is imperfection. But when we speak of God as the infinite, this refers to universal perfection. And so, in a remarkable blending of motifs, it is always simultaneously specificity of form in God's creation and, on the other hand, distance and contrariety between God and the world, that demand limitation of the real! There can be nothing in common between God and creatures, says Albert the Great (in opposition to pantheistic attempts of his time to conceive of the world as eternal), hence they cannot both be beginning and end. According to an old principle, an effect must be less than its cause. Hence for Thomas total incommensurability between world and God expresses itself precisely as that of finite versus infinite.

In spite of all the new emphasis on the real world as God's image, the late Middle Ages continued to maintain this contrast between the world as merely finite and God's limitless being. Even the Franciscans, who (according to Cantor) had always been in the vanguard in conceiving of a new actually infinite being in the subsequent period and on into the eighteenth century, remained mired in that antithesis. As Bonaventure had said: Movements of the heavenly bodies must have emanated from a starting point in time (because, after all, it would be impossible to organize something that is numerically infinite in a definite way); hence he held fast to the old identification of organization with limited form. In like manner even Roger Bacon opposed temporal endlessness of the world, for the world would then be infinite in power and would itself become God! To be sure, William of Occam, who cast doubt on traditional concepts (at least insofar as they were demonstrable) in so many respects, declared that an infinite regress in the order of efficient causes—which Aristotle had so dreaded (and with him Thomas and others) and on the basis of which Christian thinkers always sought to prove a beginning of the world—was not inconceivable! But the great step toward the infinity of the created world (which had to come, of course, if God's perfection was supposed to be totally revealed in the world and if the creator himself was supposed to speak perceptibly in the book of nature) was first taken by a later figure.

The first thrust in that direction (which was fully inherent in development of interests and of feeling about the world) did not come from speculation about the cosmos but from the concept of the soul and its relation to the creator. Indeed, it had always been said that the world bears traces of divine power and wisdom but that the soul bears the image of God in itself. Thus at least the animate-spiritual creature cannot be finite simply and in every respect, hence totally inadequate with regard to the infinity of the creator! Can we not then also clearly sense the infinite in the finite itself insofar as men know about God, turn to him, and feel his activity working within them through grace? People had always acknowledged that much of course. But dualism regarded it merely as encroachment by the infinite-supernatural into the finite-natural sphere of existence. Just as in Aristotle's view nous enters from the outside ''up to the door'' in the sentient soul, so the action of grace in experience of God is a higher intervention, which the ''nature'' of the individual being permits to happen in complete passivity.

But Duns Scotus was not satisfied with that. Even that supernatural elevation presupposes something thus far insufficiently noted: the soul's capacity to receive the infinite! And this capacity to receive infinite power must therefore be its natural prerogative; it must already belong to its essence by nature. On the part of the recipient subject, even the supernatural act of God's gift must be a natural one. God can descend to us only if our nature has the capacity to receive him. Thus the purpose for which God made us harmonizes with our capacity. God's activity in nature and God as creator harmonize with his activity in grace, the work of the Holy Spirit. If God created man

93

in his own image to the end that man should know him, then God also endowed him with infinite receptivity for the infinite from the start.

It is in this sense that Eckehart also says, "Nothing reveals itself to the soul except what already exists in the soul." The mystic goes farther than Duns Scotus: In "the ground of the soul" is God himself; at its root the soul itself is infinite, "without form and unenclosed," "without measure." Dietrich von Freiberg, drawing on Aristotelian-Scholastic doctrine of the *intellectus agens* [active intellect] and on Augustine, provides the transition: In creating the rational creature according to his own likeness, God has implanted in the soul's innermost recesses the Godlike element of intelligence; thus eternal ideas and rules and truths that guided God in creation lie within us, and if we look for them we shall find and behold them within ourselves.

This then passes like a fundamental theme into the history of modern philosophy. Everywhere the Renaissance (e.g., Ficino) emphasizes the soul's infinite longing and the infinite power to know and to will. Everyone knows Descartes's doctrine of the innate idea of God in the finite-limited self and the decisive role of this thought in the deductive process of his arguments. Here, indeed, the idea of the perfect infinite crosses over into theory of knowledge. Through his very questioning the doubter already knows about the nonlimited, about the existence of the whole truth. We do not first arrive at the idea of the infinite on the basis of the finite which we then intensify; on the contrary, the idea of the finite always includes, as its objective *prius* [presupposition], the infinite out of which this finite being has been carved. Whatever positive and real element exists in finite understanding, as the capacity to distinguish true and false, is merely a narrowing down of the truth that infinite understanding represents. In the most general terms: if I talk about a finite thing without considering whether it is infinite or finite, it is the infinite that I aim at. Hence in a certain sense "the idea of the infinite is in me prior to that of the finite, that is, the idea of God before that of myself!"

In just the same way Descartes regarded finite being's freedom of will as a direct impression [*Abdruck*] of God's infinity. Indeed this was always recognized as the chief characteristic by which God stamped his image on the soul; and it seemed that the immeasurable importance of this gift of the highest degree of likeness to God eclipsed and appeased even sin that arose from misuse of the gift. Descartes's theory of knowledge emphasized that here we find infinity in the finite. We err in research and think incorrectly in life, not because we do not know about everything, but because our will— which is essentially removed from any limitation of vision and always has the freedom to say yes or no, to sally forth or to pull back—lets itself be bound by something finite. In itself free will, in contrast with understanding, is an unlimited power, in me as well as in God. Here, too, the infinite is

II. Infinity in the Finite

original in us, and limitation is only secondary! Both primordial thinking and primordial willing—even of the *res cogitans finita* [finite thinking being]—are infinite in content or capacity. Hence, as Malebranche said, the finite also participates in infinity. With that, a peculiar transformation in the ancient concept of participation occurred: whereas in the Platonic system objects that emerged out of the unbounded-indeterminate participated in eternal form by becoming bounded, now in reverse order the finite, as something created by God, participates in the perfect infinity of the creator.

This idea continues to assert itself right on to Fichte and Schelling, wherever the absolute-infinite breaks through and comes to consciousness in the freedom of the particular individual, in the knowing and willing of the truly free person. For the time being, however, we shall not pursue this line; we wish only to add a word about Leibniz's infinity-of-souls. Here, too, it is spontaneity in thinking and willing that is the simply Godlike element in the existence of monads: the soul is a substance, just as God is, because it is "selfhood" ["*Selbststand*"]. Not that it arises from itself (for God created it), but that, once created, it leads its life from its own resources alone. The soul mirrors everything that exists in its entire fullness—the world as well as God, spatiotemporal reality as well as eternal ideas—even though not everything (in fact only the fewest things) in clearly conscious form. It pushes all this forth from itself, indeed according to an ordering that transcends all time and worlds! It is the infinite (we shall come to this later) that the soul conceives and represents here in every moment of time, and even the series of moments in time through which inner Godlike spontaneity impels them is endless. In the process the law of this endless development prevails in the entire life's work of the individual soul—the special law that specifically determines its individuality for all eternity. According to this law the "series of the soul's operations" courses on in rigorously ordered fashion, just exactly as all the meanderings of an infinitely running curve are determined by a single functional law that expresses its essential makeup. Thus, even as a created and limited individual being, the individual soul is truly infinite, and yet it is not without "form," without determinacy and fundamental comprehensibility! Whereas Thomas Aquinas still held fast to bodies and recognized a possible principle of individuation only in something finite-bounded and strictly circumscribed, here, on the contrary (following the model of mathematical determination, which is not an intuitively clear form, but rather functional lawfulness that applies even to the infinite), we have in combination the strongest inner determination of individual soul, with all the limitation bound up with its particularity, but at the same time completely real infinity of God's image. God-given order of creation need not be only an ordering of the finite-bounded, as the Middle Ages continued to hold; on the

95

contrary, if one properly pursued the idea that God has revealed himself in the world, above all in the human soul, then one must necessarily encounter the meaning of infinity in the creaturely finite, in other words therefore, finite infinity and even the "form" of the infinite.

But it was not just a question of the soul alone, regarding whose characteristics of infinity the waning Middle Ages had come to see a new path; what people discovered at first only with reference to it quickly spread to all other creatures and to the whole world in space and time. In that beautiful passage that we cited from Suso [p. 54 above], it was palpably obvious that the idea of infinity now had to push forward from the soul in all directions. And in fact the Leibnizian monad (to which point we have just anticipated) is not just the human soul but just as truly an element and archetype of all other being also. Here again it is Nicholas of Cusa who made the first determinations that pointed out the paths to all further development. In his description of the world as expression of God, he says it plainly: "Every creature is a finite infinity, as it were." All the more, therefore, must the totality of all creatures, the universe, be something infinite. How could the world as the best of all possible worlds, one that clung as closely as possible to its infinite creator, be limited in space and time! Must one not accept with complete rigor what had already been said earlier (in the period of the Church Fathers, e.g., Gregory of Nyssa): that in the immense vastness of the heavens we see a reflection of divine infinity?

Mathematical considerations were the first to lead to the link betwen finite and infinite. Whereas Aristotle always regarded the infinite as the merely potential and all actuality as finite, Nicholas now said that a neverending line is actually everything that a finite line describes in potency. Although the ancients always viewed measure and anything it measured as the limited, pure and simple, now infinite line stood for the proper, "most adequate measure" and *ratio* [proportion] of the finite line! And so, in general terms: Absolute infinity is the ground and therefore also the most adequate measure of all that exists. We always know the finite only through contact with, in and through, the infinite. Thus an old idea—which said that God, who is infinite being in the logical order, was the *primum cognitum* [first thing known] (in the Middle Ages Bonaventure, in particular, building on Augustine developed this), that is, God was the presupposition for knowledge and the full definition of every created being—was now reformulated and transmitted to the epistemology of the Modern Period. In the Modern Period in fact this doctrine of the priority of the infinite then recurs everywhere— in Campanella and Patrizzi, in Descartes, Malebranche, and Pascal, in Geulincx and Spinoza. How peculiarly Spinoza's famous dictum contrasts with Aristotle's logic of being: *omnis determinatio est negatio* [every delimitation

II. Infinity in the Finite

is negation]! Divine substance is now *ens absolute indeterminatum* [absolutely indeterminate being]. Hence it is not setting a limit that is the positive element in being and knowledge, in contrast with the non-being of potentially infinite matter; instead the absolutely positive ground of being and knowledge is always the actual-infinite, of whose being everything determinate and limited can only be abridgement, partial negation.

According to the new conception of Nicholas of Cusa, then, one must measure creature and world alike by the norm of infinity. But God is now, as we saw earlier, in this new sense the "ground" [*"Grund"*] of the world: he comprises within himself *complicite* [compactly] what the world then unfolds. It is therefore not just the spirit of man, "the noble image of God, that participates to the maximum in the fruitfulness of creative being" and accordingly possesses within it an infinite longing for knowledge, a power that with every step of progress fructifies itself anew and is thus creative-infinite (so that all human knowledge, in spite of all its limitations, is nonetheless caught up in infinite approximation to perfect-infinite truth and reason, which every step forward in research, every "conjecture" and hypothesis presupposes and has in mind as its goal); no, the universe in space and time must be infinite too, because it expresses and unfolds infinity!

Thus Nicholas's metaphysics and philosophy of nature were the first in the Christian era to teach the infinity of the world. To be sure, he does link up with the old distinction that permeates the entire Middle Ages, especially on the basis of Augustine's discussions and which we mentioned again with Thomas: The world is privatively infinite, not absolutely and "negatively" infinite like God! But the ancient-Aristotelian denigration and reference to deficiency of matter is totally abandoned here! The world is not God himself and cannot claim for itself that infinity without parts and potential division that people have always praised as the incomparable element in the divine being. What one could call the "parts" of God, his attributes, is itself in turn infinite. In contrast, the world in space and time quite obviously contains finite sections, limited parts. After all, as Plato emphasized so much, there is always a more and a less in it. Hence it is not the absolutely greatest thing— which is God—but only the "concretely greatest" thing, concrete infinity: one in which unity does not exist without multiplicity and composition, in which "the infinite is limited"—finite infinity. For the universe is not all that can exist, but it simply exists without a limit to it; it is not infinite but indefinite; nor is it eternal but merely of unending duration. But if this is supposed to be a "defect," it is no longer in any way a defect in form and limit and actuality, but only its contrast with divine being itself. And as we already saw, this opposition also signifies a valuational framework: fullness of God is unfolded in the universe. Hence concrete, privative infinity of the world is the "image," and the indeterminate is the "greatest possible imitation" and immediate expression of that absolute negative infinity of God, of the infinite. Even privative [*private (sic)*] infinity (the boundless in space and time, which everywhere admits a going-beyond and "transgressions" into more and less, and has neither beginning nor end) carries the full value of something perfect. Since there is nothing that could limit divine power, it must be possible with respect to any given magnitude to think of a greater or a smaller one. Thus ancient valuation has now finally completely turned into its direct opposite, even in the concept of the privatively infinite.

It is a well-known fact how—on a path through Bruno, who was also able to turn Copernicus's research to good account—this act of the great German determined the picture of the cosmos for the whole of modern science and metaphysics. Copernicus himself remained entirely under the sway of the ancient picture of the world on this point: he, too, viewed the realm of the fixed stars as the boundary of the spherically shaped universe. But for him, who now taught the motion of the earth, that realm was unmoved. And with that, therefore, as Bruno and Galileo saw, Aristotle's argument for the finiteness of the world based on the circular movement of the heavens fell apart. But whereas the more circumspect Galileo still left open the question whether the universe was therefore unbounded, Bruno's cosmic fantasy enthusiastically snatched up the new confirmation of Nicholas's metaphysical ideas. And he then also brought to light every sort of initiative that pointed toward the idea of actual infinity in Antiquity, especially the theory of the atomists concerning infinitely numerous worlds in infinite space. He expressly disputed Aristotle's identification of the perfect with the finite as unproven prejudice. It is precisely divine perfection that forces us to assume infinite existence in the world too. "I teach an infinite universe, the effect of an infinite, divine act," begins his speech before the Venetian inquisitors. With Nicholas he considered it incompatible with the perfection and goodness of the creator that God should not also exercise his omnipotence infinitely in infinite work as well, which is preferable to finite work after all. Space full of worlds is infinite, becoming in time is endless, the number of beings is unending. And because the universe (as we saw earlier) has now become homogeneous, it follows that other stars are not the locus of Godlike intelligences and angels, but instead are inhabited by living beings like ourselves. This entire universe, made up of an infinite juxtaposition and succession of worlds, is a unity of existence and life, the expression of one divine universal being in the form of multiplicity. Religious pathos in the idea of infinity—something altogether new when compared with ancient doctrines about infinite worlds—takes possession of the concept of the world here.

And it has remained victorious in metaphysics from that point on against

II. Infinity in the Finite

all residues of ancient finitism. Kepler still shied away from it. It still caused a secret shudder in him—in contrast with the heroic jubilation of Giordano Bruno—to imagine oneself wandering about in such infinity, where there is no border, hence no middle point and no definite places: he, too, was able to think of "harmony" of the world only as ordering of something circumscribed! But Bruno's world organism already emphasized, as Leibniz's monad was to do later, the inner law that can bind even the unbounded. And so, with Descartes, with Leibniz and Newton, with the youthful Kant, and with all the others, this external spatial-material nature, too, is infinite, just as soul and knowledge are; and each one of them also emphasizes the connection with God's infinity and the meaning of creation. Descartes, to be sure, still distinguishes between infinite and indefinite so that he can still contrast God and world from one another. Only God may be called infinite in an absolute sense; with respect to objects there is still always imperfection and boundary (thus boundary is now a deficiency, even in the world!). But for him, too, as well as for Nicholas (to whom he expressly appeals), the indefinite in world and knowledge is the expression of divine infinity. Even this expression of the indefinite appears in this context more as conditioned by the perspective of finite understanding—understanding that cannot say any more here than that the number of objects or their parts or the expanses of space transcend any assignable boundary in principle and that there are absolutely "no grounds" here for positing limits; whereas in the case of infinity of divine being, which we likewise cannot naturally grasp through understanding (*comprehendere*), we nevertheless have grounds to see (*intelligere*), that is, clearly and distinctly know, that there can be no limit here! The greater we conceive God's works to be, says Descartes, the better we observe the infinity of omnipotence. Hence no matter how much Descartes distinguishes both thinking and extended objects from God as "finite" substances versus the infinite, nevertheless there is infinity in souls as well as in the corporeal world. Because Descartes regards body as coinciding with the space it occupies, he also views infinite magnitude of the universe and infinite divisibility of the material as immediately implied by essential infinity and unending divisibility of mathematical space. The finitism of the atom, which all previous centuries had still followed, now began to unravel. Leibniz carried this through with particular emphasis.

Thus God and world drew ever nearer to each other, and the danger loomed that both would ultimately coincide completely. Giordano Bruno tottered on the brink: pantheism was always at the door in his works, and though he sometimes very sharply rejected it, it nevertheless came back again in completely undisguised form. The distinction that Bruno adopted from Nicholas between absolute maximum and concrete maximum often threat-

99

ened to evaporate, and God appeared (as in those Arabic doctrines that the Middle Ages so fought) as nature itself in its creative power (*natura naturans* [literally, nature naturing]). Spinoza took this path to the limit: thus he viewed not only divine substance but also the world of space (as well as that of thought) as completely-infinite [*voll-unendlich*]. Later on, Newton also no longer viewed endless space as merely created being but as something that belonged to God himself as his "sensorium" (as a Newtonian, Kant preferred to speak only of space as "infinite expanse of divine presence" in his early work); but Newton nevertheless regarded the world in space as God's deed and work. Spinoza, however, felt justified in directly attributing spatiality and materiality to divine substance itself as one of its attributes. What Malebranche and other students of Descartes saw as a dangerous consequence of his teaching regarding substances and infinity and tried carefully to avoid, Spinoza carried through without hesitation. The universe is infinite because God himself is nature. Both series are infinite, that of objects and that of ideas—infinite in their effect, their fullness, and their division. World is eternal, just as God is; time is only apparent. Parmenides' doctrine of universal unity returns again, but this time applied to the infinite [*ins Infinitistische*]. A thing can be finite only if it is bounded by something else of the same nature as it is; hence never substance, the One Being! Finiteness is, "at bottom, partial negation"; absolute affirmation and positing of an entity always signifies its complete infinity. And so the young Spinoza concluded that God cannot leave undone anything that is good; therefore the world must assume the attributes of God. Correspondingly, in his mature work perfection-infinity (the absolute maximum of valuational qualities) and spatiotemporal-infinity (infinity of quantity) are absolutely identical. The attribute of infinite spatiality directly expresses the essence of divine substance as inhering in itself and belonging to its own proper being. And what appears to us as endless time is in truth eternity of timeless succession in God's own Being itself.

God-nature is "the absolutely infinite being." And this absolute infinity—positing pure and simple, without any negation—now no longer stands in opposition to "privative" or boundaryless infinity; there is no more talk of that. Instead, its counterpart is infinity like that of the attribute of space, which as an infinite thing remains nevertheless restricted, so to speak, to its own dimension. Divine substance, on the contrary, is not just space-infinity but at the same time infinity of thought and still more besides. As if there were not enough to praise in God-nature in the infinities that Descartes's theory of substance had discovered as comprehensible to us or as if there were still too much "determination" and therefore negation in this duality of attributes (and God is nonetheless supposed to be absolutely indeterminate

100

II. Infinity in the Finite

being!), Spinoza now demanded infinitely numerous attributes for infinite substance, "absolutely infinite" attributes. Each of these in its own dimension and in its own way "expresses" infinite being in just the same way as boundless spatial extension and unlimited realm of spirit, the only attributes that we know as human beings. Absolutely infinite attributes, each of these in turn completely infinite in its own dimension and kind, infinite concatenation and organization: thus "the infinite in an infinite manner" follows from God's necessity. In such a complex of infinity even the finite becomes essentially infinite. Just as attributes "express" substance, so do modes (finite "stimuli") in turn express those infinite attributes in their "specific and determined way." The individual *exists* only as a member of a necessary order of being, an endless chain of modifications; hence it also shares in true, absolute infinity. There is no such thing as the merely finite or the contingent.

But it was not the privilege of pantheists alone to be able to claim complete actual infinity for the world also. On the contrary, Leibniz—who sharply distinguishes between God and the world, completely in the spirit of Christian theism and also more sharply than Bruno or Nicholas—drew this final consequence from the ideas of infinity-perfection and the best of all worlds. That it is precisely an actually infinite world that "expresses" God's infinity can also be a feasible position even if one does not identify God with world. Of course Leibniz does waver on many occasions between expressions of the infinite and the indefinite (regarding the latter one can maintain transcendence only beyond any assignable limit). But even more clearly than in the case of Descartes, it is always only the difficulty our understanding has in conceiving the actually infinite that makes it seem more appropriate to him to use the second expression. Thus Leibniz always preferred—above all in exact science and especially in infinitesimal calculus—definition of the indefinite sort. Yet his metaphysical conviction always remains firmly on the side of the existence of the actual-infinite even in the world! To him, it is not only God who is infinite; there is also infinity in the sense of the greatest thing of its kind: totality of space, maximum of everything extended, and eternity as greatest for all succession in time. In contrast to this he then posits as an example of the indefinite only the asymptotes of the hyperbola and anything else that transcends merely assignable limits. As much as Leibniz thereby emphasizes the possibility of conceiving an infinite whole on the one hand, he nevertheless constantly battles against the medieval, that is, "merely syncategorematic," infinite. What Descartes inferred from the identity of space and body was a conclusion—one against which he struggled in fact— that flowed just as readily from his own conception of space as from a way of ordering objects: If space is infinite, we must assume that the world is also infinite. Only in this way is the world, too, commensurate with the power of the creator. No matter how slim the possiblity is for us to conceive infinite totality, it is just as difficult on the other side for us to think an ultimately finite whole! In a letter to Foucher Leibniz expresses this entirely unmistakably: "Je suis tellement pour l'infini actuel, qu'au lieu d'admettre que la nature l'abhorre, comme l'on dit vulgairement, je tiens qu'elle l'affecte partout, pour mieux marquer les perfections de son Auteur. [I am so much in favor of the actual infinite that instead of admitting that nature abhors it, as people commonly say, I hold that (nature) everywhere favors it, all the better to testify to the perfections of its Author.]"

But the altogether special significance of Leibnizian metaphysics for the problem of infinity consists in the fact that he now extended the new pathos of infinity, which had already animated all those other thinkers, to consideration of the world of the minute and divided. The tendency toward finitism in atomism of the old and new observance was something that Campanella in the Renaissance and then later Descartes's extended matter in particular tried to overcome. But Leibniz now seized on this with new verve and with express emphasis on the idea that it must be possible to pursue traces of divine infinity into the tiny as well! That passage continues: "Thus I believe that there is not a bit of matter existing that is not, I do not say merely divisible, but actually divided; and therefore we must regard the minutest particle as a world filled with an infinity of various creatures." What elated Bruno above all in the macrocosm, the world of the heavens, now comes back once again in the world of the most minute. In every dust particle, every supposed "atom," there is once again a world, innumerable creatures, which in turn themselves encompass worlds within them and so on *ad infinitum:* this is the new expansion of the idea of infinity that moved him so deeply. What most (Nicholas and Bruno no less than ancient atomists) had hitherto taken for granted, Leibniz regarded as an error, namely, that the discrete and the bounded—made up of points [*punktuelles*], so to speak—exists somewhere in space; absolutely nothing discrete and indivisible exists there. Nor does he allow even (Aristotelian-Scholastic) restriction of oneself to the *possibility* of endless division: as Leibniz sees it, endless divisibility always presupposes actually existing division of the thing itself! The objection raised in Antiquity and always repeated ever since, that unless one assumes atoms every finite piece of matter would consist of infinitely many parts—hence there would no longer be any difference between smallest and largest—no longer frightens Leibniz. He holds that, in fact, not only do infinitely numerous entities actually exist in the world (indeed ancient atomists themselves assumed this) but also that actual infinity in turn lives in every tiniest part and individual object in the world. The world is a mechanism in which every part and little cog is in its turn a world and is infinitely composite: this

II. Infinity in the Finite

is how the universe—as the work of the infinite creator and the best of all possible worlds, which actualizes the maximum of real content—distinguishes itself from any sort of human work.

Of course none of this is invalidated by the fact that Leibniz regards everything spatial as having only phenomenal reality, because every "part" in the quantitative-spatial realm has an exactly corresponding counterpart in the nonspatial-intelligible order of the world of monads. If we are to think that a speck of dust is infinitely divisible in the sphere of appearances, this means that for the metaphysical-real world (with reference to which those appearances have been "well founded") this phenomenal image, in its derivative fashion, expresses an "aggregate" of infinitely numerous monads. That is why Leibniz always says (not very precisely and therefore often misunderstood) that an infinity of living beings exists "in" every particle of matter—just as a pool of water that from a distance appears to be dead and uniform-indifferent is full of fish in reality. Even what the microscope shows us is always after all just a spatial phenomenal image. Monads do not exist in a drop of water—indeed, that would be to think of them as atoms or ultimate units in space, which is, indeed, infinitely divided in principle; on the contrary, *corresponding* to infinite particles of the drop of water and even to particles of corporeal living beings that the microscope can still detect, there are infinitely many infinite groups of elementary beings in the real world.

Now the fact that finite being can also participate in this world that is actually endless with regard to greatness and smallness, a world that in addition is caught up in constant evolution for a never-ending duration of time; that we human beings are related to that world in knowledge, will, and feelings; that other beings, too, in spite of all self-contained completeness that characterizes monads, nonetheless belong to this infinite system and are related to it with all existence and life: all of this is made possible for Leibniz precisely through the fact that even the core of particular real being, no matter how elementary and primitive, embraces actual infinity! Even the "minutest" and most limited of finite creatures is perfect-infinite in its own way. In Zeno's discussions about infinity the stock example of the bushel of corn already played its role: A grain of seed that falls makes no noise, but a bushelful that falls does. How can that be? The ancient thinker did not distinguish in this case between objective occurrence of "noise" and our perception. (Thus Aristotle looked for instability in the qualitative aspect of objective events.) Leibniz turned the question on the subject: he is certain that when waves crash on the shore each droplet of water for its part vibrates the air and that all these effects have a cumulative effect. But how does it happen, he now asks, that we do not sense anything of those tiny effects and

103

that we actually perceive only the whole surf? His answer is that even those tiniest movements have their counterpart in the sentient soul. We have perceptions that are so "tiny" that we do not notice them individually; it is only their accumulation that crosses over our threshold of consciousness. And since particles in motion are further divisible and divided, we must accordingly conclude that there are infinitely tiny perceptions in the soul! But this now also explains the soul's knowledge of the world (and even its knowledge of God) and explains the world system of every single monad (for each of them has its own kind of perceptions): the actually infinite element of the universe—in extension and division, in time and space—is mirrored in the actually infinite element of each individual being and in the infinitely multiplied infinite fullness of perceptions that exist and follow one another in each finite monad's being. But what makes these beings finite (in contrast with the divine central-monad that is actually infinite in every respect and comprises itself, the world, and every creature) is the circumstance that in fact not all these perceptions are knowledge, that is, clear and distinct intuitions, as is the case with God; on the contrary the overwhelming majority of this inner life remains in a state of confusion, oversight, and slumber. Every individual being differs from every other, although all of them are mirrors of this same infinite world of God. For in every single creature there exist others in turn of the infinite moments of the world's existence that are maturing toward clarity; thus every being carries within itself its image of the whole that is perspectivally shifted in a completely special way (i.e., illuminated with different accents). Actually infinitely numerous monads and infinite gradations of beings (whereby there are always infinitely numerous steps situated between any two given steps) are all distinguished from one another in this differentiation of their actually infinite inwardness. Each one of these beings, therefore, in itself totally reflects the infinite world—and yet in a finite, individually limited way. Individual being is not a mere mode of divine attributes but rather its own, specifically independent, contraction of and reflection of infinity itself. And in this way Leibniz fulfilled the demand he posited over and over again: to conceive of the world as work of God and as commensurate with the ominipotence of the infinite creator! His theory of creation formulates it graphically as follows: God, the infinite one, surveys infinite possibilities for world constructs. From these infinitely numerous possible worlds he selects one that is actually supposed to come into being. And his goodness then posits the best of all possible worlds, one that comprises within it the maximum of simultaneously possible (compossible) realities. Hence the world of creation is infinitely great. But "inasmuch as he now rotates the universe from all sides and in all ways, the result that issues from each aspect of the universe that is viewed from a specific standpoint,

II. Infinity in the Finite

as it were, is a substance that expresses the universe in conformity with that view.'' In this way, then, one infinite world is mirrored an infinite number of times. (That this world, as the reality of actualized viewpoints [*gewordener Blicke*], is fundamentally identical with that universe on which the creator looks—turning it on all sides, as it were—is a special difficulty of the Leibnizian system that we have no need to pursue at this point.)

Thus in this Leibnizian philosophy of infinity the ''finite'' has itself attained a character of infinity that was never to be surpassed in this direction. And yet here, in spite of the theory concerning infinite development of monads and the world, the question regarding endlessness of time had taken second place behind the mighty effort that overcoming all finitude or mere indefiniteness in extension and division of the coexistent demanded! At this point the young Kant took the decisive step in this direction as well.

Regardless how much the main work of the first half of his life and the entire metaphysics and view of nature it expressed was filled with the new pathos of the infinite; regardless how he deduced infinity of the world in every line as an immediately necessary consequence of the idea of creation; regardless how great traditions created by Nicholas and Bruno (and which had now penetrated beyond metaphysics and science into poetry and general world consciousness of the eighteenth century) echoed in every passage; regardless, even, how much this world picture defined the later Kant's feeling for life and his pathos of ''the starry heavens above me''—we are not going to discuss these things any further at this point. The only point we wish to focus on here is the infinity of time.

We have seen how the Middle Ages (Scotus Erigena notwithstanding) and even the period of the Church Fathers (Clement and Origen notwithstanding) always believed that a decision in favor of a temporal limit to the world process was required by the doctrine of creation. To assume ''eternity'' of the world and of motion (which was natural enough, since Aristotle after all had adopted precisely that position) seemed impossible without obliterating the distinction between God and world. Because Plato's demiurge became superfluous for one who assumed with Aristotle that the world is eternal, people also believed that the Christian creator was incompatible with temporal infinity of the world *a parte ante*. And on this basis they also assumed time and time again that there was a limit for the world at the end of the process. To be sure Thomas, under the impression of that very Aristotelian system, taught that reason was incapable of deciding this question and that absence of a beginning of the world was in any case entirely compatible with the Christian idea of God. In contrast with his teacher Albert he emphasized that in any case one could not deduce beginning in time from the idea of *creatio ex nihilo*. Dietrich von Freiberg, in particular, agreed with

105

him on this point, and building on Dietrich (whereas Duns Scotus still preferred to leave the question open) Meister Eckehart conceived the world and
its process as an eternal moment in God's self-unfolding. In the modern
period from Nicholas on, despite all caution regarding the question of infinity
of time for the world *a parte ante*, one hears the motif of future infinity ever
more clearly. Descartes often speaks of the *durée infinie* [infinite duration]
of the universe (hence one should not restrict the process even to the merely
indefinite!): faith teaches us that heaven and earth shall not really pass away
but only change their forms and that the world, that is, the matter of which
it consists, shall never perish. It follows from this that faith really promises
resurrection and eternal life also for our bodies, "and consequently also for
the world in which they will exist." Leibniz, too, then linked the doctrine of
immortality with the concept of infinite development.

The young Kant saw clearly that this signified actual infinity for the
temporal process. Indeed it seemed to him that this temporal infinity was
even more evident than spatial infinity. Some of the metaphysicians and all
the scientists of his time fought stubbornly against the concept of the actual
infinite (a concept that had just become a very acute issue through Leibniz).
Kant opposed them in a footnote: "If these gentlemen cannot rest easy with
this idea on account of the supposed impossibility of a multitude without
number or limit, then I would just like to ask for the time being: whether
future continuation of eternity will not encompass true infinity of multiplic-
ities and changes, and whether this unending sequence is not totally present
already and all at once to divine intelligence. . . ." But just as truly as God
thinks this infinity of time, he could also "represent the concept of another
infinity in a context confined to space and thereby make the extent of the
world without boundaries." Just as for his predecessors it had been more a
matter of spatial infinity in extension and division, so now it was for Kant
especially this infinity of never-ceasing development that became a direct
expression of God's infinity. His work *On the Structure of the World* deals
"with creation in the entire extent of its infinity with regard to both space
and time!" In expositions of his famous theory of the development of the
world he says:

> But this is the important point, which is . . . worthy of the greatest
> attention, that creation or rather formation of nature begins first of
> all with this middle point and then broadens steadily, little by little,
> into all the more distant expanses to fill up infinite space with worlds
> and orders in the course of eternity. . . . I find nothing that can el-
> evate the spirit of man to more noble wonder by opening up a vista

for him into the infinite range of omnipotence than this portion of the theory that deals with successive completion of creation.

"Creation is not the work of a moment. Once it has begun by producing an infinity of substances and matter, it then remains active with ever increasing degrees of fruitfulness thoughout the entire course of eternity. Millions and whole mountains of millions of centuries will pass by . . . infinity of future succession in time whereby eternity is inexhaustible, will completely and absolutely enliven all places where God is present and bring them . . . to order." "Creation requires nothing less than eternity to fill with life the entire immense expanse of infinite spaces with worlds without number and without end." "And while nature is embellishing eternity with changing appearances, God stays busy in never-ending creation, forming the stuff [den Zeug (sic)] needed to build still greater worlds."

With that, the infinitism of the ancient theory of incessant evolution of periods of the world is also verified for the first time and is turned into something positive in a way that corresponds completely with the idea of creation. We are not talking here about an endless process in which every world as such is really always merely finite and totally separated from the others (where possible, repeating itself as one and the same world in an ever new identical processs). No, we are talking about a single, continuous succession of events permeated by a single meaning that works itself out forever; this is the new doctrine of never-ending development of systems in one infinite universe.

Fichte then carried this further. As one who felt quite far removed from all systematic cosmic speculations from and by nature, Fichte set out instead from the later Kant's idea of infinity. After his turn to critical philosophy with its conviction of the inadequacy of finite-sensible knowledge vis-à-vis problems about infinity in the world of appearances, Kant wanted to restrict himself to human-intellectual infinity in unlimited progress of knowledge and moral perfection; in that way he arrived at the "true infinity" of the moral realm and of the unknowable intelligible world. The entire immense universe of nature, at the thought of which sentient man recoils in terror, is for Fichte nothing but "a dull reflection in mortal eyes" of our own proper spiritual infinity, of our existence that is infinite in its origin and its vocation and is to be developed for all eternity. He regards creation as identical with incessant forward progress of humanity, of the totality of all spiritual beings forever and ever. He, too, speaks of the eventual end of this world that we now inhabit and the beginning of a new reality that will follow it. But he regards this new world as the immediate continuation of the preceding one and of the development begun in it; in other words a further, higher stage in

107

the univocal comprehensive process of spiritual-metaphysical events. Hence for Fichte, too, there is "not *one* future world," as the religious person caught up in the sensible-limiting mode of thinking imagines the future, "but an endless series of future worlds on top of worlds, which differ as a whole from the present, first world not in kind but only in order of succession." We are not to understand "judgment day" as establishing the end and boundary for the unfolding of time. In the creative mode of life of people who effect progress in the realm of the spiritual, the living creative power of the infinite itself is continuously working toward the "exaltation of God" and toward the visible emergence of his image from eternal invisibility in ever new, ever higher clarity.

Eckehart's old concept of the world now came back to life again. Schelling and Hegel joined Fichte in teaching self-development of infinite deity in building up worlds of nature or mind that reflect that deity and enable deity to attain self-consciousness. The finite is itself a moment in the infinite process of the absolute. Infinity is everything, even the finite. In the unending activity of the absolute, apparently merely finite products of the world of nature and souls are formed, but these products are continuously overcome, overtaken, and surpassed through themselves and the endless, impelling drive of productivity within them. The limit is continuously pushed back: indeed this is the way that the absolute-infinite reveals itself. It views itself as endless becoming, as producing that never exhausts itself in any finite product, but rather lets infinity shine forth in these very products. Finitude and infinity are placed in constant reciprocity, not only with each other but in each other; everything real hovers, so to speak, in interpenetration of both entities.

Hegel's logic, in the marvelous power of its intelligibility, then, summarized this entire final phase of the history of the metaphysical idea of infinity and at the same time let sound forth fully again the new valuation, whose emergence we have been following from late Antiquity and earliest Christian times. According to this logic the self-sufficiency of the finite in which the ancients had believed was a self-contradictory concept. The finite is not defined and definable in itself but always only in transition to something else; as a defined-delimited thing it has its boundary with respect to something other (either quantitatively or qualitatively). Otherness is accordingly not an indifferent "outside-it," but its own proper moment. Hence one can never rest content with the finite, for it *exists* precisely only insofar as it goes beyond itself. "The finite is something that is posited with its immanent boundary as the contradictory of itself, through which it is referred and driven beyond itself."

The finite is therefore always the bounded and the transitory. Finitude, "the most stubborn category of the understanding," presents itself to reason

II. Infinity in the Finite

as a moment that is never self-sufficient. Every true definition results only from logical interplay between a thing and its opposite, from constant overturning of concepts. With that begins the march toward the infinite. "It is the nature of the finite itself to go beyond itself, to negate its negation and to become infinite itself." According to Hegel, both Kant and Fichte ultimately remain stuck in this privative infinite. The Ought only drives one anew, over and over, beyond given boundaries and each time only by a step, at which point it is again stuck fast for a moment in something finite. The Ought is thus itself only finite going-beyond, even though it repeats this endlessly. Here, therefore, the infinite is itself always related to the finite thing opposed to it, but that means then: defined by it, bounded by it . . . as something that is itself a finite infinite thing! The error consists precisely in regarding finite as intolerable for, and incompatible with, infinite and in holding that the latter should be absolutely and "perennially" opposed to the former. Kant and Fichte persist with their Ought, with striving toward the indeterminate-infinite element in finitude and with that with contradiction in "understanding."

Thus understood, in its reciprocal relationship with the finite, infinity is merely "bad or negative infinity" (because it is only negation of the finite), infinity of abstract, one-sided understanding. It is only the true concept of infinity, the "infinite of reason," that effects concrete unity, which embraces the finite too and along with it that infinity of obligation, never-ending progression. This actually infinite being (of which that infinite process is always merely an externalization) does not stand by itself *above* the finite as something complete, so that the finite would have its locus *outside* or *beneath* it. It is also not the case that the infinite would stand as indeterminate emptiness, as the beyond of the finite at an unattainable distance from it in contrast with the finite, the sphere of existing, definite entities or realities. On the contrary, this infinity is precisely the affirmative determination of the finite, that which the latter really is. "Thus the finite vanishes in the infinite, and what exists is the infinite alone." "The finite is not the real; the infinite alone is the real." Both the finite and the "bad" infinite—bounded and boundless—are only moments in the motion of the actually infinite being, whereby the latter always works "to return to itself through its negation." Truly infinite being exists, just as both these moments of it, essentially only as becoming: as merely turning back to itself and being turned back to itself by crossing over into its other; through this process it becomes concrete reality. The absolute in itself is just as finite as it is infinite. Thus according to Hegel the "main principle of philosophy" is that of idealism: ideality of the finite and of finite process. The "basic concept of philosophy" for him, however, is "the truly infinite," in which concept absolute reality itself has found a new definition.

109

III.
Soul and External World

Connected with the changes we have thus far described in the concept of the world as affected by the concept of God is the development of a problem that is just as important. The driving impulse behind this development is the question concerning the soul and the relationship of the soul's existence to external nature. On this issue as well, the Middle Ages and the Modern Period share a common ground of life and differ sharply from the fundamentally different kind of feeling about the world that classical Antiquity had. Thus here, too, as later thought becomes stronger in its own right, a thoroughgoing settling of accounts with certain traditions of Antiquity becomes necessary. And though it was not until modern philosophy that Descartes settled the transformation with complete systematic clarity, nonetheless it was thereby fulfilling demands that from the age of the Church Fathers, above all Augustine, permeated the entire Christian philosophy of the Middle Ages and altogether essentially defined its controversies with the philosophical tradition. But here, too, that "period of decline" of waning Scholasticism was of decisive importance in attaining new independence. It was here at last that theory about the soul (as Siebeck emphasized, in full accord with the general philosophical/historical thesis that we are presenting) really began to free itself from ancient tradition. The origins of modern psychology are to be found here, not first in the Renaissance period's reflections on life.

Ancient philosophy regarded the soul first and foremost as an entity in the world, in nature, as part or member of the cosmos. Physical world perspective dominated and classified views of the nature of the soul; from the start people conceived those views as in harmony with concepts of matter and bodies. Soul was an object of nature; psychology was the physics of this particular object in nature, an excerpt from theory of external nature. What people saw and sought for above all in the soul was an explanation for motion, life, organic development in the world, in what is given in space. Thus Thales assumed a soul in a magnet, which has the power to cause motion without itself being pushed or moved. And, quite universally, natural philosophers of his time regarded matter as living-animated (''hylozoism''). ''Everything is full of souls'': people felt and meant this at that time in a way that is completely different from how one would probably understand it today. At that time one did not yet separate matter from the psychic, the conscious, the thinking mind; at that time there were as yet no subjects in opposition to objects in our sense. In the living, moved world man was an entity among many others, and so was his soul. Just as people conceived of forces of nature in soul-like fashion without occasioning a split in the picture of nature, so did concepts of soul for their part easily take on material character. The lightest and most delicate materials were what made up the existence of the soul. The soul was fluid or airlike, warm and firelike. That is how it still was for Heraclitus and Empedocles.

Although Anaxagoras separated the moving-ordering principle from matter and as a result, in opposition to hylozoism, dualism surfaced between a material and intrinsically inert carrier and a moving-formative nous, nevertheless even here people saw both of them as simply existing on the single plane of objects! Nous was not ''mind'' in our sense; it was the purposefully operative, harmoniously ordering world force that exists alongside world matter. In spite of the distinction, the connection between them was so close that one could raise the question whether Anaxagoras's nous did not itself signify a kind of matter. That is also why at that time the transition to the materialism of the atomists was not such a harsh step and why their description of the soul's processes as movements of atoms did not mean a leap into a sphere that appeared at first to be completely heterogeneous to the soul as it did for those, say, who in the Modern Period crossed over from the dualism of Descartes (who characterized everything intellectual through the *cogito*, in contrast with anything extended-material) into materialism. Democritus's soul, consisting of fire-atoms as the liveliest atoms of all, still remained closely related to the fire-soul of Heraclitus. Hence in the subsequent period not only the Epicureans but even the Stoics themselves could remain materialists in their own way or renew the old hylozoism. Their divine pneuma, from which even the soul of man derives, the world force of the fire that permeates all things, was corporeal-physical in nature, just as everything else is that is real.

With Plato's philosophy a completely different direction in the ancient concept of soul came up for decision. Although in their concept of the soul—say, in the Homeric poems—people always thought of soul only in connection with living body, conceived soul's powers essentially as living activities alone, and virtually identified them with parts of the body, and although then the soul after death stood for nothing more than a gradually disappearing (because bloodless) shadow; nevertheless, Orphic mysteries and Pythagorean theology of the soul had taught immortality of the soul. They saw the body as a trial for the soul, a prison, a transition phase in the migration of souls! Thus here the soul was not merely a moment in the process of nature but something independent, which remained such in contrast to all matter and corporeality; it was separable from the latter and of higher rank, for at bottom it belonged to a superworldly and hyperphysical existence. Plato's doctrine of the soul stands in this tradition. Now we have not only dualism between ideas and matter but dualism between immortal soul and corporeality. Plato regarded the soul as an intermediate form between pure immortal ideas and the material-sensual world with its coming to be and passing away; soul is immortal but not eternally unmoved like the ideas themselves; it simply remains alive without perishing.

But even so the soul is nevertheless just a member of the world, more precisely a mediator between two worlds, two realms of objects! For the world of ideas is a world, immaterial to be sure and in no wise objectlike, but nonetheless objective for all that. This immaterial element of the ideas is no less distant from "spiritual" ["*Geistigen*"] in the modern sense than Anaxagoras's nous was; it is intelligible, but it is not an intelligent thing! Plato's "idealism" does not rest on a concept of the soul-like-subjective nor on primacy of consciousness over external being nor on self before objects, as is the case with idealism in the Modern Period! Ideas are true being; and just as objects of spatial reality are composites of the non-being of matter and those form structures, so existence of souls establishes a bridge between that world of pure being and this tottering existence of appearances. Soul is like a mixture of objectively conceived rational being and bodily existence. Hence despite all his religious premonition of a specific inwardness of the soul and despite his doctrine of immortality of the human soul, Plato sees the soul as totally harnessed to the existence of the world. It is not something in contrast with the world or worlds, but is rather a member in them and among them. And this is just as true for him with respect to the close binding of all the soul's functions to bodily organs as it is in his theory of the world as a *zoon* [living being, animal], a doctrine that then became the source of all ideas about world-soul in later Platonism. The world-soul was always a principle of life, the inexhaustible, primordial, and meaningful evolution of the world as a whole. The soul was not thereby something that would be

112

conscious of the world as its opposite number and would influence it only from such a distance, as it were; on the contrary, soul is a driving moment of the world's existence itself, just as the principle of life in every organism is not at all set off at a distance from its spatial-corporeal existence but is instead completely interwoven with it, even though it is not itself spatial and is not a body.

Thus Plato's great student, combining doctrines of philosophy of nature with concepts of his master, then defined soul precisely as first entelechy, as power and actuality of the body. Aristotle is the father of soul theory [*Seelenlehre*] as a special philosophical discipline, but his psychology is itself an excerpt from physics—it is physics of living being or biology. His treatise "On the Soul" investigates manifestations of life in plant, animal, and man, from the merely vegetative up to deliberative thought that develops in the service of life. "Endowed with life" and "endowed with soul": both things point in an entirely single direction insofar as one does not mean something absolutely identical by the terms. Soul is purpose, form, and cause of movement for the body; hence it exists only in constant correlation with matter. It is form that organizes body; it is the immanent goal of nature in the living thing, the goal of its development, the invisible, inner life force. All life means passing beyond matter, which is capable of becoming anything, into determinate, delimiting-ordering form. [Aristotle] emphasizes the body-formative function of the soul so absolutely that one can no longer speak of immortality of individual soul as Plato taught it in accord with those religious traditions. Soul is inseparable from body, whose form it is, and its affects are always at the same time those of the body. Higher functions of the soul, those directed solely to the intelligible, can never exist without lower ones, through which the soul is completely interwoven into the system of nature. When body dissolves, soul also must perish. All that remains is universal form, which indeed as a principle is imperishable. But as an individual being a person is a unified, organic whole, of which the soul is only a particular, not really separable, side. Thus Aristotle's psychology never really deals with the soul's inwardness as such but only with a person's reciprocal activity with external nature and society! Soul remains within the cosmos, not opposite it; it is not a world in itself. Self is swallowed up in outer world.

Nevertheless there is an eternal element that resides in the individual human soul: in this regard Aristotle follows [earlier] religious promptings and Plato's thought. For in his perception and behavior man does not merely function in reciprocal relationship with surrounding nature; on the contrary, he also knows the highest principles in purely conceptual thought. This thought lies higher than any reflection in practical life, which for its part still belongs with achievements of the organic soul-principle. With respect to its

113

content, scientific and purely theoretical knowledge of the abstract and intelligible has nothing more to do with the body; it no longer belongs together with biological reflections. Whatever there is of purely theoretical reason in man does not come about through generation nor is it affected by death; it does not mingle with the corporeal, although thought can influence the body. But for Aristotle this means: it has nothing to do with the individual person. As far as the individual is concerned, his highest thought is still essentially bound to lower functions and the body, and that is where it stays. Thus if reason as such transcends corporeality and death, nonetheless it has nothing to do in itself with being restricted to the particularity of the individual soul. When an individual person dies, the rational element in him reverts to the immaterial, lively ether of the celestial sphere. Thus it appears even among the living as though from the outside [thurathen] as something that per se is totally different from it. Reason is One [Eine], unique, and universal; and rationally active soul shares in eternal reason only for the duration of its transitory existence, but that eternal reason of itself has nothing to do with singularity or individual life. Hence for Aristotle also there is in the human soul a peculiarly spiritual element that is distinct from the mere principle of life, but insofar as, at the same time, it blends into the universal element of unitary reason, it also entirely loses the character of specific inwardness and subjectivity toward which religious ideas of immortality tend of themselves. Hence even Aristotle's concept of divine nous still remains far removed from the concept of "spirit" as later ages have understood it. To be sure, the unification for which Plato's theory of ideas first paved the way is already actually carried out here: that of the spiritual with the immaterial; and it is also declared of this God that he is aware of himself [daß er sich selber denkt]. But just as Spinoza's substance (which numbers among its attributes that of "thinking" also) as causa sui [cause of itself] nevertheless remains at an unbridgeable remove from the "self-positing" of Fichte's self—as an objective-substantial entity even in its activity of thinking in contrast to this absolute inwardness and active [aktmäßigen] subjectivity—so also Aristotle does not think of the self-referral of nous as a subjective soul-like event nor as a kind of personal self-consciousness, but instead merely as an expression of its self-sufficiency and freedom from anything worldly. This "thinking" by the divine nous does in fact not think the world, nor does it see the cosmos as its opposite or in itself. For that would then somehow contaminate the purity of this highest eternal form with matter and relate it to the transitory-manifold! Instead it remains within itself, and it revolves within itself alone. As highest unattained ultimate purpose, nous transcends every existing thing that longingly strives for it as its fulfillment, as archetype of every truly existing thing. Just as the One Being of the Eleatics and Plato's Ideas did,

III. Soul and External World

so likewise does this God of Aristotle put itself forward as ideal being, as archetype and substantial form. There is no real breaking through the circle of objectivity here either.

It was not until the concept of soul in Alexandrian and Neoplatonic philosophy that a transformation began to make its way in this matter; here, too, there was decisive influence from the influx of oriental religiosity and attitude toward life. To be sure, in the case of Philo the soul was still one of the forces that God introduces into matter to inform it [*um sie zu formen*] without tainting itself with materiality, in other words, primarily a moment in the objective world process. Plotinus, too, understood his concept of soul entirely in the context of metaphysics of being conceived according to physical categories; his psychology arose in the framework of mystical philosophy of nature! From the One emanates the nous and from the latter the world-soul, which contains all individual souls. Here, too, the soul is only a weaker reflection of rational being! Nevertheless, however, it is still not a moment and a member, like any other, in the world process, but rather—in accordance with religious traditions—a true pivotal point of cosmic events. In it the process is twisted around: *proodos* [a going before] becomes *epistrophe* [a turning about]. And the soul can play this special role in virtue of the uniquely special character of its spiritual being that now really comes to philosophical awareness for the first time.

In Greek thought of the classical period there was absolutely no real concept of the subjective or of the subject, insofar indeed as one understands this expression to mean not merely "attributed" ["*untergelegte*"] substantial element or carrier of predicates, but rather that special element—so hard to describe—that everyone nevertheless recognizes in the existence and life of his self and in the deliberate activity of his own inward being. To be sure, Heraclitus had said that in his research he was really looking for himself, and Socrates of course had advised everyone to know himself. But with the preponderance of physical-biological motives as well as of concepts of supersensible being, people never really arrived at the point of genuine reflection about the soul as subject, as self, as independent sphere of activities and facts of consciousness that is just as separable from any reality of nature as it is from the sphere of the ideal-immaterial and is posited opposite to both of them as subject is to objects. Plato's theory of perception contained the first significant impulse toward a concept of subjectivity or consciousness; it juxtaposes the *psyche* as a unified-comparative function to contents communicated to us through bodily organs. But despite how much this epistemological motif was intrinsically destined to distinguish soul as subject from outer world and from all objective being in general, nevertheless it was the struggle of moral-religious inwardness that first led to a complete grasp of

115

the problem. The Stoics discovered conscience as "co-knowledge" ["*Mit-Wissen*"] of man about his own condition of soul in moral struggle that proceeded alongside knowledge of the externally given; it was the experience of conscience that stimulated the concept of consciousness. It was not until then that a breach was made in the objectivism of theories about reason, the nous, and the spiritual. The *dianoia* of the Stoics pointed more clearly to consciousness than did the *noein* of Plato. The later Stoics in particular refined the motif into the individual-personal and contributed decisively to the emergence of the concept of the self.

Thus with Plotinus, who combined initiatives of Plato and the Stoics with experiences of oriental mysticism, the special character of the soul as subject broke through at that turning point in world history. Precisely this, that the soul knows about itself, that it "accompanies itself," made the transformation possible and freed it from its bondage to body and matter. The higher, special element of the soul is that inner element in which we know about ourselves. In this inner core the human soul is its own activity, grasping everything else, even its own contents that are transmitted to it perhaps through the senses or in some other way. The special spontaneous unity of consciousness stands in contrast with everything manifold-objective as its mirror. The outer is reflected in the inner. Thus the soul, which is itself a member in the cosmic process, can nevertheless independently oppose the process in its own inward contemplation and, turning its back on the body, can prepare a path toward the One through self-reflection.

But now Christian thinkers posed the problem of the soul and the world completely anew and on an entirely different basis. Although even Plotinus (who after all had pressed forward the farthest toward insight into the special character of the soul as something distinct from everything external and existing—something subjective, conscious, and self-aware) viewed the soul as one form [*Gebild*]) among others in the cosmos, in a world-process conceived in essentially physical terms, so that even questions about the human soul still occupied a place in the general framework in which people speculated about the world-soul and souls of the stars, the Christian perspective freed the soul entirely from such a naturalistic context. The center of gravity not only of all theory about life but also of reflection about the world shifted completely away from the physical-cosmic into the personal. The all-important thing here was the moral-religious process alone, and whereas even the latest thinkers of Antiquity still confined this process entirely within the great physical activity of the world and the tensions of existence, now this objective element receded completely, was scarcely considered at all, and counted as something entirely secondary. The important thing now was no longer objects and substances, bodies or ideas, but only individual souls as persons with inner conflicts and inner destinies. The mightiest of challenges was posed to their pure inwardness: It was not the place they occupied or the share they had in a visible or invisible universe that decided the issue of their existence or value, but rather how they were related inwardly to the spirit that was separate from, and superior to, all world objectivity—a spirit that was also person, a personal God who knows what goes on in human beings. The doctrine of creation by itself already implied absolute preeminence of the spiritual in this new subjective-personal sense. Here one did not regard understanding and will as higher functions in a natural order that rises up from matter to living activity and even beyond that to rational behavior; instead, all of external nature, the cosmos itself, is ultimately the product of a personal act that is accomplished through thinking and willing! Whereas Antiquity, to the very end, thought ultimately in natural concepts and objective categories of being (e.g., the world was an ascent of life or an emanation of light), here everything flows from the central concept of person and "categories of inwardness" (the world is a creation, indeed one that in complete contrast to Plato exists entirely without any preexisting being or ideas or matter anteceding the spiritual act)! The primordial principle, the One Good, is not being in Parmenides' sense. It is not the "idea" of good nor the nous, even as perfect form and as unmoved-yet-moving goal, but a divine person who knows and wills, loves and forgives. The subjectivity of this personal God does not "mix" with the material and the particular when that subjectivity thinks the latter or inwardly relates itself to it in the way that form and idea mix with matter when they relate to it in their activity. Hence this God does not have to turn away from all else and revolve within himself all alone in order to maintain his sublimity and purity.

But the crown of all creation is precisely man, the individual soul; everything hinges on him. Of course, even as focal point and purpose of the whole, man still stands "in" nature, in this world of external existence; but now this no longer means that the world in itself is a natural-soul-like complex and that the soul is, so to speak, a product of the cosmos just like any other. On the contrary, the world is only an arena or an environment; bodies and objects are just means toward the development on which everything depends: the process of the soul's salvation! Thus the soul is far superior to all of

117

nature, the whole world, and any objectivity; here existence has importance only in relation to the inner element of personal experience. Nature is a product of spirit for the sake of spirit, of the soul. Freed in its profoundest being from the system of nature, the soul is essentially subject and person, like the creator himself in whose image it was created. *How it relates to God* and what its consciousness and its conscience see, feel, and seek: these are what first determine its "existence"! Inner spontaneity in acts of love and hate, of repentance and submission, in the act of free will above all, defines its being. Mind and will, rooted in the innermost core of subjectivity, achieve preeminence over knowledge and "reason," in which people were inclined to emphasize an impersonal relationship of man (as a mirror) to the outer world and from the standpoint of which one did not always properly understand the subjective uniqueness of the soul—in fact knowledge and "reason" often even lent themselves to being understood in an objective manner as a form or function of existence in the nous. But now truly existing being was no longer a system of intelligible figures, no longer substantial form, most especially no longer the cosmos of orbiting stars or concentrated atoms, but instead a realm of spiritual persons, intelligences, willing and feeling subjects, all of whom are related to one another and to the person of God in spiritual relationships of love and commitment, spontaneous devotion or aversion. Soul is immortal, but not, as with Plato and the Platonists of Antiquity, taking second place (because it was still living and akin to becoming) to the purity of eternal ideas; instead, as an immortal person with its living activity of mind and will, it is the most accurate image of divine existence, which is itself personal existence; this kind of immortality cannot be surpassed by the eternity of another being other than one from God himself. Hence immortal soul exists in closest community with the living God, not just in a dependency-relationship of cloudy "participation" or waning emanation. In comparison with it, then, all objective existence, especially everything natural-worldly, is only something external and secondary which, in separation from the soul, is entirely nugatory. In the welling up of purely inner acts of consciousness the soul lifts itself in the last analysis above the entire objectively conditioning world structure. People now no longer evaluated the soul's path of salvation in terms of the universal course of the world process, but rather the other way around: it is only on the basis of inner knowledge of the essence, meaning, and goal of the soul that we first come to know what we are to hold regarding external being, the cosmos, and forms in general . . . regarding their worth and even their existence! The world process and the destiny of all objects depends essentially on the behavior of subjects; world law is not cosmic but ethical, and the goal of the world is to unite souls with the creator. Hence we can no longer define the soul essentially as form of the body: the body is means, instrument, or expression for independent, spontaneous special life of the soul, hence we must raise the question in an altogether new way as to how the connection between body and soul and their obviously existing community is possible.

The philosophy of the Church Fathers demonstrates this new order in its characteristic struggle with ideas of Antiquity. No matter how much moral and theological questions came to the fore in the patristic period, compared with interest in the external world, and no matter how much that period's entire struggle toward a concept of the human soul revolved around the question of immortality, immateriality, and freedom, this period nonetheless could not quite shake itself free from ancient formulas. We can observe this in a most unusual form in Tertullian (and similarly in Arnobius and others), who as the first philosopher of the soul and of inner consciousness in the Christian era nevertheless remained completely under the sway of Stoic hylozoism or materialism and the old subordination of soul to the spatial-worldly system. He still saw the soul as gentle, airlike matter that permeated the entire body. But on the other hand, insight into the special character of the soul-like–subjective was increasing on all sides. People recognized the inward intertwining of passive perception and spontaneous thought with one another, whereas they had diverged so widely (especially in the Aristotelian tradition) in spite of mediating instances, that the nous strove to free itself from the living particularity of the individual person. People increasingly emphasized spontaneous activity of the soul in all its functions and at the same time the point that on the basis of this inner power and activity we have an absolutely unique kind of perception and inner knowledge. But the more this went on, the more the new concept of the soul also broke free from speculations about the world-soul that had asserted themselves so much in late Antiquity.

Aristotle's definition could no longer suffice now. Gregory of Nazianzus in particular expressly fought against it. To describe the soul as the goal of bodily development and growth was the same as to make its own special calling entirely dependent on its being conditioned by the body. But in reality the soul is its own end; it is a being independent in its own right. Later on Nemesius in particular stressed this point: how seriously the old conception failed to do justice to the substantiality and immortal life of the soul. In trying to reconcile the motifs people (carrying forward Aristotle's old theory of the special position of the nous as well as some Hellenistic distinctions) then attempted to understand the essence of man in tripartite fashion: not just body and soul—but body, soul, and spirit work together in it. From the psyche that gives life to the body and that exists in animals also (governing their instinctual activities and then perishing when they die), pneuma stands apart

119

as something higher, something immortal and spiritual. The expression that the Stoics still used to designate precisely the motive breath of the divine-material world force, and accordingly corporeal-animate life, now—in association with Philo and the New Testament—becomes the principle of the inward-animate element in which the special nature of the person is contained and is linked to the concept of nous. Psyche plays the role of mediator here between spirit and body, essential immortality and natural mortality. This is what Tatian had taught and later Irenaeus, Origen, and many others. Manichaean dualism indeed used it to base its doctrine of two souls in man's breast, the light-soul and the body-soul [der Lichtseele und der Leibeseele].

Augustine was decisive on this question. It is precisely in connection with the problem of subjectivity that he has been called, without exaggerating the expression, the first modern man. With his doctrine of the self-certitude of consciousness, in fact, he laid the foundation for thousands of years of development. The enormous power of the new religious life in this man, who otherwise still belonged in many ways to late Antiquity, fully expressed the great transformation in this area at a time still previous to the entire Middle Ages and twelve centuries before Descartes's famous starting principle. Indeed the soul became the focus of metaphysical interest in an entirely new way through the fact that Augustine, following suggestions from Gregory of Nyssa in particular, time and again linked speculations on the Trinity with immediate self-givenness of the soul and the trinity of its inner being. Man, that is, the soul of man, is the image of God; therefore one must be able to sketch out the mystery of the deity on the basis of soul. Just as in the soul the all-encompassing basis of memory is united with activities of thinking and willing; and just as, according to our immediate inner experience (which is not subject to any sort of deception), the soul is itself also existing being and self-knowledge (and as such existing being and knowledge is self-affirmation and love): so are Father, Son, and Holy Spirit bound together eternally in God's being. Thus the soul's knowledge of itself leads it to knowledge of God and thence also to a true concept of the being and meaning of existence and the world; but such knowledge is impossible to us through physics, in our experience of the world itself! Augustine could not wonder enough about how it was possible that men nevertheless have always looked outwards and, forgetting themselves, were always in awe only of the magnitude of the cosmos, mountains, seas, and stars; yet that they did not sooner discover true infinity and primordial magnitude in themselves and in their own inner lives. Truth resides in the inner man; we must seek knowledge about God and the soul, not about the external world.

With this perspective on the interior, Augustine saw the essence of soul in altogether new clarity. He did not reject what he knew about the graduated

III. Soul and External World

structure of Aristotle's doctrine of the soul's functions. The soul does in fact also have to do with the body. But over and above that the soul nevertheless resides in its own existence-in-itself and in its opening to God. It is from this perspective that man first grasps the total incommensurability of soul and body. There are no similarities between inner processes such as feeling, thinking, or, above all, willing and spatial-physical events! In the soul's knowledge of itself it never encounters anything corporeal. To be able to observe and understand the soul's proper function correctly, we must also really consider it entirely without reference to the external; and this is all the more true with regard to the ultimate substantial being of immaterial souls themselves. With Augustine psychology is now no longer teaching about the body-soul connection or about activity and influence between man and outer world in nature and the state; instead the focus is on the truly innermost element of the life of the soul, on impulses of the heart and of conscience. Augustine immersed himself into the most subjective life-core of mind and will in a way that no one before him had ever done, leaving relations to body and external world altogether aside. The element that positively characterizes the soul for him and elevates it unequivocally above all objective existence is the soul's unique capacity to turn back on itself, to know about its own existence and meaning, and to will within itself in inward spontaneity. Something that is the subject of thinking and experiencing in this way can after all not then become merely the appearance of another objective-material carrier. Even in the body-soul context the distinction is still sharp and clear: As bodily organ the eye can never direct itself to itself nor can it sense its own proper affect; it is only the perceptive soul that is aware of its own existence and its receptivity even as it functions.

But it is at this point that Augustine took the great step that brought him into complete opposition with the universal habit of thought of Antiquity. Antiquity saw the most immediate and most primordial of all certitudes in the existence of the cosmos, in objectivity (conceived of either spatially or ideally); soul lives as a special member in it, shares in it, mediates between those spheres, and is the nodal point of the world process. To be sure, the Sophists and then above all the Skeptics of the late period had shaken the security of the foundation and tried to dissolve the givenness of the world and all absolute reality along with it into relativities and appearance. By logical necessity this led them to the concept of consciousness and gave them a glimpse of the prerogative of certitude that had to devolve on the subject on the basis of doubt concerning the world. But in their investigations the center of gravity always lay in a negative and destructive direction; in that respect, too, interest still remained fixed on the external world. But now Augustine, whose youth had led him through all the paths of doubt of the

121

Academy, discovered the decisive point of a new indubitable and immediate certitude (and with that at the same time the point of departure for all certain knowledge in general) in the soul's knowledge of itself. Whatever appeared to be uncertain and relative in the givenness of objects and forms, no matter what it was that one might call into doubt, nevertheless in doubt itself, indeed even in manifest deception, there is still present as a first and unshakable certainty the existence of the soul that is considering the doubt and of perceptions that have been unmasked as appearance, as inner determinations of soul. He concedes to the Skeptics that the external world is really not absolutely certain and immediately guaranteed; this is something we can learn from them. But he denies in order to affirm: the soul, whose existence seems at first to succumb to doubt along with the cosmos in which the soul resides, now reveals itself as immediately certain reality that people have merely sought for in the wrong place. One may not look for the soul in the external world that has grown so uncertain. Quite the reverse: one must pose the question about the existence and meaning of the objective-real world on the basis of the self-given and immediately experienced reality of the soul! Inner experience has unconditional priority of evidence before anything external: this is the Christian thinker's epistemological expression of a new attitude of life. The long-underestimated primordial givenness of consciousness has now been clearly attained and facts of consciousness press completely to the foreground. What exists and lives and has eternal validity is above all the soul and the spiritual that is soul-like; anything else that still claims to exist must first prove itself on this basis.

From this inner self-knowledge of the soul the path leads first of all to God. This is so not simply according to the analogies of functions within the soul to the spiritual-personal essence of God and to the Trinity; no, it is already based on the fact that all doubting reflection necessarily points to the certain and irrevocably eternal truth one finds lacking in that reflection. In fact, doubt implies the idea of God as absolute truth and presupposes his existence; hence we always think and judge in God! Both on the basis of the inner uncertainty of conscience and likewise on the basis of the knower's search [for truth], the path leads directly to God, not first to the world and to bodies. God is the only being we can grasp immediately and with absolute certainty on the basis of our soul that we inwardly experience as actually existing. External world on the other hand and even the body are further removed from us. Augustine does indeed consider them as real and as having their separate existence alongside subjects endowed with souls, that is, persons; it is not just the world of spirits but the cosmos too that has real existence. But in contrast with the eternity and self-worth of those substances, the world's existence is for Augustine after all merely a transitory means to spiritual and moral activity; it is in fact a sphere that we must overcome in the long run by force of will and action. A soul that is elevated to the highest good leaves object-existences behind. Indeed our knowledge of the world does not rest on immediate self-givenness, but only on a kind of faith whose truth value lies in that moral relationship. The external has meaning and real certitude for us only insofar as it is an arena for the life of reflection and its effects.

Furthermore Antiquity's other world, that of the intelligible, was now also subordinated to the idea of subject, just as the corporeal-spatial world had been. Plato held that the soul existed only on the borderline, as it were, of that realm of ideas; it is only insofar as it seeks the ideas and duplicates them within itself, only insofar as it loves and intuits the ideas, that the soul really participates in genuine and authentic existence. Even the world-craftsman was stationed below the sphere of those eternal figures toward whose power of existence (which was entirely independent of him) all his creation was directed. But now Augustine took over something that people had already taught in the religious-mystical currents of orientalizing Hellenism and that Eusebius and others then took up, and he made it the very center of the relationship between God and the world: Plato's Ideas now stood for thoughts of God! The intelligible was subsumed into the intelligent. From now on ideas no longer appear as pure entities from an ideal realm, but rather as contents of spiritual and personal acts, as products of divine intellect! It is not the **idea** of the good that is the "father of ideas," but rather the personal God, divine intelligence; and so now the origin of the ideas coincides with that of the world, and the demiurge becomes the creator of the world whose omniscience is the origin of everything intelligible-ideal, not just its reflection. Hence from now on all pure rational knowledge and all knowledge of the intelligible is for its part vision of God, contact with, and groping for, divine intelligence in its eternal structure, as it were. Now the nous has become entirely subjectivity. And this then became the common property of Christian thinkers, so much so that subsequent periods, that is the entire Middle Ages, quite unabashedly understood Plato's Ideas themselves in this sense.

Augustine's doctrine about absolute primacy of certitude and metaphysical superiority of inner life, which was so new and so profoundly revolutionary for the entire concept of the world, became decisive over broad stretches of the Middle Ages. Again and again, cultivation of inner experience, demand for self-knowledge, and investigation of the soul's functions in their ascent to the vision of God became the focal point of thought. The concept of soul, subject, and consciousness was clarified in controversy regarding religious goods. It was the mystics of the period, from Bernard of

Clairvaux on, who most profoundly understood the ideas of Augustine and kindred spirits from Christian Neoplatonism. In contrast with the biological gradation of Aristotle's concept of the soul (whereby the active-rational element of the soul ultimately came "from outside" and was rigorously distinguished from lower functions), here one always sought to understand the inner unity of the soul as continuous transition from lowest activities of consciousness on up to the very highest. The stages of history of the soul in the evolution of salvation were laid down and the rest was also developed as well; indeed the seed that leads to something higher, a kind of spontaneous activity and thought, was already planted in perception and in all sensual experience. Soul cannot disintegrate into sensuality that is totally foreign to its ultimate purposes and a purely spiritual part of its inner life.

The Victorines, especially Hugh, brought this Augustinian impetus to its richest flowering. The distinction between soul-like–subjective and spatial-material emerged ever more clearly. The core of the distinction was the inner freedom of the human subject. In man, as the image of God, the essential occurs not through pressure from outside or from blind necessity, as in the case of corporeal objects, but from inner direction and activity! The essence of the soul is now freed from the cosmic system of external necessity, in which it had still remained even for Neoplatonism. What is true of moral life, namely, that the good cannot be something externally forced on us, but rather can only be something that wells up from our innermost core, is now extended to the rest of the soul's life. Even knowledge in all its degrees is a special kind of making! The soul's reflection of the image of God manifests itself nowhere more clearly than through this creating-out-of-oneself, this activity of the self. A wall or a mirror can have an image impressed on it from without; but the soul must obtain its ideas through its own internal activity—it has to generate them inwardly through its own power. At the same time this also sharply distinguishes what belongs to the soul from anything corporeal: that for the latter the decisive thing is that it has a solid form that rejects every other, for an object cannot simultaneously have another form than the one that it has; whereas in the soul's knowledge there is always a mixture of many, indeed often opposed, forms, and the soul is able to grasp both the one and the other simultaneously. But the more sharply we distinguish soul and body in this way, the more urgently a question presses to the fore, which for the ancients—when it happened to come up (from a religious source)—achieved no real metaphysical importance of its own; it is a question that entirely lost its special importance for Aristotle's definition of soul and that crops up for the first time again with compelling force in the intellectual milieu of the Fathers of the Church: the question is how the connection between body and soul is possible! Hugh of St. Victor's insight into the

124

essential incommensurability between the soul's and the body's existence was so deep that, following Augustine's lead in this matter also, he could regard the connection between them only as an incomprehensible miracle of God.

The way of salvation, that is, the path of evolution of the soul, also goes therefore from the external to the internal and only thereby to God. In everyday life the world and the external are so preponderant (so that it can appear to be the truly real into which the soul itself is inserted as a member) that in natural knowledge it is always the eye of the flesh and the world that asserts itself, and this is something Hugh regards as the consequence of sinful perversion of what is "natural" in a higher sense! And the task of one who is striving for truth is precisely to turn this orientation around through a resolute new way of looking at things: through introspection and self-knowledge ultimately to arrive at the wisdom of God. He, too, sees the material world essentially only as a means for developing and initially stimulating inner life. Thus we can first achieve clarity even about the world only by way of knowledge of self.

But at the same time, however, the Middle Ages never succeeded in freeing themselves from the ancient conception of soul and nature. Time and again Aristotelianism prevented full development of the Augustinian initiatives. In spite of all new insight into the special character of inner life and in spite of all conviction about the unique primacy of soul and spirit, people still tried to conceive the relationship of body and soul under the objectivizing conceptual schema of form and matter that wiped away the specific opposition between them. Body is mere possibility, given life by and shaped by soul in order to become full reality in union with it; its own actual existence must come from the soul. That removed substantial existence from the body, and thereby essentially drew the soul also entirely into the physical process. And this direction of thought not only did not steadily diminish in the advance of Western thought; on the contrary, as in so many other points, it was the influx of Aristotelian tradition and writings, growing ever greater right on up to the very summit of the Middle Ages, that first produced the whole preponderance of ancient tradition and the conflicts it entailed. And with the influence of Arabic scholarship especially (which by the way also contributed very significantly to theory of the soul), the objectivistic point of view (in many ways even with materialistic and naturalistic tendencies) came fully to the foreground once again. To the same extent as interest in external nature revived once again, the concept of the soul also threatened in many ways to surrender itself to it again. People were disposed to view the soul's powers in Aristotelian fashion as the full development of the body's organic functions, even to the point of "receptive" [*empfangenden*] reason; and the purely spiritual element in reason that clearly manifests itself in the process, namely "active intellect," in turn has the tendency to break itself free from individual existence and then becomes—in strict opposition to Christian doctrine of the immortal individual soul—all-encompassing universal mind. And with this concept in turn, just as with all concepts about the world-soul, the character of subjectivity threatens to perish entirely. That was naturally an outcome (developed in "Latin Averroism") that Scholasticism, whatever its dependence on Aristotle, was bound to contest on the basis of religious dogma. Albert and Thomas led the fight. But they still remained under the sway of Aristotle's concept of the soul in the matter. Along with Aristotle and the Arabs, they, too—just as William of Auvergne or Alfred Angelicus did earlier under pressure of the same influences—defined the soul as general entelechy, full actuality of the body, principle of organic life. According to Thomas, then, even the union of body and soul in man is in no way a miracle, but rather a natural combination of form and matter. In his theory there is no need to look for special connecting links between them (such as certain concepts of pneuma or of ether sought to describe).

On the contrary, in opposition to all tendencies to separate the inner soul-like element from the body's principle of life, Thomas posited his doctrine of "unity of form." According to that theory it is one and the same form that makes man living being and also rational being; the soul that nourishes and senses is one with the soul that thinks. As he sees it, this is the only way that man can be a substantial being and a substantial unity; otherwise he would be one only *per accidens*. In itself the body is not yet substance, not full reality; it becomes such only through the soul: immaterial soul is the substantial form of body. Hence the body always conditions human knowledge; it begins with the senses and cannot think anything without sense representation. Even the purely inward self-knowledge that Augustine had brought to light is nevertheless possible only through self-observation of activities of the soul that are accomplished with given sensible content. Thus the connection of the body and the outer world is a moment that thoroughly conditions the entire life of man's soul. Just as Aristotle's theory of knowledge did, so too does Thomas's theory emphasize throughout the passive dependency of the knower on what is given externally. Whereas all attempts made since Hellenism and Augustine up to the Victorines to free the inward life of the soul from the spatial and corporeal pointed ever more strongly to the soul's spontaneous activity and sought out spiritual activity even in sense perception conditioned by the body, Thomas reverted to the passivity of ancient doctrines. That passivity had once found its most untrammeled formulation in Democritus's theory of tiny images, which said that knowledge of objects came about when filmlike material-objective images broke off

126

III. Soul and External World

from objects and penetrated the soul through the senses as though through canals. To be sure, it was only within the materialistic doctrine of the atomists that one could maintain this crude version that turned the soul into merely a container and arena for the mixture of tiny particles that had penetrated it in this fashion and that regarded the soul as a spatial entity, an object among objects. But even apart from this, another basic feature of Antiquity's theory of knowledge and its continuations in the Middle Ages was always the analogy to corporeal processes of activity. Based on reflection about perception, which always seemed to demonstrate direct incorporation of soul into world system, people always somehow regarded the soul as a kind of wax tablet on which objective reality stamped its forms. Thus Thomas did indeed transform the doctrine of images and accommodate it to the conviction of the immateriality of the soul; but he still held on to the passivistic and objectivizing feature. He viewed sensible species that come from objects as incorporeal and immaterial; but they impress themselves on the soul just as strongly as a seal impresses itself on wax. Yet the operation of active intellect and self-knowledge can be triggered only on the basis of such filling up of consciousness with cognitive material as is effected through the outer world and the body's organs. Hence the soul, as the form of unity, remains completely and essentially harnessed to the outside world.

The soul then also takes its appropriate place—just as with Aristotle and with Plotinus—in a comprehensively graduated framework of the world's being. This stratification of objects proceeds in more or less homogeneous progress from bare object through plants and animals (with their kind of "soul") to man, and from him to higher intelligences all the way up to God. The human soul occupies a central place in this schema; it stands at the transition point between living-animate and purely spiritual. And here Thomas now tries to combine Augustine with Aristotle, that is, to do justice to the Christian idea of the immortal and therefore substantial (even in its bare spirituality) soul that is separable from everything corporeal—in spite of the Aristotelian-oriented doctrine of unity of form. The difficulty is great and inner conflict of motives is pervasive; Thomas can rescue himself in the manner of Scholastic methodology only by making further distinctions. Accordingly, there are also forms that do not first attain their own proper substantiality in forming matter (hence as "inherent" forms) but that are already actual substances ("subsistent" forms, separated forms) purely in themselves. Of this kind are intelligent beings at all levels. They are pure forms without matter, yet subsist for themselves; their knowing is therefore not dependent on sense images. Among these beings man is the lowest. He is at once the highest creature in the series of form–matter substances and is composite substance himself. In contrast with pure higher intelligences, the body

127

must still be assumed into the definition of the human soul. In its "unity of form," intellectual substance is at the same time also the soul-giving form of a body, hence connected with it and the world of bodies. Although the soul is a real substance in itself and to that extent transcends anything corporeal, it is nevertheless also the form of body, which first attains full reality through it. It is immortal in itself, yet it attains full life only in community with the body. Thus ancient dualism still persisted in the opposition between transitory-sensual matter and pure unfettered spirituality as well as in the hybrid intermediate position of the human soul; and the ancient world-bound concept of soul in the theory of the soul's formal unity, despite the substantial uniqueness of its immortal-spiritual being, was still at work along with Augustinian tendencies. This artificially produced unity of motives could not indeed last for long.

Thus the subsequent development of the "period of decline" of Scholasticism fought no aspect of the Thomistic system more bitterly than it did this doctrine of unity of form! At the focal point of the struggle stood the Franciscans, qualified champions of the Augustinian tradition. Roger Bacon, the prophet of the new science of external nature who appealed for experience and experiment, nonetheless was also already directing attention with entirely new force toward the immediacy of inner experience, in which the soul grasps itself and everything supermaterial; and in the process he emphasized very sharply the fundamental difference between the soul's dimension and the spatial-material dimension of nature. The total inadequacy of the form-matter schema with regard to this duality was made visible again. He emphasized more strongly than anyone had ever done that there was absolutely nothing inherent in the soul as such that classified it with spatial existence, and that spiritual substances have no location [*Ort*] in space, neither in totally divisible body nor in some indivisible place in it. Just as readily as one could say (as happened so often in form-matter theory) that soul exists everywhere in the body, one also had to admit that it exists nowhere in it. If soul is the form of body, endowing it with life and form, nevertheless its original and proper nature does not consist in that. Thus Roger Bacon preferred, just as Bonaventure did in the old Franciscan school and just as Duns Scotus and many others would do later on, to subscribe to the point of view that under the influence of Avicebron admitted duality of matter and form even for the soul in itself alone (as everyone otherwise did with regard to purely corporeal existence). In this view the concept of matter shook itself free from its bond to space and signified merely a principle of finitude, changeability, and passivity. Now duality of matter and form exists in the soul itself, apart from the body; hence this conceptual pairing can no longer one-sidedly bind the soul to biological functions. With similar direction and emphasis on the spe-

III. Soul and External World

cial character of inner experience, Henry of Ghent now came forward in opposition to Thomism and in favor of a plurality of forms in the corporeal-animate nature of man. One can speak of unity of form only in nonliving and organic nature; but in man the *forma corporeitatis* [form of corporality] exists alongside rational, immortal soul and is fundamentally inseparable from it. The ancient tripartite division emerges once again: man is made up of spatial-corporeal matter, of body-form, and of a proper soul. Duns Scotus developed this further. He did, indeed, regard the soul as essential form of the body; but alongside it, mediating between it and matter, functions the *forma corporea organica* [corporeal organic form]. Just as the latter is form for organic matter, so is it also in turn matter for the soul. Thus the body is in itself already a totality composed of matter and form and through its own proper completeness [*Geschlossenheit*] provides foundation and occasion for the soul's own proper activity: for perceiving, thinking, and willing. Accordingly, Duns attacks Thomas's view that the separation of soul from body that occurs at death is something "violent"; on the contrary, it is then that the soul first completely comes to itself, to its essence and fulfillment. With truly extraordinary energy, however, Duns now emphasized once again the thing that was so decisive in freeing the concept of soul from objective being: the moment of spontaneity in knowledge at all levels, from sense perception and feeling—which he thought of as active functions of the subject that were merely occasioned by external stimuli and impressions—on up to participation by will and free consent in judgment (about which we shall have occasion to speak later). Prior to the Modern Period no one contributed as much toward bringing the vanishing initiatives of Augustinian psychology of knowledge to execution as he did. The importance of *species sensibiles* [sensible species] was now totally weakened; they become mere ancillary causes alongside the actively engaged principle of the soul. Intellect is not merely potentially active, nor is it first activated through the species; on the contrary, it is as a whole an active force which received impressions merely directed toward specific contents. In all sensible-intuitive knowledge, activity of the understanding and achievement of the subject are the decisive moment, but just not so distinctly as in higher, specifically rational knowledge. In general, Duns now ushers in not only a new phase of insight into the special quality and preponderant importance of the life of will and mind for the essence of the soul (in contrast with the major emphasis on process of knowledge and on intellect in Antiquity) but also and especially a new phase of investigation of the previously neglected sphere of feeling. And with that came an ever-clearer grasp of the special character of the spiritual-subjective. As Siebeck has stressed, Duns Scotus's conception of the soul contained the decisive emancipation from the supremacy of Antiquity in these questions and the first beginning toward the psychology of the Renaissance and the entire Modern Period.

Then William of Occam also, in his fight against the theory of form-unity, sharply distinguished thinking soul that is separable from the body from form-principle of the body and the *anima sensitiva* [sensitive soul], which is itself extended and linked to the body, part for part, in spatial extension. Nevertheless, insofar as he accordingly drew the line of separation within conscious soul itself, Occam still remained undecided and in a transitional phase; the separate existence of the Aristotelian nous carries forward here into the individual. He does not yet recognize that consciousness or subjectivity is the distinguishing note of unity of the soul (that which clearly demarcates that unity from anything spatial-material) at all levels of experience, even sense perception. But the nominalistic theory of knowledge of William of Occam and his followers then became of great importance in developing these questions. For it was here that a break was made with the old view that held that the external world impresses its image somehow on the soul. Sense images and perceptions are not imitations of real objects and events, but merely signs of them and of merely symbolic value! The ancient theory of tiny images, with all its consequences for the conception of the soul (which Duns Scotus had already so strongly discredited), now fell entirely by the wayside; and Thomas's theory was also expressly rejected. One now separated represented existence of objects totally from existence in themselves and put heavy emphasis on the heterogeneity of the psychic construct in comparison with the spatial-corporeal object that it is supposed to represent. Inner element differs totally from outer world! Up until Berkeley's (nominalistically oriented) spiritualism and even beyond that, this new twist in theory of knowledge in the "period of decadence" of Scholasticism worked in the direction of total separation of the psychical from the physical and toward clearer insight into the peculiarly closed inwardness of any soul-being, one that will absolutely resist being simply classified into the spatial-causal system of the world.

In the transition period of the Renaissance all the motives, ancient and modern, were mixed together once again in motley change. Revival of ancient theories encountered new, rich, living interest in the inner distinctiveness of personalities, in the manifold of the soul's affects, and in the special dynamics of heightened inner life; and, all too often, things newly felt had to clothe themselves in ancient categories and concepts. At the same time the religious question concerning the soul continued to be influential and to divide schools according to their attitude regarding immortality. Natural philosophy, Italian as well as German, everywhere resorted to the old tripartite division; it distinguished between body, spirit, and soul, whereby it described

130

III. Soul and External World

"spirit" as something like a subtle body of cosmic origin that links soul with body and man with the entire universe. In this direction, the theory of life spirits [*Lebensgeistern*] or *spiritus animales* [animal spirits] that mediated the influence of body on soul and of soul on body—a doctrine which derived from the Stoic view of the pneuma and permeated the entire Middle Ages— assumed especially great importance. Everywhere there was a constant tendency to incorporate the soul into the cosmic system and to conceive of the transition from corporeal world to spiritual world as nevertheless somehow in continuity. Correspondingly, old and new concepts of the world-soul sprang up all over; and with that it became quite easy to surrender the already attained insight into the absolutely special character of the soul's inwardness: once again people sought the universally important element of the existence of the soul primarily as a function of force—in giving life and motion to corporeal bodies.

It was not until the victory of the mechanical view of nature that a great new clarification came about. Throughout this entire period a tendency fought its way through to restrict the old ambiguous concept of matter (whose Aristotelian stamp in particular permitted the most multiform application, including into the very soul as such) to existence marked by the fundamental characteristic of spatial extension. Thus, for example, in developing the medieval doctrines mentioned Marsilio Ficino had contrasted immortal soul as indivisible-active essence from divisible and inert extended existence of the corporeal world. But here, too, he still looked within the soul for the motive force in corporeal processes and generally in all motions in the extended world. Kepler was the first to make the transition into purely mechanical thinking, which then finally freed the concept of soul also from all the objectivizing onus of the tasks of providing motion and animation. At first he was still entirely under the sway of ancient ideas; he saw soul operating in the activating magnet and he explained the orbit of planets on the model of ancient and medieval animate-spiritual star movers. "In later writings, on the other hand, with full deliberateness he replaced the *anima* [soul] that moved the planets by the word *vis* [force] and designated this force as corporeal, since it was subject to geometrical laws." It was only a step from this to Descartes's clear separation between consciousness and the world of extension. Modern science was also driving in the same direction: if, according to its view of nature, external objects were formed purely quantitatively and the book of nature was written in purely mathematical letters, then our perceptual representations of reality with their fullness of sensible qualities could not be images, little pictures, or *species intentionales* [intentional species], that is, something simply taken over from the external world in an impression and homogeneous with that world; on the contrary, the relationship between sense representation and spatial object is instead merely a nominalistic sort of representation through symbols! Even Democritus had once denied true existence to sense qualities; but he was still a long way from drawing motley images into the subjectivity of the psychical realm, such as now became the solution for Kepler, Galileo, Descartes, Locke, and others. For Democritus soul was a body among bodies; but now with the doctrine of the subjectivity of sense qualities, soul was more sharply contrasted with spatial and material existence than ever before.

As is well known, it was Descartes's ruthless determination (which indeed also led him to brush aside some important problems) that produced the great clarification and ultimate intensification of the opposition between inner and outer, the conscious and the extended. Now for the first time the body, even with all its life functions and movements, is a proper substance, unrelated to any soul-"form," a full reality in its own right. And with that the soul was now also free from any essential link with external world or with corporeal form and pneuma or spirit of life. Descartes's concept of the *spiritus animales* [animal spirits] sets aside all indeterminate interaction of the soul's inward element with the body-permeating element in this postulate of a psychophysical system; as extended entities they belong totally to matter, are subject to mechanical laws, and form no essential transition to the immaterial. There is no more talk now about star-movers, world-soul, or universal animation. The external world rotates self-sufficiently within itself according to mechanical principles. An absolute abyss separates it from the inwardness of consciousness and from thinking, willing souls. No gradual ascent—such as one finds in Aristotle, Plotinus, or Thomas—wipes away the specific difference between the two substances. Life is mechanics, and in order to remove all possible ambiguity Descartes forbids even the concept of force, for to him it smacks too much of something like the soul. But now, in a much more fundamental way than for thinkers of the patristic and medieval periods, the union of heterogeneous and essentially separated substances that manifestly occurs in man becomes a great puzzle—one that has exercised not only Descartes himself but all thinkers of the following period. The absolutely special character of subjective-conscious inner life was now recognized. Whether I think ideas and principles (as the "active intellect" of Aristotle did) or I am conscious of taking a walk, or whether I perceive something sensible or feel bodily pain, what is identical in every instance is that I know and feel, that I have consciousness. This fundamental moment of inner consciousness, of "thinking" in the broadest sense of the word, is something we can never think of as separated from the essence of the self [*Ichwesen*]; by contrast we can quite easily conceptually separate everything bodily or belonging to the body from what is really soul-like. The *"res"*

III. Soul and External World

cogitans [thinking "thing"], whether it be the infinite one of divine being or the finite one of my individual soul, is not an ideal, intelligible-objective being, but rather subjectivity or consciousness.

No longer saddled with the counterforce of the ancient world concept, the Augustinian principle now breaks through clearly. Over against the dubious existence and nature of the outer world that we ourselves have to establish, we have immediate self-certainty of soul, the conscious self. Descartes himself was at first apparently not aware of the great tradition in which he stood with his "discovery" of the Archimedean point for all knowledge and certainty. Indeed, even to this day the historical connections have been explored only inadequately. To be sure, the comparison with Augustine has been drawn often. But as yet no one has described for us how Augustinian tradition in this matter (carried forward in the Middle Ages most especially through Hugh of St. Victor and later through William of Auvergne), bucking the high tide of Aristotelianism, acquired entirely new importance in the "period of decadence"; no one has described for us how, from Roger [Bacon] and Duns [Scotus] on to William of Occam, Pierre d'Ailly, and Gerson, the threads ran on to Raymond Sebond, Montaigne, Charron, Sanchez, as well as Campanella (all of whom were immediate precursors of the Cartesian foundation); or how the great theme of the special character and primacy of certitude of inner experience everywhere expressed itself in a variety of ways.

With Leibniz's principle of the monad the new concept of soul then attained its highest peak. As monad the soul is perfect existence-for-itself [*Für-sich-Sein*], an entire inner world unto itself, complete in itself, in need of no external influence or spatial-corporeal world system. In contrast with the old passivity according to which the soul—which was above all a receptive organ for external impressions, as Aristotle or Democritus or the Stoa saw it—was a meeting point and a gathering point for tiny images transmitted to it via its connection with the body and the external world, now the conviction of the soul's inward activity that spontaneously asserted itself against all worldly existence (a conviction that first came completely to the fore in Christianity) was carried out to its ultimate conclusion. According to Leibniz the soul is a creative force, spontaneity uncurtailed by any outside resistance whatsoever. This is so not only in the mental attitude of a free, moral-religious person but also—something that others have conceived in totally different fashion—in knowledge of reality through sense perception itself. Development of the idea of spontaneity from Augustine on through Hugh and Duns Scotus had already pressed forward in the case of Valentin Weigel, the German mystic and natural philosopher, to the view that Leibniz's concept of the monad now described with total clarity: Nothing comes from outside

133

into our inner substance, and we should not assume external influence on the soul even as merely an occasion or a trigger [*Auslösung*]! On the contrary everything the soul thinks, feels, and sees, and the entire immense manifold of the world "in" which man lives his existence arises for the soul entirely from its inner resources. Whereas Descartes's matter was merely spatial-objective being without any activity or force even when it is set in motion, the soul, in utter contrast with that, is activity through and through; continuous transition from its own power, its own impulse; change that occurs entirely through itself alone! It is impossible still to conceive of this soul as fitted into the spatial external world, although Descartes went on thinking of soul linked to body in reciprocal relationship and even assigned an entirely specific locus to soul in the body's central organ. Soul is no longer "in" space in this external world of daily experience in which objects affect each other; on the contrary, the outer world as spatial and even one's body as a spatial construct is a phenomenon in the soul, manifesting itself uniquely in the inner spontaneity of consciousness that is totally contained within inner life.

Questions regarding how the succeeding period struggled with the concept of the inner world, or how in the course of epistemological reflection the ever more clearly developed idea of consciousness strove to free itself from the concept of individual soul (with the religious problematic that this entails), or how Kant's theory of transcendental unity of apperception and synthetic spontaneity of all knowledge paved the way for clarifications by Reinhold or Maimon, or the great further development through Fichte, who now brought the moment of freedom of will into the context of the center of consciousness and of subjectivity in a completely new way—are all issues that we have no more intention of pursuing here than we do the question of the gradual development of inner experience or the emergence of modern psychology. Instead, our abiding main concern is only to show the inner context within which the problems of a new world and life gradually matured toward modern philosophy on the basis of a tradition that developed early and was carried forward through the entire Middle Ages, especially its late period. With respect to this insight there is still one more moment of special interest in the theories we have discussed.

In the patristic period there developed, out of the attitude toward life we have just described, the idea that our thus inwardly directed knowledge grasped God immediately but the world only mediately, through him. All rational knowledge of the external world, said Augustine, is grasping of ideas; therefore—because ideas are merely moments in divine understanding—we have contact with God and, only through that, knowledge of the world! Thus Plato's theory of anamnesis is carried forward into an epistemological metaphysics that says that the decisive element in knowledge arises in an inwardly spiritual contact between intelligences, the finite and the infinite. The world and the kind of pictorial impression on a subject that was the view that Antiquity (indeed, even Plato himself with regard to both sensible and intelligible knowledge) maintained above all else now receded completely. In the Middle Ages the Augustinian mystics, especially Hugh of St. Victor, carried this forward, and then so did Bonaventure and the Franciscan schools, then Dietrich von Freiberg and Meister Eckehart. For all of them the path was the same one that we commonly recognize in the form of the Cartesian chain of reasoning: from consciousness of self and inner certitude, to the idea of God and its all-encompassing infinity and truth, and only then to the external world of corporeal being. Dietrich von Freiberg says that really to know an object, to see it in its *ratio* [ground], that is, to grasp it according to the eternal rules that man discovers within himself and develops from himself, means to see it in the light of first truth which is God himself, for in such knowledge we are immediately united to God. And this viewpoint became all the more sharply pronounced to the degree that people recognized mental representation, as something psychical, as heterogeneous to the physical dimension of external world—especially therefore with the nominalism of William of Occam. According to nominalism, when we know something we never know objects (or tiny images thereof) but only our own ideas as states or activities within ourselves. This increases still further one's confidence in the primacy of inner experience. Knowledge of the world is fundamentally self-knowledge and through it knowledge of God as well. Hence inner experience is not merely knowledge about existence that is more important and closest to the knowing subject (but which in the final analysis is still coordinated with external experience of nature that is a given); on the contrary, the upshot of the matter here is that all experience is originally inner experience and that inner experience is also the source of all so-called outer experience. In other words, knowledge of inner sense always lies at the basis of knowledge of outer sense. (It is well known how this problem of ''inner sense'' in precisely this context assumed such a complicated form in Kant.) According to this view, to find the world in the self, going by way of God, is not only a mystical experience or (as in Descartes) a demonstrative path for the doubter, but is the obvious path of all knowledge in every one of its acts.

   This is something the seventeenth century manifested in exceptional fullness (the influence of the motif reaches right on into the theory of knowledge of the German Idealists); Geulincx and Malebranche and Leibniz are heirs of Augustine and of those thinkers of the ''period of decadence'' who built on him. A well-known catchword (but one that has not been satisfactorily evaluated and researched) is Malebranche's theory that continued to have a direct influence even as far as Kant's Inaugural Dissertation, namely "that we see all things in God," that in God (with whom we stand in closest union when we direct our attention inwardly toward ourselves) we see not only "ideas" in the ancient sense of eternal truths but even contents of senses and images of perception, and it is only through this way—mediately, in other words—that we know the corporeally real existence of objects. In this connection, people have thus far paid all too little attention to Leibniz's theory of knowledge also. And yet Leibniz expressed his views on this question often enough and clearly. Leibniz, whose concept of the monad developed precisely from full insight into the special character of the conscious and who drew the consequences of that to the fullest limit, completely rejected any contact between self and object, that is any sort of influx or wandering of the external into the internal. There cannot be causal mediation or a bridge between outer world and inner world in a sense impression. The soul remains closed up within itself in its pure inwardness for all time. Ultimately, outer world cannot be the outer limit and envelope for the soul; instead soul grasps outer world only in its own given richness of life. The original form of all knowing is reflection, the soul's view of itself, its knowledge of its own inner makeup. It is only in this way that knowledge arrives at reality itself and grasps it directly. The idea in me is the "immediately inner object"; but we know of the external only through the mediation of these "ideas," or representations in us. "It is within ourselves and in our soul that we see the sun and everything that exists!" For these pictorial contents of the sensual power of imagination as well as the concepts of our thinking refer for their part in a representational way that is univocally oriented toward existing being "outside of me" (no longer understood in a spatial sense!). This ideational correspondence, however, through whose mediation therefore our self-comprehension also becomes (mediate) knowledge of existence that transcends the proper existence of soul, is based on the real connection of the soul with God as its creator. God is "the sole immediate external object" in the sense that in the soul's self-intuition it is precisely God's work and influence of which we are aware. Even in its knowledge about God the soul does not really reach beyond its own self-sphere, which is "without windows"; here too the path of knowledge runs through the mediating representation given in me—and to that extent God, too, is just a "mediate" object! Individual soul does not grasp the divine person in itself but only its projection on a limited plane, that is, on the mirror of its own inwardness. The difference, however, is that here a real connection exists and is experienced: the soul, as a being that is limited and imperfect in itself, points beyond itself to infinite perfection as its primordial ground. It is on the reality of God and his real creating and conserving action that the system of objects also depends, together with their harmony and the mutual correspondence of all that exists. It is this system, harmony and correspondence that first make it possible for an individual soul, in grasping what is given to it [inwardly], also indirectly to know "the external," other souls and beings, and in its self-knowledge of inner world also to see the universe itself, as though by looking at a focusing mirror. Hence we do not see objects and truths "in God" (as Malebranche taught) but in ourselves. But it is the reality of divine-spiritual substance that establishes the bridge between ourselves and everything else in the world. Whereas Plato's soul was classified under or incorporated with sensible and intelligible world, it was the other way around with Leibniz. Not only the entire infinite external world that we perceive through sense images but also the totality of ideas in the ancient sense (eternal truths, as he himself calls them) and the universe of essences or intelligible possibilities and possible worlds are drawn into the soul, even though they still maintain their own proper existence apart from individual soul. Soul exists in the world; but world also exists in turn in the soul! The old notion of the link between microcosm and macrocosm (which was otherwise essentially related only to the identity of matter and forces analogous to processes and structures in the world and in man) derived new meaning from this matured concept of subjectivity: individual soul mirrors and uniquely concentrates the great world.

This metaphysical theory of knowledge and the new ordering (on which the theory rests) of soul, God, and world demanded by Christian experience is connected with the fact that modern philosophy often makes such an insufficiently sharp distinction between inner experience in the sense of empirical inner perception of individual psychical data and in the sense of an inwardly spiritual grasp and intuition of the intelligible, that is, of metaphysical or logical-ideal being. The ambiguity already inherent in Plato's theory of recollection attains an altogether peculiar and often fateful importance. Indeed "inner experience" is always at one and the same time empirical self-consciousness of the individual person and (above all in the mediating path of "conscience") religious-metaphysical link with God and the entire spiritual world. To be sure, people saw quite early on that the evidential advantage of inner life relates essentially only to the "that" of one's own existence, but not in the same degree to its "what" (for what the soul as a whole actually is, is quite obviously not a self-given!), that self-deceptions lead us to distinguish even in the case of inner experience between representation and being, appearance and existence. This is something that people stressed continually, especially from the time of Duns Scotus on. Indeed it must have become particularly clear in the epoch of modern natural science, when now all of a sudden all reliable and exact knowledge of being was overwhelmingly, even exclusively, related to corporeal world, a world which one nevertheless simultaneously removed so far from the proper, immediately intuitive knowledge of existence that one finds only in self-consciousness of the ego. This was a paradox of the consciousness of the age, which one can review with special clarity in the case of Malebranche, who also emphatically refers to the distinction between the That and the What. But matters remained therefore in the context (and also often in the confusion) of the soul-like factual and the logical-metaphysical intelligible. Duns Scotus himself, for example, included in inner experience the idea of what the concept is or the idea that in every investigation we must discursively develop the unknown on the basis of the known. In the double meaning of ''intelligible'' as something imperceptible through external sensation it was easy to confuse empirical self-perception and intuition of the timeless essence of knowledge, of concepts, and of ideas. This is what happened with William of Occam and all the others. For the most part the ''supersensible'' in the religious-metaphysical sense was still to the fore here (as it most especially was also in Roger Bacon's concept of inner experience). But to the degree that the Modern Period turned toward experiential reality and nature, both outer and inner, the danger emerged that essential insight into ''the intelligible'' or the grasp of metaphysical-spiritual realities would be drawn into the empirical realm of psychic self-perception. This becomes particularly clear from Locke onwards, but even the rationalists became entangled in serious confusion on that basis. Descartes calls certainty regarding one's own existence ''intuitive'' in the same breath with the intuition of mathematical axioms. He says that each of them is ''clearly and distinctly'' known, in contrast with all sensual-external data of experience. All the uncertainties of the subjective-idealistic tendency in Descartes are connected with this point. And even in the case of Leibniz (who, after all, in express opposition to Descartes, turns the *cogito sum* [*sic* = I think, I am] into a principle valid only for factual and experiential truths) the concept of ''reflection'' is peculiarly ambiguous: for Leibniz (even independently of the metaphysical epistemology of representation in the inward self) the soul's capacity to look at itself and observe its own life is automatically also the capacity to intuit essence through abstraction, to turn purely toward eternal truths and toward knowledge of ultimate categories of being, such as substance, unity, power, identity, and so on. In itself the knowing soul first knows these ontological essences. Kant makes a sharp division: inner appearance and substantial existence are separated even for the soul itself! But even there, lack of clarity still exercised a many-sided influence and it then introduced new difficulties in the metaphysical epistemology of Fichte and others.

138

III. Soul and External World

It is quite obvious what importance the maturation process we have been tracing in the concept of the soul's inwardness in conjunction with the concept of soul, God, and world must have gained for the development of the world picture that was becoming dominant across wide stretches of modern metaphysics, a world picture that people have styled, with an all-too-indeterminate meaning, "idealism." Plato's Idea is "existing being" [*seiendes Sein*], which stood in contrast with soul's subjectivity (something he himself did not yet truly recognize in its unique character) and which aided the latter, so to speak, toward being; his idealism is completely independent of the concept of subject. But the Modern Period, which now became aware of the great contrast between knowing-willing subject and objective being, attempted on the one hand (as happened once in materialism) to continue the ancient orientation toward the objective, letting the soul be completely swallowed up in being; but on the other hand it tried to draw being or the outer world completely inside the subject, turning them into "idea" in the modern subjective-conscious sense, that is into a phenomenon within the subject. The priority of the animate and spiritual over nature, of person (God or the soul) over the objective was now intensified to the point of maintaining the sole reality of the subjective. The great opposite pole in this subjective-idealistic movement of the modern era was Spinoza. His God was existing substance in the ancient sense, with attributes of extension (which of itself concedes sovereignty to the "world" in an objective sense) and thought; for its part, thought totally relinquished its special character of subjectivity and lost its connection with the conscious-personal dimension developed in Christianity. Thus Spinoza defines the soul once again as formal existence of the body, as a coordinate (now no longer superior) objective moment of being for the body, as it were. Here soul is the "idea of the body." This is no longer Plato's Idea; on the contrary, the concept really stems from (Cartesian) theory of consciousness and representation and was supposed to refer to mirroring representation of the corporeal in the psyche (psychophysical parallelism); but here instead the idea was turned around once again into something objective, and the real concept of subjectivity was abandoned. The special character of self-consciousness that Descartes had made his focal point was then attenuated along the same path: Spinoza made self-conscious ego into merely an idea of an idea, whereby of course (in opposition to the entire fundamental tendency of the modern concept of the soul) self-consciousness is also essentially attached to body and to corporeal consciousness. Spirit knows itself only insofar as it perceives the ideas of bodily affects. For Spinoza thought and being now once again came together almost as closely as they had for Parmenides.

But for most other great metaphysicians of the Modern Period, development occurred in the direction of the new "idealism." The doctrines of the Church Fathers had already hinted at idealism. What Neoplatonic philosophy contained of spiritualistic and objective-idealistic tendencies, the Fathers complemented with special experience of the individual soul, personality of the creator, and relative unimportance of objective world in comparison with exchanges between mental activities. Thus Gnosticism manifested not only an intensification of ancient dualism but also a strong attraction toward Idealism. Origen considered the external world and matter to have been created subsequently, as it were, for the sake of the Fall (that split the realm of spirits) of free souls, who were then supposed to find new unity and community in the sensible world and its corporeal connection and then to soar once again out of that world upward toward the kingdom of God. In this view the cosmos is merely a means of punishment and improvement, a means and path of spiritual education; and once that education has been accomplished, the existence of the cosmos vanishes. And although this theory attributes special and compact reality to the corporeal world during the period of education, nevertheless Gregory of Nyssa also clearly intended to understand this reality itself, and especially the body, as "spiritual" in nature, as a complex of immaterial qualities. He did this in order to make comprehensible something that otherwise appeared to be an enigma, namely, that God as spiritual person created this completely different kind of reality of extended material objects. He viewed sensual body as a product of the soul after its fall into sin. Scotus Erigena then carried this doctrine forward into the Middle Ages. For all that, this view still stayed very close to the immaterialistic tendency of the Platonic theory of Ideas, and it was left to the Modern Period to be the first to try to resolve the entire existence of the world into subjective appearances (whereby even this concept of appearance undergoes a total transformation into the subjective when compared with the Platonic-objective concept). Nominalism of the waning Middle Ages first taught us to distinguish sharply between object in external nature and object as appearance in consciousness, as "intentional" existence between world in itself and world as idea. In that same fourteenth century Nicholas of Autrecourt was the first person seriously (and on this very basis) to raise the question whether anyone could still assert the proper existence of external world at all, that is, existence in itself apart from world as idea within us. From

140

III. Soul and External World

that point on, the new idealistic motif matured in the direction of the fundamental concept that developed from Descartes's adoption of self-consciousness as his point of departure.

Descartes himself was not a pure idealist in this modern subjective sense of the word any more than Augustine was. He viewed extended objects as real and completely independent in their own existence, just as soul-endowed subjects were; God created the world of space just as he did the world of spirits. Indeed, the great successes of modern science of the spatial and material world and its discovery of the laws of nature must have underscored the special existence of the external world. But later thinkers were not satisfied with this sort of coordination between such heterogeneous substances. Malebranche, who was so profoundly convinced of the preponderance of the spiritual over anything material, was inclined—as only one of the successors of Gregory of Nyssa or Augustine could be—very clearly toward spiritualism, but on the other hand he could not declare that the external nature of *res extensae* [extended objects] was unreal. His mediating doctrine of intelligible extension stood in the middle between Augustine or Descartes and Berkeley. Leibniz, too, was certainly not univocally an idealist in the modern sense. To be sure, he held that nothing material, but only the immaterial, exists in the metaphysical-real world; the spatial-corporeal realm is merely the appearance of units of intelligible being and of intelligible orders of the same. The existence of "outer world" in the sense of Descartes or Spinoza or Malebranche was thereby dissolved. But that did not mean at all that now external nature is subsumed into the subjectivity of souls; nor was that the case with Gregory of Nyssa's immaterialism. The immaterial element is not at all identical here with the subjective soul, even though it means something entirely different than it did as immaterial element in Plato. [Leibniz] still thought of the objective-immaterial units that "compose" reality and everything that is apparently spatial—in other words the monads—in accordance with the exemplar and analogy of the soul's subjective-conscious reality. More forcefully than anyone had ever done it before, Leibniz here introduced the primacy of soul before thought. (Heraclitus had offered the first hint of this in Antiquity, just as Plato had provided its early development; then at the threshold of the modern age German mysticism in particular and natural philosophy of the Renaissance, Nicholas [of Cusa] especially and Bruno, had made it urgent.) Leibniz's point was that in the soul's inner reflection we possess the key to the nature of the world and of all reality. Whatever exists, says Leibniz, must be a unit or must consist of units. But we never encounter true unity in the spatial-material realm. By contrast the soul comprises in itself something simple and indivisible, something that is unity in multiplicity. We must therefore understand all reality in accordance with the model given to us in such self-intuition. It is not as though souls and subjects are hidden everywhere behind objects and radiate them, as it were, or are supposed to conjure up images of them for themselves. On the contrary, one should guide the concept of substance in its universality by the immediate self-givenness of the soul's substance and the fundamental moments within it, on the basis of which its consciousness and its subjective inner life are established. Monads are in no way all "souls" in our sense, that is, centers of consciousness and persons; on the contrary, they are subjects only in the ancient sense of supportive substances. But here objective reality is so closely linked with subjective soul (whereas in Antiquity soul's existence was assimilated to the objective as much as possible) that once again a series of steps seems to lead upward in homogeneous progression from stone (i.e., the non-spatial aggregate of "sleeping" or "naked" monads that underlies it) through plant and animal to the human soul. Here too, in Leibniz the classification of the soul into the graduated progression of existence is an objectivistic feature (which sharply distinguishes it from the subjective idealism of someone like Berkeley). But he then partially paralyzed this by his monadic concept of being, which he conceives in analogy with the soul! So there is no regression into the ancient concept of the soul here when in contrast with the Cartesian tendency to take things apart, [Leibniz] ties in soul with the force of motion and the form of life; for now these latter elements are more a kind of vestibule to the soul rather than that soul for its part should be merely a special class of objective existence or a form of the organic-living! Leibniz uses the Aristotelian concepts of energy and entelechy once again to apply to the soul; but as he uses them they have completely changed their meaning. They are no longer originally objective principles but have been drawn from reflection about the soul. Soul is no longer the form of body, which is assumed to be an object that we know; instead, in the theory of monads the body itself is an order of substances that one must conceive in analogy with the soul (although not precisely as souls themselves)! The case is very similar later on with Schelling, say, who also classifies the soul in a great graduated structure of reality, preserving the special claim of subjectivity through the fact that he thinks of nature itself not merely as something fundamentally intelligible, not as ideally grounded in the sense of Plato or created in accordance with ideas in the sense of Gregory [of Nyssa] or Augustine and Malebranche, but as "unconscious intelligence"!

At this point we no longer wish to pursue the development of modern idealism from Descartes and Leibniz on, with its broad metaphysical and epistemological foundations and consequences; with its culmination in the metaphysics of the absolute ego (as a point located at the greatest possible distance from the ancient concept of being, the "ego" as a philosophical principle belongs exclusively to the Modern Period since Descartes and Leibniz); also with its attempts to fuse "objective" idealism into itself, as happened with Schelling or Hegel. From among all the idealistic systems and tendencies we should still make special mention here of just two world conceptions which remained particularly close to the religious origin of this entire problematic and to ancient Christian consciousness regarding the unique importance of the individual soul, and which dared to draw an ultimate metaphysical consequence out of that feeling about the world: the Idealism of Berkeley and that of Fichte.

Leibniz viewed "external world" as still possessing its own proper reality, though not in the form of space that our sense experience wants to ascribe to it. Animals, plants, and even "dead" matter have their own special value and existence in the hierarchical structure of the universe, but the point is that all this is fundamentally structured in a monadic way analogous to soul; "matter," however, means only a moment of finiteness or inner boundedness of individual beings of each kind and rank. Things exist in the world of monads as the beautiful dream of Henry Suso once described them: the entire universe of creatures, from sand in the sea all the way up to man, mirrors and praises the perfection of the divine, so to speak. Part of the splendor that people have otherwise sought only in the human soul also falls on all objects; every monad is an immaterial unity, spontaneous power, and imperishable substance; even animal "souls" and individual principles of life of organic beings in general are "immortal" in their own way! But that does not mean (as we have said before) that we are entirely reinterpreting the world here as a realm of souls or of subjects. The analogous dimension between lower monads and souls proper, between indestructibility and personal immortality, between "representation" and "perception" in the preconscious objectively intended sense of "presentation of the many in the one" and conscious understanding and knowledge—should not wipe away the difference at all. Thus the human soul truly has its body also, but it is not hidden "in" it as in a material realm of space [*Raumstück*] (as it was for Descartes); it lives instead with the body in a relationship of intelligible association only. Thus bodily existence also and all existence of a subhuman nature has its own proper reality and fulfills the great task of the world in its own way and with its own value, which is irreplaceable by higher levels, for example, by conscious souls.

Berkeley's idealistic metaphysics, on the contrary, concludes from the new attitude toward life that the whole of external nature—with all its beauty, variety, and life—and that matter, stars, plants, animals, and even the human body exist only "for" the human soul and the process of salvation that leads upward to God. The problem implicit in the spiritual first principle of a personal world creator and recognized earlier by Gregory of Nyssa—namely, what this spiritual person of God could possibly have to do with unspiritual matter or anything spatial—combines here with radical doubt about the "outer world" that surfaces for every thinking and conscious self, doubt that had grown out of the Augustinian discovery of the primacy of certitude of inner experience and out of the nominalistic-subjective conception of the process of knowledge among thinkers of the waning Middle Ages and then with Descartes. It remains to inquire what direct threads connect, say, Nicholas of Autrecourt (people had labeled him the medieval Hume on account of his dissolution of the traditional concept of substance and causality which was so surprisingly reminiscent of English critique of knowledge in the period of the Enlightenment) with Berkeley, who expressly appealed to "some Scholastics," or with some of his contemporaries similar to him in their systematic orientation, such as Robert Greville, Norris, and Collier; that there must be historical connections to be found here clearly stems from the nature of the problem, especially also from Berkeley's pronounced nominalism.

Now Berkeley totally rejected the concept of corporeal substance along with that of independently existing nature and "external world," that is, to the extent that one understands thereby more than the real existence of other animate-spiritual persons. Bodies are nothing more than complexes of "ideas," a word no longer understood in any sort of objective sense of the intelligible (which was the sort of sense that, despite the fusion of the Platonic Idea into divine intellect, nevertheless had been alive during the entire development from Gregory of Nyssa to Malebranche and Leibniz), but rather purely in the subjective sense of representations, of changing contents in conscious, actively thinking subjects. The world of objects and organisms, of heavenly bodies and elements, is nothing but our idea, appearance in individual souls. Souls do not exist in the world, but world exists only in souls. Leibniz's two-faceted concept of appearance totally loses its objective nuance here, the one that had characterized the concept almost exclusively in Antiquity (appearance as a lesser, intrinsically pale and shadowlike kind of objective existence); now one takes it exclusively in the new sense of appearance in subjects. In the process it also shakes off its objective origin at the same time: the object that appears to me. *Esse = percipi* [to be = to be perceived] is Berkeley's formula: to assume being that would exist independently of subjects and their perceptions, as the existence of nonthinking objects in themselves and apart from spirits, in other words *res extensae* [extended beings] "alongside of" *res cogitantes* [thinking beings], is nonsense in his view. Just as Descartes and Locke recognized sense qualities as purely subjective, so now he wanted to draw into the subject those primary qualities also that one otherwise always ascribed to objects existing in their own right, whereby the very concept of object itself would also disappear.

Hence only souls exist, that is, indivisible, immaterial, and always active substances (thus for Berkeley also—as he explains in detail and tries to prove in his research into a theory of seeing, continuing the tradition of Augustine-Duns Scotus—all representation and thinking is above all spontaneity of soul): substances that are only of the sort to be found in Leibniz's hierarchical ordering at the level of true subject-monads beginning with the human soul and upward to God. The true world is entirely and exclusively a world of ''spirits''! The capacity to produce ideas and to be active with regard to them shows these spirits to be will-endowed beings. That these appearances are largely independent of personal will, however, and that they demonstrate inner stability and agreement of ideas in differing souls that give rise to our false assumption of a real material world existing in its own right, is something that points to God as the universally comprehensive and infinitely active subject under whose influence we stand when we perceive ''something objective'' within us in that way, that is, something free of subjective will. The whole of external nature—with its inner lawfulness discovered by science and with all the abundance of creatures and the incomprehensibly artistic mechanism of organisms and all the beauty of plants and animals—is only a world of appearances that God has placed in us. Through this kind of insight, as Berkeley emphasizes, we do not lose a bit of nature as we really know it: the distinction between the real and the fantasized or a dream-image is not diminished in any way. (Regularity and inner lawfulness of processes of representation that we call nature or external being remain in full force and beauty when we conceive of their existence not as that of material being, but rather as the influence of divine-spiritual activity taking place within our inner self). On the contrary, it is only in this way that we first grasp the immanent meaning of the ''book of nature'' with total immediacy. Nominalism calls sense representations in us ''symbols''; and they are symbols, not of external existence, of a ''stupid and thoughtless'' Something (which would itself be then, in turn, the product and expression of the power of God and of God's wisdom), but immediate signs of God and his activity in us. Faith in the objective substantial reality of nature is a ''heathenish'' chimera, for that would be to insert nature as a blind, nonthinking representative and mediator between ourselves and God, only pushing us farther away from him. Such a nature, made independent, would all too easily lead to atheism and fatalism, to faith in the special power of objective existence and its eternal laws that would tower over the entire life of will and mind; it would lead ultimately to materialism. What we commonly call nature is nothing other than the language God speaks with us, his finite subjects; through which he teaches us about his own perfection and morally necessary paths of our inner behavior! Just as in other books words are composed of letters and sentences of words and everything depends on divining inner meaning from these signs, so is the book of nature an endless manifold and chain of ideas linked with one another in ingenious arrangement, unfolding in all of us with the highest degree of lawfulness and meaning. The task of life is to read this system of symbols and comprehend it in its orderly arrangement, to grasp it in its divine meaning and to order our own behavior in accord with it. What good would a detour by way of a really independently existing nature do us in this matter? We grasp God and his language immediately in these symbols of our world image just as we read the invisible inner life of a man in the sensible image of a human countenance. Thus for Berkeley true reality is exclusively animate-spiritual in nature, a cosmos of subjects under the commanding and obligatory influence of the divine person; but objective being or visible nature is really only ideational language between God and finite subjects, language that draws together the threads that reveal will and understanding and points out paths of life and material for moral development, so to speak, for individual souls.

It is in this last spirit, which provides such direct metaphysical expression to the Christian attitude toward life, that Fichte's idealism then builds further. We shall pass over here what a change (compared with Berkeley's) his speculation with its point of departure in the principle of selfhood produced in the relationship of particular individual selves to divine being and consequently in the concept of the latter! Nor shall we speak any more about how this idealism of Fichte strove to incorporate realism within it or how nature (which quite logically appears now only as non-ego) thereby appears to end up in many ways as a reified production of absolute intelligence. Here we wish to restrict ourselves only to that fundamental tendency in Fichte's doctrine that, totally in the spirit of Berkeley's metaphysics, sought to make outer world into a representation of individual subjects (especially important for this is his *Facts of Consciousness* [*Die Thatsachen des Bewußtseyns*] from 1810–11).

Fichte's idealism, like Berkeley's, also fought against faith in the independent reality of the objective that drove one to fatalism and to atheism as well as against naturalism and "dogmatic" realism, which he saw incorporated above all in Spinoza's system. No matter how consistent and how impervious to any sort of logical rebuttal such a system of being might erect for itself, it is condemned, because it would absolutely destroy the freedom and independence of the human subject and with it the core-meaning of our existence, namely moral life. We can never understand a free soul as a member of the objective world, as just a phase in the development of reality when

146

nature becomes aware of itself. If one thinks of self as just a mirror of previously given, unconscious-inert being, it cannot have or signify any genuine
inner spontaneity at all. In that case I do not act; in my moral development
I do not assume an attitude toward what I will be or should be; I do not
become master over nature, as is demanded. Instead, I am completely dominated by objects, by nature and its infallible laws of being. One denies the
most certain, most important, and most holy element in all existence—
namely, free will, living love, man's moral-spiritual deed—in favor of a
sensible external world that one assumes to be absolutely real.

But closer examination of knowledge and of consciousness of the supposed given shows that things simply cannot be thus. Consciousness is a
special kind of life that is independent and complete in itself; it simply cannot
be a dead, passive mirror of something external but rather (as Leibniz had
already taught) is something that is alive and powerful in its own right,
developing contents purely out of itself. Hence all knowing, even so-called
external perception, is really not knowledge of an object but only of our own
inner determination; it is self-intuition of inwardly confined activity of the
self! In all perception we are first of all and immediately aware of ourselves
and our own determination (compare this with Leibniz's "immediate inner
object"). I am not first and foremost aware of objects but of my seeing and
my feeling.

And this is not just "at first"; no, knowledge throughout its entire extent
simply remains locked up in the inner self. In reality there is no such thing
as what one commonly calls "external sense." On the contrary, even this is
only a particular determination of inner sense, labeled merely as special affects of the self. "Consciousness of an object is only unacknowledged awareness of my having produced a representation of an object." "Hence all consciousness is only something immediate, consciousness of myself." Objects
do not appear to me through their representatives (as in the theory of little
images and all the other common theories of perception); no, the object I
grasp is my own mind, exposed outside itself, so to speak, in an image.
Objects and the entire world of bodies around us are our own phenomenal
products; they are representational creations [Vorstellungsgeschöpfe]. No
matter what I see outside myself, I am at bottom always just myself; in all
consciousness of being I am but looking at myself in a specific limitation of
my innermost capacity, in the active life within me.

But this does not mean, now, that existence is but a dream or that we
would reject "world" as mere illusion without significance and reality. It is
true that the world does not possess "reality" in the way that is used by
"common realism," that is, as if as a material being existing in its own right,
it would determine knowledge. According to Fichte, knowledge cannot be

determined "from the outside," but this does not therefore turn it into a dream any more than it did so for Berkeley! What I experience as the outer world "in" which I am active is not a question of my arbitrary whim; on the contrary, I find that I am determined therein without any cooperation on my part. The "reality" of this outer world or this worldview lies in the spiritual meaning and the spiritual purpose of these specific inner appearances, these images produced out of my self in a completely determined course. "Significance" and "purpose," however, point beyond the sphere of mere knowing into willing and our inner "vocation" ["*Bestimmung*"] in the moral-religious sense. According to the doctrine of Fichte (who thereby metaphysically exploits the basic Christian feeling of the central and unique importance of the life of salvation of souls more profoundly and clearly than Berkeley does), the reality of the phenomenal world is a practical one. My special vocation, the talent I am supposed to make the most of, expresses itself in the concrete individuality of my representations of the world, of the idea of my body, and of the environment; out of these, so to speak, starting points spring up for my activity, for my moral striving and planning. The inner determination of which I am conscious when I have knowledge in the form of intuition of an object is a determination of my freedom, a particular constriction and forced direction of my primordial independence, an independence that cannot be externally abridged through any confinement by given objects. As a truly active power and as a moral being possessed of absolute inner freedom (which is directed into certain paths, however, and becomes specific volition only through specific tasks), I have "reality" in the proper sense. It is only through me that the world of objects, or nature, also acquires its own kind of reality—it is "appearance"—not of "things" in themselves but of my own moral "vocation." From this point of view all positive content of knowledge is self-consciousness of the knowing subject about itself, not as "*res*" *cogitans* [thinking "thing"]—that would still be too objectivistic-substantial in concept—but as individual striving, specially focused drive toward spontaneous activity; consciousness of oneself and one's moral vocation.

Thus the world of the senses is only the "sensualized material arena for fulfilling obligation." And this is so in the strict sense: It is not just that this is the only way the external world comes into question for us (as Augustine and many others emphasized earlier), but that it is simply nothing else; it is an appearance in individuals, one that "sensualizes" their life's obligation and turns it into a "worldview," just as for Berkeley also objects were nothing but spiritual conversation of the creator with souls. Free spirits (and their spiritual connection in God) are the only real thing; an independent world of the senses through which they might influence each other does not exist. The

148

III. Soul and External World

freedom of these spirits is restricted in a special way for each of them, yet
for all of them together there is harmonious unity in a system of meaning;
from the outset that freedom is restricted, bound to specific paths, particular
tasks and resistances that it must fulfill or overcome. "My world is object
and sphere of my duties and absolutely nothing else." "I have these specific
duties that present themselves to me as obligations with regard to and in such
and such objects; these are specific duties that I am unable to imagine or
carry out in any other way than within such a world as I imagine for myself."
Hence my consciousness of world and with it my behavior do not begin here
with the world and the existence of my self within it—that is the position of
"dogmatism"; on the contrary, it is from the necessity to act that consciousness of "reality" and my place "in" it, or consciousness of my body and
possibilities for acting, proceed! It is in immediate consciousness of my moral
vocation that "faith" in the world of senses and its "reality" arises; it is in
struggles with that world and its opposition to the supersensible that my
moral-spiritual being and my knowledge about true spiritual reality, about
the realm of spirits and the life of God that supports them, then asserts itself.
Hence nature, in which I have to live and to work, is not some alien, self-
sufficient being created without any reference to me; no, through the special
laws of spiritual activity formed within me, nature everywhere expresses
nothing other than "proportions and relationships of myself to myself"; but
there is just one fundamental relationship to myself, and all others are sub-
species of it: my vocation to act morally. In every "existing thing" in all the
"world" I always see myself and my place in the moral world order, particular oppositions and limitations that encumber my intentions and my plans.
Thus the naive realism of living-acting persons is really correct in its belief
in the "reality" of the world of the senses. Just as Berkeley thought that it
was really first through fabrications of philosophers that people made a special existence and an independent substance out of the "language of God,"
so Fichte also believed that unspoiled moral consciousness first becomes
aware of the external world only as material for obligations and as opportunity for action, that the faith of moral man in this external "reality" is
ultimately nothing other than faith in his own moral calling. It is only erroneous speculation that first turned this into the concept of a dead, inert,
independent, ego-alien being.

With this the problem of the union of body with soul, which had weighed
so heavily since Descartes, was also supposed to be resolved. In fact the body
is not an independent reality but only the most central and most personal
moment in the worldview born of duty [in der pflichtgebornen Weltan-
schauung]. Body is not merely means and instrument for soul, but it is soul
itself, the individual spiritual-moral self—only looked at in sensualized rep-

149

resentation, in a phenomenal embodiment of its strivings and powers, its paths and obstacles. Here, too, in sensing and perceiving body, the immediate object of my intuition is my freedom and my moral vocation. "It is only within individuals and through self-intuition of their power that sensible worlds first come into being," and it is within them also that the bodily element ("in" which the soul is hidden, as the common man sees it) first comes into being.

The individual is therefore never really limited by externally given reality, but only from within and through membership in the "realm of spirits" insofar as he is only one free individual alongside many others and has very specific tasks to fulfill that differ from those of others. The ultimate moral goal is divided up, so to speak, broken up into vocations of individuals; thus others are really my "external world"! They are not merely phenomenal creatures of their own moral reality; instead they live alongside me and outside me—on the selfsame fundamental basis of the One spiritual stream of life that comes to self-consciousness and to full development of its own richness in individuals (cf. Eckehart's process of divine self-revelation in the evolution of creatures). "No individual sees the essences of his peers in himself and his self-intuition, but he sees them in the immediate intuition of the One life. But whatever else exists in nature, physical power, and so on, down to materiality is something each individual sees within himself." Thus in the case of Fichte also the ancient principle of seeing things in God or through God is still valid with regard to knowledge of other spiritual-animate beings outside me. And insofar as the "world" of free individuals—the great moral community, the realm of individually differentiated purposes—is the uniquely real world and all its individuals spring forth from the One stream of life. Fichte also holds that ultimately God is the sole object of our knowledge and experience. The basis for the commonality and systematic unity of the idea of the world in individuals also lies in this God-connection, however, despite all special perspectives of each individual and his special relationship to the part of the spatial world or worldview that he experiences as his body; here, too, is the reason why everything that we do changes and influences not only the world represented in us but correspondingly also in all other individuals. What Fichte sees as creating accord among self-enclosed personal beings is also a kind of "preestablished harmony" as in the Leibnizian monads. But God's creation does not stand here foreknown once and for all and for all eternity; on the contrary, "vocations" develop and differentiate themselves in the flow of his divine stream of life itself: they do not destroy the freedom of individuals but first attain form through their acts. The spiritual-moral meaning of everything I do influences that eternal realm of spiritual life to which I belong. And whereas in Plato's objectivistic world

150

concept the action of the soul remains without influence on the intelligible world of eternal ideas (indeed it can be accommodated only within the realm of the senses), Fichte's metaphysics of the absolute ego, which completely transforms the intelligible into intelligence, attributes ever-lasting influence in the realm of the eternal itself to spiritual activity, to the struggle of the soul in search of God, and to loving fulfillment of personal vocation.

IV.
Reality and Life

Among the ultimate problems of all given existence and among the primordial oppositions in all expressions of our "metaphysical need" belong the intermingling and mutual opposition of constancy and change, rest and motion, static-permanent reality and ever-changing life. There is scarcely a moment that more universally designates the structure of what is immediately given around us and in us than that of constant change, of alteration in time. Coming to be and passing away, living growth and decay, are fundamental facts of all daily experience as well as sources of all pleasure and all pain. And to the degree that we come closer to objects around us or those within us, even moments of stability and of rest seem to dissolve and turn out to be unnoticed, gently flowing change. But there is much in us that opposes this tendency that tries to draw all objects into the stream of becoming. The ever present experience of the permanent and the fixed, past which external change rushes by—something that asserts and maintains itself and shows no sign of beginning or end—is profoundly corroborated by demands of reason and mind. For knowledge, what elapses is unknowable; knowledge is always intent on finding solid points of departure, something that lasts in the face of evolution or even within evolution itself. In every epoch thought has looked for substance in this sense, that is, for what lasts, what one can lay hold of, what does not evaporate before the outstretched hand of reason. Real becoming (emergence of being out of nothing or disappearance of being into nothingness), even if it seems plausible to sense experience, seems inconceivable to understanding. Understanding tries to help itself out (not, by the way, primarily by forming concepts of principles of scientific "conservation") by trying to grasp the changing as a

152

IV. Reality and Life

"mere" external modification, as it were, of something that in itself has neither come to be nor will be destroyed, namely "substance." "Nothing comes from nothing" is the watchword here, as well as: "What exists cannot cease to exist." This does not really solve the puzzle, to be sure, but it merely shifts it back to a different plane. Next comes the longing of the soul: that which changes constantly, which is often the source of heightened feeling of life to the point of jubilation and intoxication, can also easily turn into tormenting uneasiness in the long run, which gives decisive impetus to our wish for a resting place in life, for something that does not change, for quiet and equilibrium. We feel this last moment with particular weight in the flux of things when they come to be and pass away; and in the face of destruction through the tooth of time and the continual decay of the transitoriness we see everywhere around us and within us, we seek for the imperishable and the immortal, for a timeless something that escapes all transformation in time; we look for eternal peace in place of changing struggle, for something that is always evenly filled in place of alternating desire and satisfaction.

From its very beginnings, Greek philosophy was very comfortable with the primordial givenness of becoming. [Greek] philosophy always looked for the principle of the soul (as that philosophy understood it) in being, as a means of explaining motion in everything that exists. From the very start, interest focused on life and on the unchanging course of the stars. As early as the time of myths, the question concerning the origin of the world directed attention to the development of even those things that one encountered in a finished and static state. Universal flux in objects asserted itself so overwhelmingly that one dismissed the idea of finality; the notion of cosmic periods endlessly succeeding one another in the process of the world's coming to be and passing away permeated Greek history of philosophy from its beginnings on into its final phase. As Anaximander put it, we must conceive the principle of the world as endless so that it will not exhaust itself in becoming.

Even the idea of world periodicity, however, nevertheless implies an effort to bring flux into line with the requirements of reason after all. People always regarded self-contained motion, such as that in a circle, for example, as more perfect than continuous, unlimited motion (a view especially evident in Aristotle). Even in movement of the stars the fact that their orbits are closed entails a moment of form that solidifies, as it were, the indeterminate-restless dimension of movement into something static. If one viewed flux as a constantly renewed cycle of coming to be and passing away (especially in the extreme form of recurrence of the same thing), one could grasp the endless flow of temporal events and reduce it in a certain way to something solidly fixed. In this way one could avoid the measure-less character of eter-

153

nal process, such as eternal development in a single direction. At the same time, together with the endlessness linked to those theories and (from Anaximander on) to process—but which also inheres in individual self-contained process in the form of progress through unnumbered moments of time (as Zeno emphasized with particular acuity)—people were prone to regard process itself as something imperfect, indeterminate, and incomplete, and therefore as not belonging to true being itself. In the Pythagorean table of opposites, motion stands on the side of the boundless and the bad. Their metaphysics of numbers, although it clearly appeared to derive from processes of motion in astronomy and music, had an obvious tendency toward the geometrical and static, toward fixed form.

The only person who came forward wholeheartedly in favor of becoming and flux was Heraclitus. In many points he went his own way, distancing himself completely from the general Greek path, and was alien to Greek development in many ways, just as Spinoza has been (in an opposite direction) in the Modern Period. A foolish tradition of late Antiquity wanted to label him a pessimist and the "weeping philosopher" because he had spoken with such powerful feeling about becoming and perishing, about the instability of all reality, and about the impossibility even of stepping into the same river twice and because he saw in war and strife the father of all things. But the person passing that judgment is merely betraying his longing for the happiness of repose, of equilibrium, of the finished and complete. Heraclitus himself affirmed struggle, tension of opposites, and life in strife. He viewed the ups and downs of coming-to-be and passing-away, of birth and death, of the eternally flowing and endlessly changing, and of the motion of the world's course as an eternally flaming fire, sublimest thing of all, harmony of life itself. The fact that the sun is not always the same old sun but is instead new every day or that the river and we ourselves are never the same as a moment ago is what constituted the core of happiness for him, the harmony of opposites, the hidden unity that is better than open unity. Cosmic order is eternally meaningful as it changes; but it does not perdure and persist as static, fossilized form. "It rests as it changes."

Greek development did not pursue the path Heraclitus took in this matter any more than it did in the question of unity of opposites. Only the resolutive tendencies in Sophism made use of his ideas. And it was not until the world-dynamism of Stoicism that some of his main motifs were fully utilized. Instead, in this area, too, Parmenides—who flatly denied all multiplicity, unboundedness, and change, and who excluded change (as sense deception) from true "being"—was the one who succeeded in winning decisive influence on forming the great systems. The thrust toward the formal and the fixed that presents itself as objectively comprehensible to thought and fulfills the

154

desire for perfectly unchanging rest here reaches its strongest formulation in the concept of the One Being that has neither come into existence nor will pass away, a Being that tolerates no motion or change of any kind, even within itself. In actuality, there can be no opposition between non-being and being, nor can there be any transition from the one into the other and vice versa; there is no coming-to-be and passing-away. Past and future are empty noises, and so are "becoming and perishing, being and non-being, change of place and alteration of gleaming color." True being is unborn, imperishable, unshakable; "it lies motionless, confined by mighty bonds without beginning and end . . . it perdures at rest within itself as the selfsame in the selfsame." Parmenides and his disciples deny every type of motion; only unchanging and rigid being has true reality.

This had a profound influence on all who came later; even when evaluating motion as a given reality, their goal nevertheless always was to trace it back to, or attach it to, the solid, the formal-static element. Plato tried to understand opposition between Heraclitean flux and Eleatic being entirely in the spirit of the Pythagorean table. Becoming exists, but only in the world of the senses, which in fact is always becoming and never is, in this world of fleeting appearances; true being persists without change. Plato addresses multiplicity, which Parmenides had so utterly rejected, with his existence of ideas: among the many Ideas, each one is in turn unity for a multiplicity of appearances. But flux remains, indeed it becomes with even greater emphasis the mark of the merely sensible and phenomenal! Whenever he talks about process, he always stresses transitoriness, instability, signs of decay. He is far removed from Heraclitus's joy in becoming. The best we can say about process is that it embodies striving toward being, and that all becoming takes place for the sake of specific being, whereas becoming in general happens only for the sake of unchanging existence of ideas. Just as multiplicity and relative character of sense appearances find their anchor in the unity of ideas, so flux and process find theirs in the static fixity of eternal forms. The demiurge of the *Timaeus* encounters visible matter in a state of unsteady, that is, irregular and inharmonious motion; it is by looking at the ideas that he brings fixed order into the flux.

Nonetheless Plato strove to go beyond this exclusive emphasis on static being. He sounds an important motif in his concept of soul, which derived from doctrines of the Pythagoreans. The soul shows that it is immortal because it is the principle of life as spontaneous movement. To be sure, the point is not so much that soul itself is essentially living and therefore immortal, but rather that it provides life and movement to something else (the body). But there is, in fact, a hint of the idea of something imperishable and living in this doctrine of the soul, so that one does not restrict events exclusively to coming-to-be and perishing in the temporal world of sense and to being depreciated along with it; on the contrary, in a special sense one even elevates them into the spiritual. But on the other hand soul does not, after all, belong to the realm of eternal ideas but—precisely because it is a living-moving thing—to the world of sense, even though it is the highest element in it; soul ranks first, but only in the sphere of becoming. Even before becoming involved with a body at birth, it ranks below the existence that it intuits; that is the only reason it is possible for it to take that sudden plunge. Hence, also, the highest life that soul can attain is eros, upward striving toward pure eternal forms; it achieves its highest existence in serene contemplation of the unchanging. Specifically emotional elements or disturbances of the soul, insofar as they are not the impetus and the path to such static contemplation, still hover close to the realm of sense.

The late Dialogues with their idea of "movement of concepts" (as the inner tendency of ideal images to crowd in on each other and become mixed together, which drags them down to the sphere of the concrete and actual) strive toward a concept of change that guarantees a certain right to existence to process itself, even on the level of the intelligible and the timeless, and thereby affirms its own proper value for every existing thing. [Plato] thereby overcame Parmenidean rigidity of the existence of ideas and paved the way for a closer relationship between being and becoming, between eternal permanence and the liveliness of the sensible and the animate. Plotinus's system of emanation built on this foundation. But his ultimate principle of being, the One, was elevated above any kind of change, exactly as Eleatic being was; it is absolutely static. As Neoplatonists argued against Christian thinkers, God himself cannot be "living"; the One cannot be energy. *Kinesis* [movement] and *zoe* [life] enter the picture, however, as early as the nous. Living movement exists even in spiritual being itself. There is a dynamism that leads from here (with the "outpouring" of levels of being) down to the sensible realm. But it still remains subject to the level of highest ordering of static rest; and as far as sensible becoming is concerned—such as bodily movement or organic development or even inner movement of personal life of the soul—there is no new valuation, just as there was none for Plato. Of a piece with this was the scorn, so characteristic of the entire ancient world and its ethics, for activity and achievement in the actual world. Silent and motionless contemplation of static being was the exclusive goal of all higher spiritual life. Even the life of the soul was but transition and striving toward being.

Aristotle is the one who most clearly maintained the transitional character and merely provisional element in all motion and life. Change and life play an outstanding role in his world system, to be sure, and with respect to the Platonic Idea he saw his own merit precisely in the fact that he introduced principles of change and did not simply assume motion and becoming as eternally inherent in material existence as Plato (and the atomists) did. Development and energy were essential features of Aristotle's concept of world. But even he still regarded becoming of every sort as a sign of dearth, of incomplete and formally unripe existence. As a special and spontaneous stream of vitality, flux was for him a foreign concept. All becoming presupposes a ''wherefore''; it is only transition to something unchanging. There can be no such thing, then, as endless motion (understood according to its essence); instead, every movement ''has its goal and its limit.'' Movement (whether it be change in location for a stone or life for an animal or even human activity) is realization of ''something unfulfilled''; accomplishment of the possible, insofar as it is indeed merely possible; transition out of matter (which can become anything) into form, which is. Process necessarily vanishes in the realization of whatever goal is placed before it. Hence there is no becoming where there is no matter; it is only because everything actual is commingled with matter that there is motion everywhere in nature. Even eternal revolution of the heavens is a sign of the material moment in them and demonstrates unrealized possibilities in them. Life cannot exist in something without parts, but only in the realm of the divisible-material. Aristotle expressly disputes Plato's concept of soul as perpetually living being. As the purpose and form of the body to which it gives life, soul itself remains motionless. It is only externally and incidentally that body draws soul along with it in movement, just as a traveling ship does the pilot who stands unmoved on it. Life is therefore not something essential in its own right, not something primordial, but only transition toward existing being, only an affect (*pathos*) of existing being. Hence it always points toward unmoved-static being as the specific note of actually existing being. In the stricter sense of the word, becoming also lacks altogether the value of new creation: nothing comes to be that did not already exist; after all, becoming merely seeks for the existing form that has been assigned it ahead of time, the form that is its final cause. And so according to Aristotle, in the case of anything caught up in becoming, science too looks only for the static-universal element at which becoming aims; and soul in this sort of knowledge of being becomes something endowed with understanding and knowledge, something separated from the sensible and material, but only so that it ''might come out of its natural unrest to rest.''

With respect to all life and movement and becoming we must ask the question regarding ''whither.'' That something ''is'' and is at rest is perfectly natural; but we must explain every kind of movement away from a state of rest. Even Plato (as Aristotle believes) has soul, which is self-moved, come

157

into being only with the world. For soul and world and for everything that moves in them, either spontaneously or through another, we must raise the question about the most universal origin of movement, the "first mover." And that is the absolute and total actuality of the divine nous, actuality that is free from any unfulfilledness of matter. Nous is itself unmoved, and that means not only that in itself it did not come to be but is instead eternal and removed from all perishing; it also means, however, that here there is absolutely and fundamentally no becoming at all, no liveliness and no flux (which Aristotle says we can understand only as transition from unfulfilled potency to a higher plane). To think of the first mover himself as moved would entail the nonsensical act of regarding him as in need of movement and as striving toward some still unattained goal! Thus this god of Aristotle is not the source of motions in the world in a causal sense, then, for that would somehow involve him, as one performing an act, in becoming! This God cannot even think the world, nor can he know about the world: that, too, would draw him into the changing-flowing plane. Free from every unfulfilled possibility, he is drawn up into absolute rest and fixity of pure form, Plato's Idea, Parmenides' being. As the total actuality that he is, how could he still be flux and life? The word *zoe* [life] does nevertheless crop up (doubtless in accord with some other religious ideas); but it no more involves the character of inner movement or of life than the concept of "energy" does, which Aristotle in fact meant in a sense that is so different from the way we understand it today. Even the thinking whereby nous thinks himself shows no trace of motion or of timeless life. On the contrary, this "first mover" is himself unmoved in every sense, and he moves the world only to the extent that he is the ultimate goal of all striving and of all self-development toward static form. He moves the world as the beloved, himself at rest and fulfilled, moves the yearning lover and restless desirer. Although the source of motion in a causal sense must itself also always entail motion, the *causa finalis* [final cause] makes room for eternally resting and completely static existence.

The Christian notion of the "living God" is opposed to this conception of the perfect in the most profound way. With the priority of personal life over objective being the question of movement also assumes an entirely new aspect. What was inherent in the Pythagorean-Platonic idea of immortality,

IV. Reality and Life

but had to take second place to the Parmenidean concept of being, now came to its fullest unfolding. Abstract dialectic's concept of self-movement even in the intelligible acquired new and deep power from transformation of the intelligible into the intelligent (Plotinus had already made this transition). Indeed the motif of creation overthrew the statics of the ancient world completely. God, who towers above all existence, is not quiescent form or the eternal idea of the good, static being confined within itself; on the contrary, he is efficacious power who first created existing beings through the power of his will. Plato's demiurge could form worlds and be active in forming only insofar as he himself took second place to the motionless perfection of the existence of ideas. But the Christian world creator stands precisely as inexhaustible vitality, as active omnipotence who comes before and is above all "existence." Here is motion (though not coming to be and passing away, not temporal change) in the one undivided being who is free from matter, movement on the basis of principle, of the eternally unchanging and all-sufficient deity! What the Greek could conceive of only on the basis of dependent ranks of the order of being devolves here on the absolute himself: God creates the world, guides and governs it, perhaps even intervenes in it through miracle. He knows about the world, comprehends it and personally takes a providential and coordinate hand in the course of things. He is also most profoundly conversant with the manifold of creatures he has created and with their life, although indeed in his own special way that involves neither time nor multiplicity. And the world of creatures is above all a living thing, just as its creator is. Its life stems from him, from the *causa efficiens* [efficient cause] of everything real. Human souls make up the proper core of creation, and they themselves are God's image, precisely because they are active powers that express themselves inwardly, and because they themselves are animated life, not just motive principles. Even when the body set in motion by the soul decays, in fact especially then, soul proves itself to be "living." Its essence is not quiet mirroring of pregiven being but rather spontaneous activity, which as God's gift in the strictest sense of all makes it like God: free will! Here too therefore, there is inner motion in a being without parts. And here there is not merely striving toward a static goal in which soul itself rigidifies; perfection attained in this case does not end in cessation of movement but in "eternal *life*." The first and highest of the new "categories of inwardness" is life. Life itself is the abiding thing. God himself is eternal love, hence the kingdom of God into which emancipated souls are supposed to come—in which they of course find "peace" and "rest" and are totally removed from the unfulfilled and restless condition of all desire and striving—is also, as the kingdom of love, eternal movement. This living love is motion without a terminus in which it would perish when it

159

reached it; for it is not desire but rather never-ceasing, never-exhausted turning toward the beloved, leaning toward him, offering oneself to him. Love
is endless movement, and it should be so. It recognizes no ''end'' in Aristotle's sense, no limit nor measure. Whereas ethics in antiquity so praised
the soul's serenity amid opposite emotions, its equilibrium and balance in
the face of every sort of passion, here the demand is for unending, limitless,
and measureless love that flows on forever and never dies of anything. The
loving person is an immortal being.

With that, however, process in the world also takes on an entirely new
meaning. As great as the role of the principle of development in Aristotle's
world system had been, the static moment had nevertheless remained dominant in it. Nothing came to be that did not already exist before; pregiven
form was merely inserted into indeterminate matter. The question of essence
had to do exclusively with what abides, never with becoming itself. The
world is always in some sense finished; it is always the present moment. The
forms of everything becoming and actual are solidly established complete
substances; in principle, becoming always remains secondary, behind what
exists. But with the total transformation from the being of nature into ani-
mate-inward being, from the cosmic into the ethical, and with the central
position of the moral-religious task of winning one's salvation, the entire
center of gravity now falls precisely on becoming, precisely on the future.
The world of becoming is now no longer so much a world of decay and
transitoriness, but rather a world in which each person must accomplish the
new birth of his own being. Just as world as an act of creation is new becoming, emergence out of nothing, as we are expressly told, and not merely
repetition of what has already existed, so also the existence of every man is
first of all a product of his own inner life, his free, creative will. It is soul
that first makes itself into what it then is for eternity. In the beginning is the
deed, not being. It is in willing and in turning itself toward love, in active
accomplishment and earnest endeavor that the soul made in God's image
attains eternal life, more so than in static contemplation, in merely being the
image of truly existing ideas, or in ecstatic abandonment to the motionless
One.

But this new emphasis on becoming and development now also received
particularly special support from the fact that evolution in individual souls
was combined with the idea of the evolutionary progress of mankind and
building up a kingdom of God that embraced all individuals. The ethical
process thereby acquired a kind of cosmic importance. Now one looked for
becoming in time not so much in the cycle of coming to be and passing away,
in eternally selfsame rhythm of natural changes or in periodic return of forms
in the spatial world, but rather in univocal development of free beings toward

the eternal kingdom. What once happens here is never lost, but is stamped into the book of eternity; on the other hand it is something that did not exist before, for it is a free act. Temporal development from the past (original sin) to the future (universal redemption) dissolves the static sense of the present and recurring, self-contained cycles; here for the first time "development" becomes truly temporal. The important thing is New-Becoming, the great demand of the future, not what is already given and abides. Each and every one faces the demand of fundamental renewal. The time in which we live, however, is the one path toward the eternal goal; the entire center of gravity of the eternal kingdom that is to be built falls on activity in this time. Every moment of life is important for the final judgment. Time and temporal process is more than a pale imitation of something established from eternity, more than an image of the perennially existing. In *history*—the history of salvation of the individual as well as of humanity in general—temporal process acquires immense importance. Creation, Fall, Mosaic Law, and sacrificial death of Christ signify the great turning points in the one path that leads to the future. The living God's creative activity continues on in the work of grace that points out the path to all of mankind and helps every loving person achieve full life. The metaphysical philosophy of history of the cosmos made up of souls stands opposite to metaphysics of inflexible being, to form-bound nature, to world locked up in a uniform cycle of eternal recurrence. In eternity as well as in time, life triumphs over being as something of greater importance.

In this matter as well, the age of the Church Fathers was marked by the first great struggle of motifs between the new and the old world. The concept of the living God and creator of the world took a long time to assert itself. Ancient opposition between static perfection and sensible-worldly movement did not want to go away. This was most sharply manifest in the teaching of the Arians: they regarded the second person of the deity as subordinate to the Father, as noneternal and created, precisely because people looked for a connecting link between eternally unchanging divine truth and temporally evolving and changing world, something corresponding to Plato's demiurge. And wherever argument raged against consubstantiality and in favor of subordination of the Son, this was one of the main motifs: A son who was himself born or who had already descended through emanation could more easily assume a connection with living-changing being; one also assigned creation of the world to him for that reason. But with the victory of consubstantiality, the demand for divine life in creating and conserving the world and in guiding mankind pushed its way through. People (e.g., Theophilus of Antioch) now understood the revelation of God himself as a gradual development; he did not complete it in a single act of creation. Whatever human beings earn in the free self-development of their lives, in obedience to God and his revealed commandments, continues what began in the act of creation. Although the old opposition still resounds clearly in Tertullian's distinction between hidden and revealed God, and although he here ascribed relationship to the world (hence also the characteristic of life) only to the latter, nevertheless both of them unite in the essential unity and perfection of one God. Indeed, Tertullian quite expressly chides the pagans for demanding a do-nothing God. He regards the true God not merely as source of becoming and of opposites in general; no, God works as the eternally living one as well in unchanging fashion, inasmuch as he intervenes in the temporal process of this world and in successive human developments. In a similar way Clement of Alexandria also spoke in favor of a living God, and Origen, in spite of all the difficulties he considered inherent in the connection and transition between time and eternity, nonetheless expressly emphasized that God's omnipotence made it impossible that he should be idle and without influence. We can also detect in him the positive valuation that at the same time devolved on process and life in the world's existence on the basis of the idea of the living God. Linking up with the pantheistic dynamism of Stoicism, he saw in the living world and in the universally vivifying power of its forms and changes, the expression and revelation of the living God—not without some unsteadiness, however, in the area of the distinction and value-diminishment between quiescent Father and creative "Word" who personally enters into what he moves. Gregory of Nyssa also insisted that there is nothing in God that does not actively express and communicate itself. The Logos of his trinitarian concept is not merely eternal and spiritual but also alive, a living power of will: *autozoe* [life in his own right], as he says expressly, not merely *zoes metousia* [participation in life]. And so Gregory understood the human soul as life that is by nature constantly in motion; in a state of dead inertia it would perish. Whereas Aristotle could conceive of motion only in the case of something unfulfilled (*ateles*), here the soul is in fact intrinsically living and never-resting movement, *ousia autoteles* [self-sufficient being]! Life does not end in some alien goal; it always lives in and from itself. Nemesius in particular, in struggling against Aristotle, tried on this basis to find the connection with immortality of living being in Plato. The eternal life of divine being was then also a fundamental theme with Augustine (in whom, nevertheless, ancient devaluation of change still continued to assert itself clearly). Creator-spirit moves himself. In God "being" is at the same time not only knowledge (this is something Aristotle had also said, yet he was able to turn this into something immobile and static, and into something objective) but above all willing and acting also. Conservation of the world is nothing other than constantly repeated, ever new creation at every moment of time. In this doctrine—which

162

of course permeated the Middle Ages and still played so great a role in Descartes, Leibniz, and many others of their century—the ancient sequence was most dramatically reversed: "being" and permanence result first of all from life, they express ever new activity.

At the same time, the valuation of temporal becoming in the sense of univocal universal history steadily gained ground. In Christian gnosis the question of the relationship of meaning between successive revelations of the Old Testament and the doctrine of Christ had already emerged in the ancient idea of emanation and cosmic periodicity. And what people still often interpret as struggle and controversy between several deities, the Church Fathers, beginning with the great foe of Gnosticism, Irenaeus, understood as gradual revelation of the one God who also made the world. The purposeful and guiding proclamation, first of the Mosaic Law and then of the inner word of life in Christ, was a promise of further development as well. A new era had arrived and a new light shone into the future, in which the entire world, including both humankind and physical-cosmic being, will transform itself. Theophilus and Tertullian explained this new meaning of evolution by analogy with the development of a single person from birth to full maturity. They projected the three stages of life to that point (they omitted the declining period of old age, hence the analogy limped here) on to three great periods of development of humankind, the last of which was supposed to have just begun. They stressed throughout the necessary slowness of this development as gradually increasing acquisition of eternal goods by free men and as gradual self-revelation of God accommodating itself to our human nature. Clement of Alexandria in particular directed attention to future, superterrestrial development and also looked there for periods that are also stages on one path to universal redemption. He presupposed throughout that all individual souls and the ups and downs of particular paths of life would effect a single universal work, whether one saw the final goal as redemption of all beings or separation of the good from the damned. The transformation of humanity through Christ's action and teaching is not transition to merely inert knowledge but impetus toward love and action, toward building up comprehensive community in the universal church. It is for this work that we living persons exist in a corporeal-sense world; but the body is not merely something that entangles static being in worthless becoming.

In a very peculiar way these Christian motives were in conflict with the ancient world periodicity of Origen, who gave signs that he was profoundly permeated by doctrines of Antiquity in other respects as well. He held fast to the eternity of the world process as well as to the cyclical alternation of world conflagration and world rebirth described most recently by Stoicism in such forceful terms; but out of each of these successive worlds and developments a new number of free beings emerged purified and redeemed and accrued to the kingdom of God. In like manner periodicity cannot mean recurrence of the same thing, because the free will of people inhabiting and building up these worlds is opposed to that. And finally: Christ has appeared only once in the great course of changing world periods; with his achievement the return to God begins for all time. Augustine was entirely free from such hesitation and mediation. "World history" is a single path of life, comparable to the triply articulated growth of a person from infant to adult or also to the successive work of the six days of creation, which accordingly also calls for distinguishing six great periods. Augustine tried to incorporate into his conception of a unique, unilinear course of history that was to flow into the eternal Sabbath of the City of God not just the graduated path from Old Testament to doctrine of Christ, but all other evolutions and creations in the life of peoples up to that point. But Augustine very emphatically rejected Stoic cyclical doctrine, because in his view it would make events appear meaningless. The teleological structure that Antiquity knew only as a permanent order of nature, cosmos, and forms of life now shifted over entirely to process, to temporal development. Christ died for us only one time. And all men have but One [*Eine*] task to perform: to build up the universal church. This living, growing, and acting church is the meaning and content of all activity and process in time.

Thus new ideas pressed forward, yet there was a lot missing before they could actually transform the entire picture of the world. The ancient cosmos, with all the static elements that clung to it, and the old opposition between what is spiritually perfect as immobile being (not merely as free from coming-to-be and passing-away) and becoming as a symbol of deficiency was never fully overcome. And so it remained throughout the entire Middle Ages. To be sure, a major fundamental premise of all theological and philosophical systems of this period was that God's existence was *operari* [acting] and his essence was *actio* [action], inner action in thinking and above all in willing, hence also activity in creation and conservation outside himself, the action of grace, and so on. One also sought for a connection with motion of the world: Scotus Erigena taught that just as we can see the existence of God the Father on the basis of the existence of objects, and just as we can see the Son's divine wisdom on the basis of their rich ordering, so we can see life of God, the Holy Spirit, on the basis of never ceasing movement of all objects! At the height of Scholasticism, Albert and Thomas emphatically stressed that God himself is constantly at work in the world and does not hover over it in alien and immobile fashion—and that means at work in the sense of causal activity, not merely as exemplar and principle. Albert in particular now really changed the Aristotelian concept of "active intellect"

164

entirely into something living-creative, something that functioned freely and creatively as will does. Pagan philosophers, he said, were in fact unable to understand the true meaning of activity of the highest being with respect to creatures: it was activity, but that did not mean change or transitoriness. And Thomas saw the guarantee for unity of all reality above all in the fact that all objects, because they issue forth from God who is essentially active cause, must also for their part be active causes that always produce effects and that are also therefore implicated with one another through causal links in all directions. The idea of life also made steady progress on the basis of the doctrine of soul. The more people abandoned ancient doctrine regarding soul and knowledge; the more they saw in the soul not merely an idle principle for mobile body; the more they stopped seeing knowledge primarily as reception of something externally given instead of as inner independence that (as the ultimately determinative feature of essence) pervaded all stages from perception up to knowledge and love of God, so much the more clearly did superiority of life over immobility assert itself. But ancient static world order nevertheless still had the last word, at least as far as nature and the motion we find in it was concerned. Supported here, too, by dualism between God and world, between perfect being and actual being, that world order resisted carrying out what the idea of the living God must have demanded. In the same way Aristotle had done, Thomas Aquinas also defined movement as transition from mere potency into actuality, as a mere *actus imperfecti* [an act of an imperfect entity]. Movement, like matter, belonged to something that only potentially existed. A body in motion strove for a point of rest at which it then is in actuality what it had previously been only potentially. Thus the entire philosophy of nature and science was dominated by the idea of "substantial forms": these rigid, static-unchanging, merely teleologically effective principles, in comparison with which all movement, including movement of the stars, and all events and organic life signified only striving and transition. Movement and life possessed no existence or meaning in themselves.

Even the historical-philosophical motif did not really break through faith in what is given once and for all. To be sure, the idea itself continued to live on and acquired major new content, for example, particularly in Joachim of Flora's idea of the currently (i.e., the thirteenth century) emerging new "age of the spirit" or through Thomas's insertion of the world state into the developmental path of humanity en route to the City of God. But there was constant opposition, based on Antiquity's still-unsubdued feeling for the world, from the conviction that truth, both religious and philosophical, was not something that we are to utilize first and foremost in an evolutionary sense, but rather as something that is given to us in finished form and that

165

we have only to preserve. Just as people regarded the entire truth of salvation (insofar as it can be accessible to man at all in this life) as completed revelation given to us once and for all in sacred Scriptures and their elucidation by Church Fathers, so at the same time—in accordance with the fundamental conviction that so essentially defined and also so severely restricted the Middle Ages—they also thought that the heroes of ancient wisdom provided everything essential in worldly and philosophical knowledge once and for all. From the very start the universally dominant principle of authority assumed this rigid character of real opposition to evolution and future progress. This is why the syllogism now became the sole dominant methodology in philosophical thought: The true principles of everything knowable have in fact already been discovered; they stand solidly unshakable and cannot be increased; all one has to do is to follow the ancients (especially Aristotle), to deduce from their basic principles whatever new particular issue happens to fall within the scope of human interests.

By contrast, Joachim of Flora's philosophy of history seemed to proclaim a new attitude toward life. When he saw the final and most mature period of human evolution as appearing for the first time in his own period—this age of the Spirit that now grew out of that of the Father (which began with creation) and that of the Son (with Christ's redemptive act)—that implied obvious faith in gradual ascent of religious insight and powers and in an ongoing and ever expanding vitality of the process of revelation. Revelation once given in Scripture has not settled everything once and for all; religious searching and acquisition has had to go beyond that and must do so now as well.

But the new age sounded forth very clearly in Roger Bacon's struggles in favor of a new method of research: knowledge is not the possession of a particular bygone era nor merely a legacy from that point on, but rather a task for every century. Aristotle and Avicenna themselves admitted that they had not been able to solve all problems, and Averroës did not merely comment on Aristotle, after all, but also improved on him in some areas! That encouraged him toward new paths. And so Duns Scotus in particular then stressed the point that the Holy Spirit still continues to live in, to act in, and to build up the church and develop its doctrines. Just as he elsewhere tried to explain how the action of grace is connected with creation and with the continual guidance of life through God's hand—seeing in that connection merely a phase and application of influence that is always at work in those latter acts, an inner movement through the Holy Spirit that does not cripple one's own activity, but not a sudden intervention as if from the outside, nor a breaking through nature that God himself has created and guided, not a contradiction in nature—so he also understood governance of the Spirit in

166

IV. Reality and Life

the community of believers not as a gift that came once and for all as rigidly established authority, but rather as something that is still active and creative, that points to the future, that commands us constantly to search for new paths to add to the old. The command given to every person and every age is to build up spiritual life still further, to continue to build up doctrine in free activity and research, inwardly guided and given wings through the never ceasing life of the Holy Spirit. From that point on, conviction regarding the ability and challenge of the new age to become and to create something new—to add to the treasure handed down, to expand and even improve doctrine, to replace what will no longer satisfy in it with something else— grew inexorably. Of course Renaissance and Reformation wanted once again to hold fast totally to the traditional (purifying it from perversion by later periods, as people thought), to the ancient; to imitate and follow it had to remain the sole task of present and future forever. But their real influence went far beyond that often so narrowly defined program; even in philosophy of the period a great deal of new will to discover nevertheless expressed itself in ''imitation'' of ancient doctrines and schools. New natural science especially claimed to be and to offer something new. Galileo saw the greatness of divinely created nature precisely in the fact that one would never finish reading in this book and the desire to explore and to discover would last forever!

Constraint was then completely broken in the seventeenth century. Pride in the ''modern'' challenged mere praise of the traditional and then also led (most especially in Descartes) to the other extreme: completely overthrowing the ancient and wishing to begin everything anew. Leibniz's reflections on *perennis philosophia* [perennial philosophy] combined both elements: preserving tradition in the broadest conceivable sense and new building that goes beyond the totality of everything already given. Whereas among the Greeks Plato, for example, praised the practice of Egyptian art, in that it forbade ''adopting novelties or contriving anything else that deviated from the traditional'' so that ''whatever people painted or sculpted there 10,000 years ago ranked neither higher nor lower than what one does today''; whereas throughout the entire Middle Ages innovation was suspect, not only in the religious-dogmatic sphere, and instead the old and permanent alone should decide and execute; so now with Leibniz the highest obligation for present and future was to understand the ancient more profoundly than it understood itself and in preserving nonetheless to transcend what has been preserved! He felt and understood in a new way the plurality, opposition, and change in the former appearance of what was now traditional; the new age in fact had to create unity through new insight. An element of truth lies in all tradition, but the whole truth lies in no tradition; one has to struggle

167

for it. Gradually, faith in the possible and even necessary progress of historical development emerged. And with that, process and historical life won primacy over the unchanging and permanent.

Just as Duns Scotus represented the decisive turning point for this question of historical consciousness, so Meister Eckehart represented the decisive turning point for the metaphysics of process. On the basis of the idea of the living God he summoned up courage for the mighty paradox: "God comes to be and ceases to be," "God's becoming is his essence." The absolute itself is flux, a "flux that has flowed into itself" (as Pseudo-Dionysius had said earlier); living, "welling up within himself." Here the concept of movement has changed totally. This welling up and flowing of God is not motion in the sense of seeking an end, one that terminates in a goal. The kind of movement whereby becoming and the thing that has become, striving and reaching the goal, are two different and opposed kinds of things is expressly excluded from the deity. *Operari dei suum est esse* [God's action is his existence]: for Eckehart this means at the same time that here *operari* and *operatum* [action and thing enacted], action and fulfillment, exist simultaneously and are one. To that extent Eckehart also calls this eternal happening and becoming *motus sine motu* [motion without motion], "becoming without becoming" [*Gewerden sonder Gewerden*], "flux without having flowed" ["*Fluß sonder geflossen*"]. But then he also positively labels this process "life." For Eckehart Aristotle's question about the Why of movement no longer exists with respect to life. "Life lives on its own basis and wells up from its own being." And whereas the ancient concept of a living thing's spontaneous movement still demanded a goal here also, the unattained form as the Why of a process, now this life that is attributed to the perfect and absolute being himself has no further basis than its own power and fullness. God's love as well as that of the "just" man, the pure man, is movement without goals toward which to strive. "Therefore, just as God acts without a Why and has no Why, in the same way the just man acts without a Why; hence just as life lives for its own sake and seeks no Why to explain what it does." "If someone should question life for a thousand years: Why do you live? If it could answer, it would say only: I live because I live. . . . It lives, therefore, that it may live unto itself. If someone were to ask an honest man

168

IV. Reality and Life

who is working for his own personal reason: Why are you doing your work? If he could answer rightly, he would say only: I am working for what I am working for.'' (Not therefore for the sake of a fixed goal at which I could rest!) ''Life is so desirable [*begierlich*] in itself that we desire it for itself.'' It is therefore a living *ousia autotheles* [self-sufficient being]! Life is purpose and value in itself, just as statically conceived forms and ideals are otherwise. ''Why do you love truth? For the sake of truth. . . . Why do you live? Indeed, I do not know! *I want to live.*'' Just as a steed jumps and bounds on the green heath ''that it can let itself go all at once with all its strength in jumping on the heath: that is what he would enjoy, that would be his nature,'' so is it then God's nature and desire to pour out all his being and his fullness into the ''likeness'' [*Gleichheit*] of creatures; and love and activity of a noble person is likewise of the same kind. On this basis, even Eckehart, the quiet mystic, can demand activity and rank it above abiding in the state of ecstatic rapture, as he does in the example of the bit of soup [*Süpplein*]. It is not one who rests in contemplation but one who loves and acts out of inner fullness of life that is God's image. Eckehart thereby distanced himself from the Neoplatonic mystical tradition in which he stood. The subsequent period, especially from the Reformation on, then actually broke with ancient primacy of contemplation over activity and, for example, with the prejudice against manual activity and labor. This attained its first fully matured philosophical formulation in Fichte's ethics.

Thus for Eckehart the immobile and nonliving no longer maintained any kind of supremacy in value and reality. The act of creation fused with God's inner movement. All creatures and the world itself live in the never-ending and nonteleologically directed process of God's self-knowledge. Event and flux are everything; and therein lies the constant ''greening and flowering'' of living being in contrast with everything ''tired and old.'' Even in timeless being—indeed here for the first time—there is true ''becoming'': eternally new existence ''without renewal'' and ''without aging or abating.''

Mystics of subsequent centuries then carried this forward, especially Jacob Böhme (with whom the ''evolutionary-historical pantheism'' of German Idealism later so readily linked up). ''Being'' is the eternal process of God's giving birth to himself; it is a becoming in the will or a ''drive'' that has only itself as its object. The more powerfully the subject assumed the position of metaphysical center, patterned everything after itself and assimilated it, so much the more absolutely did life also assume primacy over immobile being. Movement and life in the world of external nature then also attained altogether new importance among natural philosophers in this group. It is not because the actual never arrives at a terminus (hence always falls short of eternal archetypical images) that everything is moving and restless

169

in nature, but because the life of God lives and acts in all creation. Universal movement with happy affirmation was perceived as the expression of fullness and perfection that characterizes this best of all worlds.

At the same time the scientific concept of motion in the narrower sense of change of place underwent the most remarkable change. Occamists of the fourteenth century had already developed the fundamental motifs of modern natural science (which is above all, of course, theory of motion) that we otherwise know about as first coming from Galileo. The new concept of motion grew out of the religious soil of the late Middle Ages, not out of esthetic feeling about the world during the Renaissance, as people commonly describe it. It was back then that people first began to question the basic principles of Aristotle's physics and theory of motion. The dynamic concept of motion asserted itself against the theological one; motion through impetus that was active in the moved object itself and that of itself would never lead to rest asserted itself against striving toward ''substantial forms.'' (On the basis of this idea Leibniz later on arrived at his fundamental dynamic principle of ''*living* force''!) The complete transformation of the concept of motion that people later formulated as the law of inertia was already accomplished here. This law said that motion no more ceased of itself and crossed over into another ''state'' than rest did (whereas Aristotle said an object in motion came to rest immediately and entirely of itself when it had arrived at its ''natural place,'' the goal toward which its striving impelled it). Of itself the impetus at work in a moving body would continue to work forever; it would never weaken and would never allow the moving body to come to rest, were it not for external opposition and counterforces. Accordingly, motion contains just as much ''being'' as rest does! Hence in this period also, as we have mentioned, the concept of the mechanics of the heavens took this form: There is no need to explain cosmic movements, with their eternal uniformity and order, through motive intelligences or higher unmoved forms (as with Aristotle, the Arabs, Thomas, and even beyond to Dietrich von Freiberg and to Kepler!), but instead, when the world was created, not only matter but also motion came into being at the same time; impetus imparted to the stars remained active, and there, where there was no resistance from the air and (as people thought) from ''gravity,'' it never weakened, hence motion never slowed down. Movements of stars occur uniformly forever and except for the universal influence of God's power that ultimately preserves all beings in existence, no special motive action from God or soul-like–formal stages would be necessary. Movement that God has once created has no natural end and no natural desire for annihilation, any more than, say, the existence of objects has. Both tendencies—that of mystical speculation and that of the new foundation for science (both of which sprang up from precisely the same living soil)—came together in the work of Nicholas of Cusa. As his writing *On the Play of the World* [*De ludo globi*] explained, the natural motion of a perfectly round sphere, for example, will never cease of itelf. Without using external forces and without becoming weary, once it is set in motion it will continue to move forever; unless it is hindered or destroyed from the outside, motion is in itself permanent. As long as it is healthy, organic life (because it is natural movement) will likewise never cease. And in general "movement in the rational human soul can never cease, which (movement) it has and exercises even without the body. Hence that spontaneous spiritual movement subsists in itself. Movement that is not self-caused is an accident, whereas self-caused movement is a substance. Being whose essence is movement does not possess movement as an accident, for example the nature of spirit, which cannot be spirit except through spiritual movement that makes it actual. Spiritual movement is therefore substantial . . . hence it never ceases." Naturally, then, although people often designate deity as absolute rest and describe the living motion of all beings toward it and one another externally in completely Aristotelian terms, nevertheless Nicholas characterizes it essentially as eternal and subsistent life. Just as God is absolute magnitude, identity, beauty, goodness, and so on, so is he absolute movement also. The Trinity, for example, is "not a mathematical but a living correlation. . . . Capacity for life must be so all-powerful that it generates its own life from itself, and from the two of them proceeds the spirit of love." Thus all motion in the universe (as "God's creature") proceeds from God, who is spirit. Movement in the universe is "created spirit." It is because everything moves itself that the actual coheres and constitutes one universe. The world's movement is the *explicatio* [unfolding] of God's rest, which is itself, indeed, subsistent life. No finite being moves itself exactly as another does; yet each of them participates in its own way in the movement of every other, just as all limbs participate in movement of the heart; it is thus that the world manifests itself as a living unity.

And on that basis Nicholas then drew the conclusion (onto which people from the circle of the Occamists and, based on their scientific ideas, Nicholas of Oresme had stumbled) that the ancient doctrine to which church and Middle Ages had sworn allegiance on the basis of the given authority of Aristotle (as they had done in so many other matters besides), namely, that the earth did not move while the heavens moved around daily, was false. Because movement of bodies was not something external to them and was not something that clung to them only ephemerally, but was instead something naturally inherent in everything actual and part of one world, then earth simply cannot be unmoved. There is no solid world center, and there is no star that persists without motion. In this manner the path to Copernicus's theory was

171

paved by a purely theoretical shattering of the ancient world system with its fundamental attitude focused on a static middle point and its conviction that all motion (not just in our concept thereof!) related to something at rest. The affirmation here accorded to movement and life finally went so far that even coming to be and passing away—which for the ancient world were precisely the quintessence of the frailty and futility of sensible-concrete being—were subsumed into the idea of divinely created perfection of the world! As explication of the living and acting God, who was after all the identity of opposites, the world must be "uninterrupted generation and destruction"! "Even all generation, destruction, and transformation stems from the fact that God (the absolutely identical one) always produces the same thing (*idem identificat* [the same creates the same]). For inasmuch as the same being manifests itself in the greatest opposition of forces and inasmuch as each produces something like itself and opposed to the other, a struggle between forces ensues and out of that struggle new generation and destruction." What is identical and permanent here is not immobile being but life, movement that takes place in opposites. Heraclitus's theses won new world importance from the idea of the living God, who as spirit is life and process. Later on Hegel consciously united Heraclitus and the stream of ideas that came fully to light with Eckehart and expanded still further from that point on, a stream that drew its certitude from the primoridally religious given of the inward-spiritual-living dimension; on the basis of the fully and thoroughly matured position of the Modern Period, he set out to explain anew every word of the Obscure One from Ephesus.

We are not going to pursue further at this point what role the new attitude then played in the world picture of the age of the Renaissance, especially with Kepler and Bruno (and also in Ficino's theory of the soul in which, as a reversal of Antiquity, matter no longer stood for something that ensnared the soul in movement, but rather as something that dragged it down into dead motionlessness). In our first theme we have already traced how people came to exalt matter more and more as God's work (which it is, just as much as any "form" is) and how matter subsumed ordering-moving forces within itself. And whereas now ancient doctrine about the plurality of emerging and perishing worlds came to life again (against whose cyclical character Albert the Great had also expressly fought from the standpoint of the Christian doctrine of salvation), Giordano Bruno tried to see in all concomitant and successive stages of such world systems and processes "the pulsebeat of one divine universal life," an organic context of life in place of mechanical-meaningless juxtaposition. And just as earlier in the doctrine of Scotus Erigena about the identity of seeing and creating in God as well as in Dietrich von Freiberg's and Eckehart's doctrines regarding creation, so here, too, the

172

IV. Reality and Life

idea of the living God pushed in the direction of eternalizing the world process, toward creation without a beginning. God could never begin a transition
from being an inactive principle into becoming an active one: just as God's
essence is eternal, so is his becoming.

Regardless how much the reversal of interest (which now set in and
often led even to naturalism) away from inner life and toward external nature,
coupled with the splendid success of mathematical science of nature, tem-
porarily drove back the initiative from animate-spiritual life, nevertheless the
new valuation of process was never lost. The new science was itself a theory
of motion. Without referring to modern mechanical principles at all Campanella had earlier defined all knowledge of the world as history, that is,
knowledge of what evolves. From Galileo onward science actually read the
book of nature not as a given system (such as the natural philosophy of
"substantial forms" had done), but as incessantly flowing universal process
that is held together object by object by the consequences of motion. Descartes provided the first overarching principle that shed strong light on the
relationship between the new metaphysical attitude and new scientific methodology. To be sure, it appears that as far as his space-matter was concerned,
movement was fundamentally (in a way not very different than for ancient
Atomists) a "state" or a "mode," that is, of substantial being, which was
also immobile. On the other hand, it was not at all decisive that Descartes
viewed bodily differentiation as arising first of all from movement and that
therefore movement first defined individual bodies, whereas [for the Ato-
mists] formed atoms did not come into being, but subsisted in themselves
quite apart from any movement; mechanical movement was necessary only
to explain the ordered world manifold. But Descartes put entirely new importance on movement inasmuch as he now posited his law of conservation
of the magnitude of movement alongside ancient principles of substance and
preservation of existence as well as conservation of matter. That was something conceived entirely in the spirit of Cusa's subsistence of movement in
a spiritual being, but here now carried over with full clarity to the corporeal.
The fundamental principle for investigating nature was now no longer substantial form but a law of motion. The archetype of the modern concept of
law (prefigured already in the Logos of Heraclitus), which dissolved the static
principles of ancient science (Plato's ideas and Aristotle's forms), was formulated by this new principle of conservation. From now on principles of
nature were "rules governing movement," laws of becoming. But the metaphysical context shone forth clearly from the rationale that Descartes himself
provided: "We also understand that there is perfection in God not only insofar as he is himself unchanging, but also insofar as he operates in the most
constant and unchangeable way." Conservation in the usual, substantial

173

sense relates to the first "perfection," and conservation of never-ending movement relates to the second. That we call God "primary cause of motion" now means something entirely different than it did for Aristotle. Laws of nature are rules of motion, precisely because God the unchanging One always *acts* in the same manner. He created motion (although it is only a mode) at the same time as matter, and what he has once created he preserves in existence. But that motion is in its own way a "being" is also clear from his discussion of inertia. As Descartes says, whereas ancient philosophers always spoke only of the fact that figure or measure or rest did not change unless something encroached on them from without (whereas they always made an exception from this basic principle in the case of motion), now he was interested precisely in motion as the thing he wanted most to understand. And he added that motion, as understood then (i.e., according to Aristotle's definition) was something altogether different than motion as he understood it.

Occasionalism then pulled together the connection that Descartes had thus established between unchanging activity of God and laws of motion to the point of identity between the divine principle of activity (the will of God) and forces of motion in the world. With Geulincx the demand for this became inescapable and Malebranche then decisively acceded to it. Although the world manifests many imperfections, in one respect it cannot be more perfect than it is: the lawfulness of its motions and events is absolute. God's unchanging, universal perfection, the permanence of his power and of his will, expresses itself directly in it, that is, in laws of nature and unchanging rules of motion! (Berkeley's spiritualism also saw in uniform lawfulness of sequence of movements, that is movements of ideas, the immediate effect of the unchanging and living will of God and of his constantly uniform behavior.) And this is not an expression that ascribes proper independence to worldly and finite existence; on the contrary, what functions in all finite motion is simply nothing other than the power of God. God creates a moving body or posits it anew, so to speak, at every point of its path in time and space; continuity of motion means nothing other than unceasing creative activity of God. Thus God who is present to all objects in their inner being moves them without ceasing. Consequently all becoming is fundamentally not only the expression or effect of divine activity: it is divine activity itself. On that basis pantheism was unavoidable. Ancient hostility to motion still seemed to play a role as well. Malebranche could conceive objects themselves—which are inactive and immobile—as something relatively independent with respect to God, but not motion! For him motion still did not really belong to the essence of matter (just as for Descartes it had been only an added modality). Motion was originally and essentially proper only to the

174

living God! Only something spiritual, something that knows and wills, can be a motive power or principle of motion.

In this connection it was Leibniz who produced the broadest and most profoundly fundamental formulation of the new valuation of living-active being. Just as in the case of Cusa, Descartes, and Malebranche—indeed more comprehensively than in all of them—tendencies of the new science of motion combined in Leibniz with basic orientation toward living-spiritual being, toward God and the soul. At the same time the theory of monads opposed the pantheistic tendency that in the hands of the Occasionalists had denied all proper motion to objects, indeed ultimately even to souls, and had restricted all activity to God's action alone. Leibniz was part of the tradition of vitalism in German natural philosophy, a tradition that from Paracelsus on to the elder van Helmont looked for its own proper inner principle of life and movement in every creature and in every single object. We have a counterpart to the dynamism of these heirs of the mysticism of Eckehart and Suso—a dynamism whose feeling about the world was oriented toward the living soul—in a very kindred English movement, the philosophy of nature of Glisson. His philosophy of nature (like Leibniz's later) sought to conceive of substance itself in an entirely universal sense as life, as activity, and as motion—not regarding motion merely as an external-modal accretion to life. *Natura substantiae in genere est viva* [the nature of substance in general is living], said Glisson. Movement is immanent in matter itself (not just in organic being); it is an intrinsically inherent principle of matter. The title of his work illustrates the direction clearly enough: *Tractatus de natura substantiae energetica seu de vita naturae* [*Treatise on the Energetic Nature of Substance or on the Life of Nature*]. But none of these philosophers was linked to the new science. There was still too much of the fantastic and the arbitrary in their reflection on nature to permit the new valuation of motion in this form to determine the metaphysical systems of the century of Galileo and Descartes. Leibniz was the first to provide fusion at this point.

Whereas Descartes considered bodily motion merely a state and modality, not an essential activity, and whereas his concept of matter as *res extensa* [extended thing] seemed to exclude any element of force and genuine effective capacity, he defined thinking substance altogether essentially by its activity of "thinking" or conscious life. The *res cogitans* [thinking thing] always "thinks"; it can never set aside this activity, for spontaneous movement and inner life are its very existence. That (along with other elements) was a questionable duality in the concept of substance: spiritual substances (including God) were essentially living, corporeal ones dead or only externally moved. The external world has no similarity with what is the most important thing in existence. But the monadology now used the self-given ego as its

175

point of departure to seek the key to the essence of all objects and thereby to attain a homogeneous conception of the world. Leibniz taught that substance is something we know immediately from our "reflection." A glance at the soul, however, showed him that we cannot (as Descartes thought) define the essence of the substantial as independence of being, for as something created by God the soul does not possess "aseity" at all. On the contrary, what makes it substance and gives it "independent status," even with respect to the creator and preserver of the universe (contrary to pantheistic doctrines), is free will, moral independence, capacity to bring itself into relationship with God in knowing, loving, or willing—not merely to be brought into relationship! Soul's substantiality is shown by and consists in its spontaneous activity. Independence means standing on one's own and doing on one's own; it means acting from one's own capacity, one's own impulses, one's own self-unfolding. Every soul is power, an efficacy different from the power of God. All rest, and therefore also all mere receptivity or allowing-something-to-be-impressed on the soul is only apparent; everything in the soul is movement, inner change, its own proper activity. Desiring and striving do not allow the soul a single moment to rigidify in a merely permanent "condition" of having a single idea; its life is constant transition, making new, self-development of inner powers. The essence and happiness of soul do not consist in "rest" but in life; every apparent perception of rest in the soul is merely failure to recognize the "tiny" ideas and impulses that in reality always keep us "in suspense"! "Even in joy there is unrest, for it makes a person aroused, active, full of hope, always ready to go still farther." "Indeed, unrest itself is essential for happiness of creatures, for happiness does not consist in full possession—which would only make it without feeling and dull—but in continual and uninterrupted progress toward ever greater goods, progress that is inconceivable without desire or constant unrest." Even in our "apparently quietest states, we are inwardly moved; for we are never without some kind of movement." "It is for that very reason also, that we never find ourselves in a state of indifference." Even the "peace" of eternity, which must not be indifference after all, would for that reason (according to Leibniz's concept of eternal life) be "unrest" in precisely this sense. Soul is, in fact, in time and eternity; it is act, not object; it is action, not inert substance. Its independent status itself is active independence [*Ihr Selb-Stand selber ist aktives Selbst-Stehen*].

Accordingly Leibniz then defined substance in general by activity! What Nicholas [of Cusa] had begun with his formulation that movement of spiritual beings itself "subsists" was now completed by identifying substance and action. He always expressly repudiated the idea that substance is just "being," to which movement merely clings and from which—as something

176

IV. Reality and Life

itself unmoved and merely capable of action—activity would flow only on account of external stimulus. On the contrary, all substances and all monads are *"principes de vie"* ["principles of life"], living and self-prompted movements, spontaneous and ever present actions. Their "being" is itself a "state of changes." Transition into action or act—together with possibility, capacity, and tendency to act—also lies in the monad itself; it is nothing other than this living tension and this constant execution. With the monad, Aristotle's concepts of entelechy and substantial forms acquired entirely new meaning: rigidity of form-substance disappeared and in its place came the "law of the constant succession of its operations"! Process of actualization is itself substantial being here. Hence one thought of it as something never finished; the meaning and, as shown earlier, all happiness of existence consists in movement. Therefore bodily substance must also be essentially action; here, too, all rest and all mere stability is only apparent, only unobserved change. Descartes's inherently static extended substance cannot be reality; it lacks living force, the principle of activity. The law of conservation of magnitude of movement itself forces us to cross over to the concept of force. But because we cannot find force in the spatial-material sphere as such, we must think of essential principles even of external being as nonmaterial. Activity of monads lurks behind mechanical events too; here too all substance is ultimately action. The spatial-static first "results" from the living-dynamic, from monadic unleashing of power. This expresses itself also in the world as we experience it through the senses, in spatial and corporeal phenomena. Everywhere there is life and movement; in the smallest apparently immobile bit of matter right on into the infinite there is living process. The world system (which presents itself to the metaphysical eye as universally comprehensive harmony of inner activities of the monads) shows itself to sense and natural-scientific experience as a system of relationships of activity in all directions, in which no event can occur in any one part of the universe without having its modifying effect on all other parts, no matter how far away they may be. Thus everything is constantly in motion and nothing is at rest anywhere in reality. Every body is always in motion, even in the "state of rest," which in fact simply does not exist in an absolute sense. Thus movement wins out over rest. And whereas the ancients tried on the basis of the concept of being to conceive of movement as an aggregate of states of rest (see Zeno's arrow argument)— a concept still operative even in Malebranche's explanation of movement through successive acts of creation at individual points along the path of movement—now Leibniz, reversing matters, defined rest as unobserved movement or more rigorously as infinitely tiny movement; inertia as infinitely minute activity; "dead" force as the start of or an "element" of living force. The law of rest was now just a special instance of the law of movement.

As early as Leibniz the central role of movement and living activity was directly connected with the principle of development. One should now no longer understand this in an Aristotelian sense as movement toward, and mere transition to, a given fixed form, but as inner ascent and growth into the infinite, which in principle is never supposed to come to rest but is the natural effect of primordial forces. But the theory of monads applied this principle to individual being for the most part, although on the basis of it and especially in connection with the "kingdom of grace" it is reminiscent of the idea of world evolution. For the external world, on the other hand, Descartes tried to provide a genetic history that is based on purely mechanical processes of motion; but for him (as well as in ancient cosmogonies) that was expressly only a means of explaining the world as it now stands in finished form. It was not until the young Kant that interest in becoming, based on the new God-and-world-centered feeling of universal life, crossed over to the question of development of the world and of cosmic world-"history" itself ["*Geschichte*": from *geschehen*, to take place, to happen (translator's note)]. Like Descartes and Leibniz he too saw the "character of permanence, which is the mark of the freedom [*Wahl*] of God" not so much in preservation of matter as in unswervingly continuous action of world-formative forces actually realized through the act of creation. Fundamental matter out of which everything cosmic comes into being for eternity is itself dynamic in nature; forces of attraction and repulsion that represent "original sources of movement" are its essential features. Everything actual is acting [*Alles Wirkliche ist Wirken*]; rest is only "lack" or "deprivation" of movement, indeed we must ultimately define it (as Leibniz had already done) as infinitely minute movement. Movement of matter requires no foreign cause nor any ordering principle; those original forces themselves lead in easy succession, independently and spontaneously, toward the erection of world systems. But this erection is not merely transition to a finished world. Rather, the life of the creator manifests itself precisely in the fact that creation is never finished! Augustine regarded all the world's perfections and the total beauty of the universe as fully existing from the very beginning, from the instant that creation occurred once and for all; nothing can be added to them in the course of the ages. Kant, on the other hand, now saw the true effect of the power of highest being precisely in endless development in time and in the ever new appearance of perpetually new orders. Although Kant speaks "of creation in its infinity," he does not merely mean infinite extension in endless space (as "infinite extent of divine presence") but also and above all never-ending process of becoming in time as the scope of the living God's activity. The ordering and furnishing of the world edifice from the storehouse of created stuff of nature takes place little by little in the course of time; creation

178

is "rather cultivation of nature." "Creation is not the work of a moment. Once it had begun by bringing forth an infinity of substances and matter . . . it continues actively for the rest of eternity." "Creation is never finished. It did indeed begin at a certain point but it will never cease. It is always busy bringing forth more natural phenomena, new objects and new worlds." The field of revelation of divine properties is just as infinite as the properties themselves are: this holds true not only for existence in space but above all for process in time. And now Nicholas of Cusa's idea also asserted itself with tremendous power: We must include transitoriness (against which the ancients fought so hard and which horrified them about the principle of becoming) as well as even decay and death in our affirmation of life. Negative element of decay and dependency of what has merely evolved were no longer the most prominent feature of existence of the world and earthly events, as they always had been in Antiquity; on the contrary, the positive-happy element of becoming, as incessantly creative activity that brings ever new being into existence, now became most prominent! "We can count the inescapable propensity that every fully matured world structure has to dissolve gradually among reasons that could support the view that the universe will, on the other hand, be fruitful in worlds in other regions to make up for the loss that it has suffered in one place. The entire segment of nature that we know . . . corroborates this fruitfulness of nature that is without boundaries because it is nothing other than the exercise of divine omnipotence itself. Innumerable animals and plants are destroyed daily and become victims of perishability; but through its inexhaustible capacity for generation nature nonetheless keeps on being productive in other places and fills the vacuum." "We should not be too shocked to admit perishability even on the large scale [in dem Großen] of God's works. Everything finite . . . must perish and have an end. . . . But we may not mourn the demise of a world structure as genuine loss for nature. Nature demonstrates its abundance in a kind of prodigality which, even as some of its parts are paying their tribute to perishability, maintains itself unharmed through countless new generations in the overall expanse of its perfection." And according to Kant not only this living conservation but also "continuous progress" belongs to the essence of cosmic process. "Regardless of all the devastations that transitoriness incessantly produces, the magnitude of the universe," that is, of ordered cosmos, grows constantly on the whole! "Creation is at work through all ages with ever-increasing degrees of fecundity." In all "future succession of eternity" the system of the world will gradually expand in the infinity of space into the infinite. If with respect to matter the created world has existed infinitely from the beginning in space, then it is also ready to become so "with respect to form or development": "thus cosmic space will be animated with worlds without number and without end.'' ''And while nature embellishes eternity with changing appearances, God remains busy in incessant creativity, building up the impetus that leads to formation of still greater worlds.'' ''I find nothing that can raise the spirit of man to nobler awe, inasmuch as it opens up his vision to the infinite range of almighty power, than this part of the theory that deals with successive completion of creation.''

From this point Kant later discovered the transition to the other kind of becoming and progress that first became a central focus in Christianity: that of the history of the human race. In the same period Lessing and Herder helped that ancient idea (which Lessing first rediscovered through study of the Fathers of the Church) to renewed life. Both of them appealed constantly to the Christian principle of the living God for their evolutionary doctrines. Lessing wanted to show that the ground for change and for contingency in worldly objects is inherent in that very principle! He was interested in God's governance in history, in gradually evolving revelation that grows into the future as the ''education of the human race.'' The old analogy with the course of an individual's development cropped up again. And just as was the case with Joachim of Flora, he sought for the new ''eternal gospel'' over and above the completed givenness of revelation in Christ. God does not provide truth all at once but in stages that are commensurate with the phases of development of men and nations and with their maturity of understanding at a given point. What he does provide, however, is always already inherent in man's innate spontaneity; people are not dead mirrors and wax tablets on which God's stylus writes, but rather their existence is activity, inner development and striving. Everyone knows Lessing's dictum that expressed the new pathos of development with particular beauty—the one that says that if God presented him with a choice in the matter he would prefer perpetually active striving for the truth, with all its danger of error and failure, to secure possession of truth. Pathos of endless striving, with which Leibniz had begun and which then played so central a role in the systems of Kant and Fichte, set itself in opposition to desire for fulfilled rest. This question, too, emerged early from the Christian era's new feeling for life. Augustine discussed it, but he still decided in favor of tranquil possession, faithful to Aristotle's dictum that knowing was more blessed than seeking.

Herder's philosophy of nature also (following in Leibniz's train) regarded all objects as independent, spontaneous forces and all existence as process and free movement. The power of God can reveal itself only in active forces. Everything static and fixed is actually only a product of generative, dynamic-organic principles. Everywhere we are surrounded by the daily ''wonder of becoming'' (here, too, not affliction of decay but blessedness of new becoming occupies the foreground). And so nature as a whole is also

180

living development, constant progress toward higher forms. Herder was the first to conceive the idea of development and progress as a single principle for both nature and man and to combine the processes of nature and history into a single universal process. Its meaning was the ancient moral-religious one: approximation of creatures to divine perfection, something that man attains most clearly in the living development of history. Man's existence is Becoming; he is never complete, for beyond events of this world the unfolding of a higher history continues to take place.

But it was the philosophy of German Idealism that produced the ultimate triumph of living process over static being as well as complete fusion of all the motifs we have seen evolving historically into one great metaphysics of becoming. Fichte laid down the decisive foundation. In his case we witness once again with especially dramatic emphasis the link with basic religious motives that we have been tracking right along.

According to Fichte's fundamental conviction, the essence of all "dogmatism," by putting its faith in the primordial character and primacy of the objective, simultaneously betrays freedom to static-necessary being and life to dead being. Hence Fichte felt that in this matter as well his own opposite pole was the system of Spinoza, who indeed—uniquely in the Modern Period—had shut himself off from the weight of the motif of life and had renewed the rigidity of Parmenidean being in his own way! Anyone who thus conceives of the absolute and everything truly existing as something stationary, stiff, and dead—said Fichte—fundamentally does not understand himself and ultimately cannot be truly convinced about the totality of his system. Quite apart from the ancients—for whether they consciously raised the appropriate philosophical question is very doubtful—almost all thinkers of the Modern Period had contradicted their life through their speculation. Leibniz alone was perhaps the sole man of conviction [*der einzige überzeugte*] in the history of philosophy. Idealism, which founds its concept of being on the active subject, is the only philosophy that fully and consistently adopts the sense of life that every morally acting person knows and lives by. Hence the idealist has nothing to do with the rigid being of dogmatism that is given once and for all or with an in-itself that would be objective-dead; on the contrary, he sees freedom and spontaneous activity as the only positive

181

thing. He regards "being" as mere negation of freedom, a concept that is not basic and original but merely derived, imagined as in contrast with activity. The idealist's entire philosophy is essentially a single great development of the idea of freedom. Now, for Fichte this fundamental orientation toward the spiritual-active was not merely given, say, by the fact that (as Leibniz thought) I attain metaphysical contact only immediately in myself. Freedom is not only the inner experience of everyone but also the absolute faith of moral man and his challenge. To be sure, every man inwardly knows of himself only on the basis of his behavior and events; the immediate element in activity is my feeling, desiring, thinking, willing—nothing but acts and the actlike; in this inner consciousness of self I am entirely "life and action," "not being, but only pure activity." But that we thereby confront simply absolute being, that we may find no limit in absolutely objective being and given necessity and rigidity that always accompanies such being, is something no inner perception and no analogical argument tell us but only the moral consciousness of our living, active person. Hence the decision in favor of true philosophy is not a question of contemplative or as it were quiescent knowledge of given world structure (even of an inner spiritual sort) but is itself a deed, an act of freedom.

The absolute in us is therefore not "being," not "something permanent," "something perduring," which one could then grasp as such in a fixed concept, but rather essentially living "action" that I behold only in helping to carry it through, as something that is itself actively in flux. "Anything stationary, quiescent and dead simply cannot enter at all into the sphere of what I call philosophy. In philosophy everything is action, movement, and life; it does not discover anything but merely allows everything to come into being under its tutelage, and this applies even to the extent that I absolutely deny the name of philosophizing to trafficking in dead concepts." One may not even call the original principle, the ego, "active being," "for this expression refers to a permanent something in which activity is inherent."

Above all, Fichte (exactly like Leibniz) also excludes every concept of active being as something that is itself a fixed essence that merely has capacity to act, whereby real action would first result from stimulus provided from elsewhere. On the contrary, selfhood is absolutely active in itself; it is pure action without any underlying substratum; its knowledge and its active being is itself "substant" ["*substant*"]! It is what it does, and without acting it is nothing. Whereas Spinoza defined God as *causa sui* [cause of himself] (something that is from our retrospective point of view at any rate a change with respect to Aristotle's teleological concept of God, a transformation toward the causal-dynamic, toward *natura naturans* [creative nature]), with respect to this issue Fichte lamented the absence of insight into the character

182

IV. Reality and Life

of activity that such self-positing must after all possess. It is not first of all static "substance" but rather selfhood that is self-positing, performing an act; existing being is always only just a "deed," product of an action, but at root is really the action itself. Selfhood exists only because it posits itself. Its "being" is inner movement, pure "agility" ["*Agilität*"], flux without "rest" and permanence. Everything that is (apparently) at rest and exists objectively is always only the outcome of an interchange within this original living being.

Method in philosophy corresponds to this concept of first principle. "All philosophical knowledge is by its nature not factual but genetic, not grasping some sort of existing being but inwardly generating and constituting this being out of the source of its life." The principle of becoming encroaches here with most extreme decisiveness on the timeless world of concepts. Using the methods of static logic we cannot establish a metaphysics whose task is to describe the "life of spirit" or to grasp "history of consciousness" in an ordered system of intelligence that generates everything actual. Hence one now abandoned syllogistic method that was still completely dominant throughout the Middle Ages—with its subordinating under fixed principles (corresponding to the concept of being of "substantial form") and its rigid pyramid of concepts—just as one also abandoned Descartes's logic and that of the centuries following him, with its double path of analysis and synthesis. For in this latter method, too, which still depended all too much on the model of Euclid with its geometrically static contents, one fundamentally presupposes that the object is a finished complex composed of simple elements that conceptual labor has to analyze into its fixed parts and then to use as building blocks. This is especially clear in Spinoza's system of immobile substantial being that is constructed "in geometrical fashion." Leibniz's new substance-principle, however, already found itself in peculiar contrast with methodology that he adopted and developed; and it is only because there were still enough static moments left over in it that the conflict did not become obvious. But for Fichte there is absolutely nothing left that is static; there is no universal or particular, no complex or simple "being" any more, but only activity and life. Thus he demands a new philosophical method: dialectical method. Plato's start in the direction of movement in concepts (which Neo-platonists carried further) and Heraclitus's logic of becoming with its doctrine of the war of opposites found their first full development here and stepped masterfully onto center stage. Self's activity unfolds before its very eyes as an endless series of tasks proliferating in all directions, with constantly emerging opposite tensions between thesis and antithesis and their synthetic resolutions that are in turn always merely relative and therefore themselves driving forward. Speculative knowledge does not have to discover, say, a

183

static substance underlying stimuli or an eternally abiding goal of process; on the contrary it is itself supposed to go through phases of development, and beyond everything that is apparently static, to detect dialectical tension and transition to new activities. Hence its concepts must no longer be "dead"; they must themselves become "living concepts" that strive to transcend themselves and constantly show that they are in transition. The tension of contradiction lives in every genuine philosophical concept and never permits that concept to become static or fossilized in itself.

In the period of the Atheism Controversy the connection between this philosophy of freedom/activity and experience of the living God first came fully to light. At the very center of this conflict was Fichte's battle against God-substance. We may not think of God as abiding, permanent, lasting being or as "substratum"; "one cannot say of him: he is substance." The ancient category of substance, derived from external experience of objective being, completely fails here. The true God is an "order of events"; "not being, but pure activity (life and principle of a supersensible world order), just as I, finite intelligence, am not being but pure activity . . . as a member of that world order." We must understand "order" itself actively, as "active ordering (*ordo ordinans*)," as "act"; thus Fichte uses all words that have the ending "*-ung*" in the sense of action [*Tathandlung*]). "One sees that here we are thinking only of acts, only of events, something moving forward, not of being and immobile permanence: creating, preserving, governing, not at all creator, preserver, governor." "Your soul is nothing but thinking, desiring, feeling itself. God is nothing but the very creating, preserving, and governing that we have to assume."

Hence the concept of "life" became the focal point of Fichte's later philosophy. Just as Eckehart had said that the question Why no longer had any validity for life and every answer to the question could only say: I am glad to be alive; so now according to Fichte "life is necessarily blessed, for it is blessedness." Again, following the ancient doctrine of Joannine Christianity, he identified love and life; self-unfolding and inner dialectic of self, its "unity in duality that is not thereby sublated but abides forever," presents itself as eternal tension and process of love. All happiness of genuine life is grounded on love, striving, impulse. But true being can in fact be nothing other than such life. "Only life can exist independently from itself and through itself; and again life, just as surely as it is simply life, carries existence along with it. People commonly think of existence as a permanent, immobile, and dead thing; philosophers themselves have thought of it in such fashion as even to express it as the absolute" (*causa sui!*) [cause of itself!]. We must understand the words being and existence themselves as verbs, actively. "Being, entirely and simply as being, is living and spontaneous,

IV. Reality and Life

and there is no other being than life; in no way, however, is it dead, immobile, and intrinsically inert. . . . The only life that is utterly of itself, from itself, and through itself, is the life of God or *the* absolute; and if we say "the life of the absolute, this is merely a manner of expression; in fact the truth is that the absolute is life and life is the absolute." "Every being sustains and carries itself; in living existence this self-preservation and consciousness of it is love of itself." Even all permanence is therefore essentially act, living activity of self-preservation.

Thus the life of history can now achieve significance as never before in any metaphysical system! Eckehart's notion of God evolving and coming to self-knowledge in forming the world—a notion that mystics and philosophers of nature after him, especially Jacob Böhme and the younger Helmont, wished to expand further in the direction of philosophy of history in the grand style—now became totally permeated with the recently surfaced (since Lessing, Kant, and Herder) idea of the process of development of mankind and of all spiritual life. Kant's claim (first raised in connection with the problem of the external world) that we must never think of creation as completed, but only as incessantly ascending development, achieved ultimate fulfillment in Fichte's metaphysics of living spirit and of freedom. "Creation of the world from God is thus not at all complete (as people commonly think) nor has God come to a state of rest; on the contrary, creation goes forward forever, and God remains the creative one, because in fact the immediate object of his creation is not inert and immobile corporeal world but free, eternally and spontaneously generating life. The genuinely true world, for which alone corporeal world exists, is the spiritual world, man's life and thought, precisely as a world, that is, as totality and community. . . . This is the world that God immediately and constantly creates in his image inasmuch as he always continues to develop his image in it with new clarity." For this and this alone is the purpose of all existence, that God should be glorified, that his image should emerge continuously and with ever new clarity from his eternal invisibility into the visible world. The world moves forward only in this glorification of God and everything really new that can appear in it is the appearance of divine being with fresh lucidity; without that appearance the world is static and nothing new happens under the sun." Accordingly, man in history, precisely insofar as he knows and creates something new, "by activating his knowledge becomes a veritable living force in the world and a motive force behind the continuation of creation." Fichte held that all value of existence rests on the fact that "new and fresh life" constantly emerges. Compared with happiness of life—insofar as it is indeed creative act, formation of ever new visages, glorification of incessantly new aspects of divine life, and ascent to ever higher purity—sadness of decay and of ephemeral being and perishability that dominated the attitude of ancient thinkers with respect to becoming now no longer played a role! Life in time, in the "fleeting" here and now, is imperishable life insofar as it passes through this process of becoming. The only thing that is absolutely consigned to decay and to non-being is dead being, mere "being" in the ancient sense—static being and inert being that clings to it! "The impulse of purely natural existence is to hold on to the past . . . , but where the divine idea . . . takes over a life, it builds new worlds in it on top of the ruins of older ones." There is *one* freedom that works in all striving persons; history of mankind, of spiritual community, is *one* life. "The entire world of spirits, understood as a single reality, is free, and therein consists its proper life that is distinct from the life of God." "There is a single universal freedom of the totality, and freedom of the individual is not set apart and restricted to itself; instead, every freedom encroaches on and affects the freedom of others, and there is a common bond between the freedom of all." "I know of no nobler ideas than the idea of this universal influence of the entire human race on itself, of this incessant life and striving."

At this point [Fichte] has also abandoned the static moment of Leibniz's system that said the system of the universe was grounded in harmony that predetermined all questions of evolution! That system held that the world was in fact already complete in advance in the mind of the creator, and evolution had merely to fulfill what had already been given and determined. Hence Leibniz also really failed not only to attain to living freedom and living activity that truly creates something new but also to the complete triumph of process and activity. Fichte was the first to conceive of the divine world order itself as activity, as life, as unlimited creative act, and not merely as preservation and governance of something already created once and for all! In the spiritual struggle and progress of human generations "the deity continuously develops toward new and fresh life." Individuals too have not been (as Leibniz maintained) created once and for all, but rather there are constantly new ones coming into being to fulfill new tasks of evolution and to take over anew the tasks of those individuals who pass on without having matured ethically. Even the world of "objects," nature, which we are supposed to influence, is not fixed and always uniform cosmic reality, but rather expression of spiritual life and of obstacles arising in it, which, as such, we are also always supposed to overcome and transform!

All true being is life, and all life is essentially free from death, immortal; hence temporal life has no end. Nor is our earthly existence followed by a world beyond, in which nothing more would occur but instead everything would merely exist and enjoy its "being." There is no future world, but rather an endless series of future worlds upon worlds that as a whole differ from the present world not in kind but only in order of succession. Eternity does not first begin in the future; it has already begun, and we are in the midst of it precisely insofar as we ''live'' spiritually, love and do what transcends the senses. Eternity and happiness exist in true life itself; they are not a fixed state but flux, not possession but striving, not immobility but action. And this succession of worlds is now no longer a succession of cycles that turn back on themselves and, as far as they can, by repeating themselves in totally identical fashion, make becoming itself something staticlike; on the contrary, what is accomplished in the entire unending series of worlds that succeed one another is a *single* process that debouches into the infinite. The individual unit, the single person, passes through the unending series of all worlds, and this is no longer conceived (as it was in ancient doctrines of transmigration of souls) as punishment for transgressions committed that had to be expiated before the soul could arrive at the rest for which it yearns. In fact the reverse is true: individuals who have not produced a moral will within themselves also do not survive into the future succession of worlds; only those who truly strive morally will grow into ever new tasks and life. Hence [Fichte] affirms life and never-ending activity and striving for their own sakes here in a more profound and radical way than ever before! ''In future worlds there will forever be tasks and labors to perform, just as here; there will be absolutely no sensate meaning in them, however, but only a good and holy will.'' To be sure, Fichte still talks about the ''final goal'' when he wants to designate the direction and content of development; but in essence we will never attain the final goal. It is in fact not the meaning of life and of striving to fulfill oneself in it, to terminate therefore and come to rest in it, to die, to fossilize. There is no final world; succession of development and ascent has no end; the absolute final goal itself will never be visible. For Fichte this conviction entails no unsatisfied, passive resignation but highest happiness of life itself.

Correspondingly, the moral imperative is no longer directed toward a being, a goal (''highest good'' as object), but rather to life and action! ''Action, action is what we are here for.'' The source of all vice is indolence, will to perseverance as inclination toward inert being and finding repose in oneself! Quiet contemplation of immobile-eternal being, which once stood for the very highest thing that the spirit of man could attain, retreats here entirely. Activity in the world, value-filled activity, is our ''vocation,'' to infuse the divine-eternal idea into everyday work on earth. Only that person can see God who lives God [*der ihn lebt*] and acts in his life. A firmly established goal of the will is not the ultimate goal of willing, but will itself is: ''It should exist in a certain condition simply in order to exist in it.'' ''The act of creation of an eternal and holy will in itself is the act of an individual's self-creation towards immediate visibility of the final goal, hence the act that thoroughly determines his own proper inner life. From then on it does not itself live any longer, but the final goal . . . lives in it.'' The creative act of moral will—which is not determined by any previously given being (say, one's own firmly implanted ''character'' as substance that merely expresses itself externally when it is active)—elevates itself into eternal life of love. This is not love like the eros of Antiquity, which longed for peaceful possession and quiet contemplation, but rather, as life itself is happiness and never wants to end.

We cannot consider further at this point how this was then later further developed or transformed, first by Schelling and Hegel and simultaneously in Schopenhauer's world of will, then by Eduard von Hartmann and by many nineteenth-century metaphysicians up to Bergson's *Evolution créatrice* (Creative Evolution] and Nietzsche's metaphysics of will to power, of Dionysian life. With Schelling and Hegel connection with the living God and primacy of the active-spiritual is still quite clear. Schelling took as his point of departure Fichte's ego as that ''which gives existence to all objects, which therefore itself needs no other being but rather, carrying and supporting itself, appears objective as eternal becoming and subjective as infinite producing,'' and he then also drew external nature (which Fichte wished to let stand merely as represented object and resistance to activity of spiritual beings, that is, as something permanently immobile and without any life of its own) into reflection about becoming and development. ''History of consciousness'' acquires its prehistory in natural philosophy. Nature is unconscious becoming, activity of unconscious intelligence, which leads to emergence of consciousness and development of history and continues forward as conscious life in mankind. Dead substances of the past then must vanish entirely with respect to one's view of nature also: nature is living and dynamic in every respect. Products of nature that appear to be firmly given are always merely stages of unresting, endless activity. The strife of opposites, real dialectic, is already dominant here in advance of any real life of the spirit. In its essence nature is *natura naturans* [active nature], now in the full sense of infinitely active! With the problem of the absolute then, from which both nature and spirit derive their life, the claim of the living God and the concept of creative life became focal points once again. Spinoza's philosophy of identity had to be transformed in this sense. Ancient speculations of the patristic period and of the German mystics, especially Jacob Böhme, attained new life in Schellings's question about the ground of all beings. Change and process in objects is a revelatory process that derives from creative love freely springing up from the divine ground. Tension and opposition between good and evil in the world are the condition of all life and all progressive devel-

IV. Reality and Life

opment; they are conditions of God's revelation because God himself is life. Contrary to what Spinoza believed, realities are not a mere "consequence" of the absolute in a rigidly mechanical sense that denies all freedom and living spontaneity even to man; rather, the living being dependent on God and "in" him is nonetheless at the same time independent being! According to Schelling's concept, pantheistic identity is "immediately creative," not mere coincidence and immobile oneness, but rather "generation." "Reflection on divine essence itself attains a much higher standpoint, for the idea of that essence would completely contradict a result that is not generation, that is, positing of independent being. God is not a God of the dead but of the living." "God can reveal himself only in something that is like him, in free and independently acting beings. . . . Even if all beings in the world were merely thoughts in the divine mind, then on that very account they would have to be living." Being that is generated by, and depends on, creative power of the living God (who is himself in his innermost being a "living ground" and, moved by a murky yearning to generate himself, passes over into the activity of eternal will) is itself in its turn, as "derived absoluteness," necessarily life and creative freedom! This gives rise to dynamism in nature (in contrast with the "lifelessness" of Spinoza's system) for lower levels of the world: everything real—therefore nature too, the world of "objects"—has "activity, life, and freedom as its ground"; and for the world of spirit there is in addition the towering reality of freedom, of independent acting. The theory of potency also underscores once again the principle of life. Platonic Ideas, with which Schelling expressly identified his potencies, are transformed here into something dynamic. The types and stages are not fast and firm, but (corresponding to the character of potency inherent in the word) strive to transcend themselves. Yet this impulse is not, as with Aristotle, transition from the merely possible, from mere matter, to actuality; on the contrary, here these potencies are precisely forms and they derive instead from the absolute! The primordial character of life, which is a property of the absolute, propagates itself further into its modes of revelation.

Thus Hegel sees the entire world process as self-development of idea. Logic of becoming and metaphysics of becoming of the fully matured system grew slowly out of the philosophy of the young Hegel whose fundamental concepts were: life and love. He, too, saw the static unity of Parmenides or Spinoza as empty, abstract unity. If it is going to preserve fullness of beings and worlds within itself and allow them to issue forth, then this unity must be life. In the religious sphere the fragmented dividedness of multiple individuals proves to be essentially unity, for "life does not differ from life, because life exists in one Godhead." "In love life discovers itself . . . in love the separated element still exists, but no longer as separated—rather as one;

189

living being feels living being." In living being, besides unity there is always at the same time tension of opposites, which pushes beyond all singularity or particular stage. "Here unity and separation are one, a living entity set in opposition to itself, but without making these oppositions absolute." In the case of dead, static being, of course we have not only empty unity but also absolute oppositions, "fossilized oppositions" ["*festgewordene Gegensätze*"], contradiction! "What is contradiction in the realm of the dead is no longer such in the realm of life." "Necessary division is a fact of life that forever builds itself through opposition: and wholeness together with highest degree of life is possible only through integration of the highest degree of separation." Unity of all "being" can be only life, only becoming and development.

[Hegel's] later system elevated this into the form of logic. Otherwise all concepts had the tendency "to express what becoming is as static being." But now we should be able to succeed in grasping everything that is apparently static as a moment in a dialectical process! Thus infinity and finitude are not opposites or contradictory, but rather "the infinite is the process of becoming finite and conversely the finite is the becoming of the infinite." There is no reason for becoming, nor does it result from any cause but from the concept, the spiritual meaning of things themselves! To grasp a being is to grasp in it the transition to something beyond it, to every other thing. The "malaise" of contradiction lies hidden in all being and is the root of all movement and life. Truth, the idea itself, is life; and "the phenomenon is coming to be and passing away, which does not itself come to be or pass away but exists in itself and constitutes the reality and movement of the life of truth." Just as Spinoza wished to posit geometrical-logical reflection *sub specie aeternitatis* [from the standpoint of eternity] in place of the temporal and causal, here, too, one was supposed to grasp the logical necessities of all being: but not as geometric and static, however; on the contrary, as living-flowing dialectic. In process as dialectical philosophy describes it, nothing is mere preparation for or transition to a solid point one is supposed to attain; rather, the meaning of the goal itself does not fulfill itself except in the overall course of its becoming! The goal is no longer fixed form or static final principle but developmental life itself. [Hegel] was strongly opposed to Fichte's endless process toward an absolute "final goal." No matter how much Fichte (as in the earlier case of Leibniz) through endless postponement shifted the entire center of gravity away from the goal of development into activity or striving itself, Hegel absolutely regarded such a concept of a goal and purpose that always remained (only at the end of the sequence of events) as totally unsatisfactory; for him there was still too much static repose and too little affirmation of event even in such moral perception of teleological process.

IV. Reality and Life

Hegel saw becoming or the life of idea not merely as means to an end nor as mere path to a goal; rather, truth is the totality of all individual stages of development; perfect being, the concrete One, is development itself! Process that endlessly strives toward a mere final goal possesses only "bad" infinity, which in itself is still finite and locked in rigid opposition; the true infinite, as life, is itself both path and goal all in one. And from divine perfection of the whole every particular stage of becoming and every step in the history of mankind—despite all insufficiency, unrest, and turbulence at work in it— receives its ray of importance from the ultimate meaning of life.

In Schopenhauer's sense of life, ancient longing for perfect rest breaks through once again. Like Fichte on this point he conceives of the infinite as eternally active, spontaneously living will; he does not view this tireless will as signifying happiness and free, creative activity, however, but rather the nameless torture of desire that is at once pointless and coercive! Our task is thus to redeem the will from the torture of becoming, to annihilate becoming in the nothingness of absolute death. All events, especially all history, are senseless, unhappy, and reprehensible. Cessation of appetitive movement is the true goal of life that has become aware of its own worthlessness. Esthetic contemplation provides an incipient note of redemption: as peaceful contemplation (understood here statically once again as describing immobile "objectifications" of cosmic will) of Platonic Ideas. Blessedness is not positive happiness of life (as it was for Eckehart, Leibniz, and Fichte), but only this negative point: freedom from pain of movement, which finds no fulfillment in any sort of goal. Thus pathos of life is converted into flight from becoming.

But then a new faith in universal life emancipates us from that once again: Nietzsche's Dionysian affirmation of becoming. Nietzsche viewed Hegel in particular (next to Heraclitus) as the great proclaimer of the blessedness of becoming, of affirmation of decay and annihilation itself, of opposition and war. He thought it was the outstanding merit of the Germans to have taught becoming while "radically rejecting the very concept of 'being'." "Change belongs to the essence of being." In the same way as Fichte, Nietzsche said: there is no "being" behind doing, acting, becoming; "the doer" is simply imagined in doing—doing is all there is!" "The fact of 'spirit' as *one process* proves that the world has no goal and no final condition and is incapable of being." This son of the people that through Eckehart and Leibniz, Fichte and Hegel have done more than all others to help the motif of life to victory felt the tradition himself: "We Germans are Hegelians even if there had never been a Hegel, inasmuch as we . . . instinctively ascribe a profounder meaning and a richer value to *becoming* and to evolving than we do to that which 'is'—we scarcely believe that the concept 'being' is justified." "Evolution is the proper German discovery and direction in the grand

191

realm of philosophical formulas.'' Hence his metaphysical formula of ''will to power'' was no striving toward an attainable-static goal, but rather self-ascent of force, power, active life! And just as for Cusa and the young Kant and then for Hegel, so here too eternal fecundity of ''life'' was the highest principle, which justified and transfigured all transitoriness of becoming and even of all perishing and annihilation. ''Life itself, this eternal fruitfulness and recurrence, conditions pain, destruction, will to annihilation.'' All opposition and struggle exists in becoming; ''Dionysian'' universal life is an ''eternal will to generation, fecundity, recurrence; feeling of oneness in the necessity of creating and annihilating,'' ''driving the entire fullness of life's oppositions within itself and redeeming and justifying it in divine torture.'' Here the idea of eternal recurrence of the same is now not diluting becoming but rather expressing an ultimate Yes to eternal process: a process that unfolds within itself and needs no fixed goal for its meaning. The world is a play of forces, ''of forces and waves of power, a sea of storming and deluging forces within itself, eternally transforming itself and affirming itself . . . as becoming that knows no satiety, no boredom, no fatigue—this is my Dionysian world of eternal self-creation and self-destruction.''

V.
The Individual

Metaphysical superiority of the universal and typical over the particular and individual also constituted an altogether decisive fundamental feature in the world picture of ancient philosophy; this feature was one that was hardly reconcilable with ultimate convictions of the Christian era later on. One can also observe a related issue in the form-ideal of Greek art. Plato's theory of Ideas provided the fundamental principle behind this conception of being. Ideas are *eide* [forms]; linked to actual being they are universal principles such as genera and species. The genuinely substantial real element in existing individual entities in the spatiotemporal world of phenomena was thus always the ideal-universal only, which always constituted unity for the many actually existing individuals. Plato changed Parmenides' unique Being (which annihilated all individual existence) into typical figures and structures that can represent each existing, particular being only in diluted fashion, in a mixture with the non-being of the material. Knowledge always aims at, and seeks to aim only at, the universal, and it is the universal that the concept grasps. Truth and genuine being exist in the universal. At one point however the individual seems to be greater: the soul is immortal insofar as it is individual and living (or so it seems at least). To that extent, therefore, an individual entity exists beyond space and time. But Plato does not put much emphasis on this individuality of the soul, nor can the soul as merely immortal align itself with truly eternal existing ideas, much less surpass them! On this point (just as with the issue of life) Plato's concept of soul was adopted from a special religious tradition into his theory of ideas. It is a foreign element in that theory in a certain sense, an element difficult to accommodate in its systematic framework.

Proofs for immortality likewise do not all apply to individual survival at all. The doctrine of the *Symposium* clearly aims at the generic and superindividual element in man and animals, and reference to a vision of ideas for a soul that is subsequently temporally bound (a reference that is particularly important in the system) does not, as has been often emphasized, prove the survival of the individual.

It is true that Aristotle then set out from the problem and reality of individual object, for which he invented his term *"tode ti"* ["this very thing"] and which he was then the first to designate as being and substance; and his newly directed interest toward sense data and experience related entirely to individual objects, especially living beings in organic nature. His theory of knowledge and of science also put particular emphasis on setting out from what sense experience provides in both areas. But his metaphysical discussion then tells us that the individual object is not an integral ultimate element, is not really substance, but is only a composite of form and matter. Form is the universal element in it, the only element that knowledge always grasps! According to Aristotle, knowledge at every level, including sense perception, is knowledge only of the universal (whereby the "only" is charged to our account, not Aristotle's). What knowledge grasps and seeks to grasp are superindividual quiddities [*Washeiten*] as the essential element in individual being. Form is a type, being is always a universal. This seems entirely clear in plants and animals: here the important thing is obviously not each individual instance but the species, the genus! It remains constant-static in the cycle of birth and death and in the vicissitudes of chance destiny; it is the unitary-formal element in the multiplicity and fragmentation of existing things. What distinguish this horse from that one are only incidental factors that do not affect essence. Universal horseness is the essential being in all horses. Science grasps this essence in the general concept, the concept of the species of horse. It is the same for all objects in reality. But the ground of individual being, about which we must expressly ask (because the essentially primordial is the universal), lies only in matter, the principle of contingency, of the changeable. It is matter that causes deviations from the universal type, eternal falling behind pure form, fragmentation of the One into many. Everything multiple within the same species of being thereby proves its material character. Matter parcels out, as it were, the one universal and essentially necessary element among many individuals with their contingencies—contingencies that really exist, not just for us, say, or owing to our abstract mode of thought! Aristotle sees this as true for every level of the real. To be sure, universal forms interweave with one another and also orient themselves, so to speak, in descent from highest universals through specific differences toward the particular; but this process of narrowing among the forms never

194

V. The Individual

reaches as far as individual self; that can come into question only when matter (with all the aspects of worthlessness connected with it) becomes involved. Hence Aristotle also allowed individual immortality to lapse once again. Form-soul is individualized only through matter and body; fettered to the individual in this way, it is itself individualized. In itself the purely spiritual is a universal! What comprises eternal principles in their universality cannot itself be contingent-limited in nature. The rational moment in the human soul, which enters into its body-bound individual existence "from the outside," crosses over after death into the universal nous, which is exalted above any particularity of actual existence. Spiritual personality in its precious uniqueness is not involved here; indeed Aristotle's psychology is altogether without any personal-inner dimension, holding instead in all matters to the generic-typical dimension of man's life in nature and society. It was not until Hellenistic Antiquity that people first noted individuality in its positive significance. The Stoics in particular recognized the special value inherent in the radical differentiation within the world system (extending even to the individual level) and in the motley multiplicity not only of species but also of individual objects; they also came to appreciate human personality in its individual features and searched for its appropriate concept. But the systematic principles of their metaphysics were still too dominated by the tendencies of ancient generalist valuation in Platonic-Aristotelian universalism to allow real development of the idea of the individual to occur. Then when Plotinus took the step that was so momentous for the theory of ideas—namely, co-ordinating ideas of individual objects also with Plato's universal Ideas, for example, the idea of "Socrates in himself" with the ideas of living being, say, or of man (because the variety in individuals was something beautiful and especially because the human soul was eternal)—nevertheless even here the universal's absolute priority in being remained in place! The individual first issued forth from the universal in a descending series of emanations. Pantheistic attraction toward the All-One combined (as it did in Stoicism) with ancient superiority of the generic-universal; the individual disappeared in the totality because it had no importance when compared with genus. Descending stages of universality are just so many stages of diminishing perfection. In the fading effluence of world principles out of the One and then from the nous, the individual almost disappears as a late, subordinate, isolated phenomenon. Even though the higher element is shimmeringly reflected in it as in a microcosm, the individual nevertheless lacks any significance of its own. Indeed in the mystical life-doctrine of *epistrophe* [turning about; figuratively, conversion] individuality seems equivalent to sin, which has to be extinguished in an ecstatic union with God that melts away individuality. The concept of personal immortality, which was maintained despite

195

that, remained isolated and no less alien in Plotinus's system than it had been once earlier with Plato.

That this axiological priority in the ancients' concept of being ran counter to Christianity's attitude toward life goes without saying. Here person is the essential thing. The spiritual world on which the sensible-temporal is dependent and toward which it is oriented now no longer presented itself as a realm of universal, conceptual entities possessing necessary-typical normative power (in comparison with material contingency) but on the contrary as a plurality of soul-endowed subjective beings who continue to exist as essentially the same individuals in time and in eternity! Here the entire concept of the world flows from the principle of immortal soul (together with that of divine creator). The individual lies at the heart of the system. The world system (to the extent that one can speak of such here, for first of all religious doctrine in principle naturally said nothing thus far about man's environment or about the cosmos apart from soul-endowed, immortal being) is simply pluralistic: "creatures" first constitute the world. But [Christianity] also stressed the uniqueness of the individual, as particularly in the passage about the talent which we are supposed to turn to profit. As a person every one feels himself personally oriented toward the Father; the destiny of each person depends altogether essentially on his free will, on the conduct of his life, on acts of the grace of God (who counts every hair on every head) that relate to him, the individual. The universal is built up only on the basis of the deeds and framework of individuals. The origin of original sin, for example, in which we all share is not a feature of the race, say, but the result of an act of will by the individual Adam; it continues to pass on from individual to individual. The redemptive act of Christ's sacrificial death is also first and foremost a uniquely individual thing and only on that basis does it attain universal significance. The more purely the new world importance of immortal person impressed itself on the idea of being in the later period, the more clearly must the individual also—and not just the human, personal individual but individual being in general—free itself from the subsidiary position that Antiquity still assigned to it. And just as, with the new substantial idea of individual soul and separation of its being from organic body, the old form-motif and its orientation toward the universal had to retreat, so also, on the other hand, the doctrine of the resurrection of the body entailed a disposition to expand the idea of individuality to "contingent"-material being.

In the period of the Church Fathers old and new motifs lay juxtaposed to each other but not reconciled; matters remained the same with Augustine. The transformative force inherent in the motif of subjectivity and spiritual life from the very beginning was not yet present at the start (nor for a long

196

time to come) to the motif of the individual. To be sure, Augustine felt the unique metaphysical worth of personality, independence of the individual, and weight and reponsibility of free will as keenly as virtually anyone before him. And the more he insisted on the life of will and mind and on original spontaneity of inner life, the more surely did the temptation return, in the manner of Antiquity to dissolve the spiritual-individual element (as something essentially cognitive, hence lost in the being of ideas and sharing in its universality) in uniform and generic reason given to all men. Indeed in his entire doctrine he proceeded from immediate self-certitude of his own self as individual subject; and his psychological descriptions, totally different than those of Aristotle, dealt with his own highly personal-individual inner life, and not merely so that he could then compare it with that of others, say, and generalize about it. But the old hierarchical ordering based on degrees of universality still remained decisively at work. The individual has full reality and is foreknown in God's wisdom as an idea beyond time (just as everything material and changeable also ultimately is). Yet matters are still such that all individual objects in materially bound being strive to return to the universal, to higher and truer being. The world order their restless, unfulfilled becoming seeks is essentially an order of genera and species; and, only by way of descent, of individuals, too. There was still no feeling of the discrepancy between the ancient world picture and the new doctrine of the soul. It seemed enough that those forms and ideas were taken up into God's mind as his ideas.

Thus the Middle Ages also stood overwhelmingly under the sign of so-called "realism." The core of the thesis of Realism was not that the universal was also real ("in objects"), but that truly substantial essence and in any case higher reality were present in the universal (the universal "prior to objects"). Platonic Ideas were models and archetypes for existing reality that imitates them but never matches them, always lagging behind their pure being; so here, too, although the independence of degrading, individualizing matter was completely abolished with respect to the creator, [Augustine] thought of divine-perfect ideas in God's spirit as archetypes God used in creating reality as an imperfectly evolving thing in descending degrees. This was just as an artist first looks at patterns and then creates an actual work of art with the natural imperfections that are inherent in the actual and the particular. In addition, on the completely changed basis of the doctrine of creation the question of the ground of being of the individual, the principle of individuation, was raised; here, too, there was thought to be a need for a special explanation regarding how something proceeds from ideas to individual being! Hence the world of individual realities always seemed to be a mere image of something eternal-universal in the mind of God, whereas

197

sensible-changing, unique, living being seemed a mere appearance of the ideational. All knowledge that transcended pure sense perception necessarily related only to the universal; science aims only at always universal "substantial forms." The decisive method of knowledge lies in the syllogism; formation and logical linkage of the universal provides everything essential. "Realism" always expressly appealed to Plato's doctrine as well. As for Aristotle, in these discussions people preferred to stress another point: reference to the individual object and experience that begins with the individual. Opponents of realism readily played off what was consistent with realism in the theory of knowledge of Aristotle and his school against Platonism. But in reality it was always precisely (Neoplatonically transformed) Aristotelianism that was decisively effective in "realistic" trains of thought. In the matter of church doctrine, with which the wisdom of the old masters was supposed to be absolutely consistent, one preferred to highlight those motives in which transcendent connections bound together the unique-personal element in representations of God and the soul. This was especially so for the mystery of the Trinity (regarding which William of Occam's nominalistic insistence on the unique-individual had to admit that, looked at from the standpoint of reason, this seemed to demand realism) as well as for the doctrines of original sin and vicarious satisfaction. But the danger of pantheism always lurked nearby (something that foes of realism time and again threw into the balance as the most important dogmatic scruple): the Neoplatonic fusion (so important in transmitting ancient doctrines to the Middle Ages) whereby the individual was absorbed as it were by the whole as well as by the generically universal element, pushed in this direction with such urgency that often one could escape it only with difficulty.

Thus, in one of the most extreme formulations of the universalistic tendency, for Scotus Erigena God as pure being (which is a predicate of every object in some way or other) is most universal being, prior to, and above, every individual being, the apex of a pyramid in which the relative and particular is always subordinated and adapted to higher-universal being. The more universal a thing is, the more substantial it is and the closer it is to God. The truth is that the particular is immanent in the universal and contained in it; every universal being contains the particular being that comes under it and allows it to issue forth from it, generating it in the process of existing. The universal exists in the particular and in the individual as in its parts. Thus creation is division, a kind of "analysis" [= a breaking down (translator's note)] of divine being and divine goodness, multiplication of unity by way of descent of what is most universal into special and individual being, into genera, species, and numbers. First the simply highest categories emanate from Being, then the less universal, and finally individuals that occupy the lowest rung in the hierarchy of the world. It was expressly asserted against the Aristotelians that individual beings are not really substance. Efficacy and power to generate and to endure always belong only to the universal, which merely makes its appearance through the individual. Thus here, too (in a matter that is obviously contrary to church doctrine), we see the Neoplatonic reversion of individual beings into the divine ground, conceived of as a re-ascent to species and genera all the way up to most universal unity. To be sure, Scotus tried to save the individual and to preserve eternal life for every creature in God. As thoughts of God all ideas are eternal, those of individuals (to which God's goodness also descends) as well as those of genera and species. In God's wisdom the individual also finds eternal stability, in spite of its return into the generative-universal principle that dissolves its individual being; the individual is not just an ephemeral appearance. Man in particular is himself a true microcosm: his mind represents all the divine ideas in itself, and he is also free and independent in his own way; thus separation of his soul should not be terminated at the end of all things. But this is not really consistent; at root Erigena's entire Christian system is simply more Neoplatonism after all; the demands of the new religious doctrine remain unreconciled in the system of being of ancient universalism.

Medieval realism did not always travel this route, and the subsequent period for the most part avoided what was bound to lead to pantheism; in general, to the extent that it was possible to do so within its fundamental vision it stood for the special rights of the individual also, especially of the immortal soul. It would be an interesting and an extremely important task to study the very different forms in which realism appeared in the course of the Middle Ages so that we might observe the way in which they tried to do justice to the individual metaphysically. In general, the universal remained in the foreground even beyond Thomas. But the universal is always precisely the essential-permanent element also, which is not subject to change at all; individual being, however, even if one thinks of it ultimately as essentially determined in its special character, nevertheless always adopts contingent-changing forms of appearance inseparable from it; as a changing entity it seems to be of lesser stature. Hugh of St. Victor's important development of Augustine's concept of person led to no change of principles on this question of the universal and the particular. Nominalism, however, was of a completely different mind. The metaphysical content of this form of thought (that emerged from problems of logic) not only stood for the special value, but even for the unique reality, of individual beings; in comparison with that reality all universality had always only derivative significance (universals "after objects")! In its harshest forms, with respect to the realist objection of the dogma of the Trinity, it did not even recoil from suspicion of tritheism.

199

But this nominalistic individualism of the eleventh and twelfth centuries did not lead to a newly developed metaphysics of its own which would have focused, say, on the newly attained principle of the individual, as the ancient system of being had focused on the universal. Furthermore: it failed to win victory! Church and school clung tenaciously to ancient universalism, merely repressing its excesses time and time again, and then as far as possible *also* acknowledging the reality of the individual.

This situation still did not change when aggressive Arabianism, especially Averroism, strongly and unabashedly underlined the pantheistic connection of the universal with the whole, as it sought above all on the basis of Aristotle's (and his successors') principle of nous to dissolve the individual in a comprehensive principle of universal being of the soul. In this sort of world system there was naturally no hesitation in defining (with Aristotle) that all multiplicity of individuals arises only in "division" of matter. Albert and Thomas fought against those doctrines and battled with utmost energy against "Latin Averroism" and the heretical consequences that many sects in that century (often drawing on Scotus Erigena) wished to infer on the basis of realism. Siger of Brabant, for example, taught openly that the *anima intellectiva* [intellectual soul], because it is free from matter, is in fact a single, identical soul for all men; it is not until it becomes linked with the multitude of human bodies that it becomes many individual souls. Nevertheless, in their newly won dependence on Aristotle they still remained faithful to the system of realism for all that! Even more so than otherwise they now stressed (while appealing to the Stagirite [Aristotle] and his critique of Plato's Ideas) that the universal has existence and empirical factuality only in the individual; but since the latter was nevertheless always paired with the imperfect, the value of the individual was not enhanced thereby. No matter how much Thomas's theory of knowledge emphasized importance of individual experience and used virtually nominalistic formulations in placing *universalia post rem* [universals after the thing] (as first abstracted by the mind from sense experience of objects, not given or implanted by God) in the foreground, nevertheless he, too, viewed the system of being as entirely subject to the metaphysical primacy of genera that are archetypes and intermediate causes of creation in the mind of God. The privilege human intelligence has before other individual beings is that despite its own singular character it grasps universal ideas of God and is in fact not related to the individual (i.e., the contingent-perishable) by way of the senses alone; but it never really attains the pure generic character of perfect mind, for it always remains in understanding and will a personal-individual thing. Individuality is the same as imperfection and limitation; the closer intelligences stand with respect to

200

V. The Individual

God, the more general they are, and the farther they stand, the more powerfully they are "contracted" toward the specific.

Thus for the Aristotelian Thomas the principle of individuation was still matter, the form-receptive moment; or more precisely *materia signata* [signed matter; short for *materia prima quantitate signata*, i.e., prime matter "signed" with quantity (translator's note)]. Matter can always assume generic forms of existence only within completely specific and defined dimensions; the one species is divided through a specific quantity of spatiotemporal matter into a multiplicity of examples and defined with respect to here and now. The specific matter that constitutes Socrates' body—*haec caro haec ossa* [this flesh, these bones]—would have to enter decisively into the definition of "Socrates" (if it were possible to supply one)! To be sure, Thomas expressly stressed against the Aristotelians (as did his teacher Albert on other grounds) that matter is not itself the cause, but only the condition of, existence for the individual and that the really ultimate cause is God, but that is above all a defense against independence of matter on the basis of the idea of creation: matter, hence also its individuating effect (in a completely different way than for Aristotle) is itself created by God and willed by God. Everything in the world, even what is relatively imperfect, derives ultimately from God's will. Moreover both Albert and Thomas emphasize that this lowest division into individuals also—not just the grand classification into the eternal system of genera and species—contributes to the beauty of the world and to complete explication of its highest fullness. And with respect to human souls, they teach naturally that death does not annul the differentness and individuality that arise from matter; on the contrary they remain fully even after bodies dissolve. Individual soul is immortal precisely in its personal individuality. Not all individual beings exist only for their species, such as plants and animals do; rational individuals contain their purpose within themselves and God wills them as ends, not merely as means. But the ancient principle of matter as principle of individuation remained nonetheless in force; and matter is in fact in itself the lower element, the source of the accidental and perishable. The contradiction appears in most peculiar fashion in Aquinas's doctrine of angels. From the time of Philo and the Neoplatonically philosophizing Church Fathers all ancient levels of universality were harmonized with religious revelation, which taught hierarchical ordering of superhuman intelligences; accordingly, except in the case of God's spirit Platonic Ideas maintained their own existence and completely special functions in the world of creatures. In the case of Thomas the question regarding the principle of individuation led to this connection also. Superhuman intelligences are free from matter; how then were they supposed to be single-individual beings? The solution is that each angel constitutes a species unto itself and is unique

201

not only in its own kind but as its own kind; there are as many species here as there are individuals! God could not create several angels of the same species, because only matter can divide up universal forms. We are to understand the difference between individual angels as difference in kind. In many respects Thomas's age turned away from this peculiar doctrine, for ecclesiastical-dogmatic as well as philosophical reasons (Dietrich von Freiberg with particular force). But for the most part people left untouched the real source of the difficulty—ancient overestimation of the universal.

It was not until Duns Scotus that a great transformation came about on the whole question. Others before him had already prepared the way. Through their younger representatives the Franciscans (whose old leaders, for example, Bonaventure, still stood essentially on the ground of Aristotle's definition of the individual, although they also sought mediation with modern questions) provided new initiative in this area as well. Henry of Ghent, who was so permeated by the Augustinian-Victorine concept of person, denied (which Thomas had, however, conceded) that in God's mind separate ideas of individual creatures existed in addition to species-ideas. According to him God knows individuals through his knowledge of classes. Universal ideas shine forth into many individual ideas just as a beam of light is refracted into many colors; in God all objects are real as universal idea, and actual individual beings emanate from it. Here the principle of individuation is negation: In the evolution of the individual, universal idea's identity and inner "capacity for increase" is taken away. This negative determination clings to individual objects only as accident; differing instances of the same species differ from one another only through the fact that one of them is not the other. Here, too, the question became particularly difficult in the case of angels. Hence Henry of Ghent can only appeal to God, who alone knows how he created angels as substantially different beings. But in contrast to that, Richard of Middletown stressed (as the others had) not only that God had created everything that he made as individual being and that he did this according to specific individual ideas in his mind, but he also stressed above all that individuals were the goal of creation. Gottfried of Fontaine also rejected the Thomistic principle, because it could lead only to accidental differences between individuals, never to substantial ones; he also demanded

202

V. The Individual

different substantial forms for different individuals, which are after all different substances.

Duns Scotus now actually introduced a form-principle for the individual also! To be sure, he remained a "realist" insofar as universals were real for him—before and in objects—just as they were for everyone else (except the nominalists, whom he also combated). They appear existentially only in individual objects but are themselves independent of them. Otherwise no science would be possible, because science always refers only to general concepts after all. A system of the reality of the individual alone, such as the nominalists seek, would logically have to maintain the impossibility of all knowledge of overarching connections, of relations, grounds, similarities, and classifications! Such a system would then restrict all knowledge in principle to verifying totally different individual objects; it would make all systematization simply the result of certain logical operations of merely subjective origin and significance. But in reality every time we think of concepts of genera and species, an existing-universal element exists as prototype and antitype of intellect. Intellect produces our universal concepts, to be sure— not arbitrarily but with the necessity of a mirroring [*abbildenden*] function. But Duns Scotus now held that it is not only the universal that is substantial-real. After all, nature is perfected in the individual! Uniqueness and essential differentness from other individuals do not indicate imperfection of creatures but rather something that God has expressly willed! The creator does not will difference in species and thereby relative sameness of individuals *more* than he wills differentness of many individuals. That God creates manifoldness and multiplicity within the same species is also an effluence of his abundant goodness, indeed, one that is particularly important: for it is primarily the individual that crowns his work; it is the individual that transcends mere genera and species as a *higher* form of existence, the highest among all creaturely beings. Individuals are the ultimate highest purpose of the creator; indeed, he wills to grant the noblest of them eternal happiness! Thus the individual element cannot be based on admixture with matter; this explanation is faulty in itself, according to Scotus, and most especially with regard to the problem of immaterial soul. Nor can it be based on some other kind of negating entity. On the contrary its principle must itself be something positive and formal! Just as genera receive their specific difference from above, as it were, so must individuals receive their individual difference from above, even though our limited knowledge might not be able to grasp that latter difference as easily as it does the difference in species! Richard of Middletown had identified the element that accretes to an "in"-dividual [= non-divisible] as exclusion of divisibility. Duns now links up with that; but he emphasizes that the individual-unit's opposition to division, as it were, is in fact more than privation of divisibility and that there is something positive in it, a positive ground for inability-to-divide. Just as truly as a real element in being must correspond to universal ideas of knowledge, so must a real, simple unity of the individual also correspond to the idea of the individual! Form is the object of a concept, hence also of the concept of the individual. That which makes Peter a man and that which makes him this particular man is in each case a positive and real entity. Just as universal principles enter into distinctions between species, so do *entitates individuantes* [individuating entities] enter into differences between individuals. It is not merely virtually (as was thought in the principle of individuation by matter), but rather formally that individuals and all single objects differ from one another. Alongside universal forms of whatness (*quidditas*) that had hitherto been the sole topic of discussion, there must also be a form of thisness (*haecceitas*) that is *ultima realitas* [ultimate reality], highest being and ground in everything that exists! Besides possessing existence-as-living-being and human-existence, Peter also possesses Peterness [*Petreitas*]; besides his generic and specific character he possesses individual character—that which is the presupposition and ground of individual and unique personality. In and of itself, quite apart from union with body, individual soul is already substance; it does not first become individualized through corporeal moments. It is only in ephemeral objects of nature composed of matter and form that matter also has a share (although in itself only a subordinate one) in individuation. Spiritual beings differ from one another individually on the basis of a purely formal principle; hence Duns sees no reason why there could not be more than one angel of the same species; here too we have still another treasure and proof of the goodness of God.

At this point the revival of nominalism began, which was to win such decisive importance. In a much stronger and more fundamental way than in the period of the high Middle Ages this theory now appeared in its new form as champion of the individual. Durandus de Saint-Pourçain declared flatly that the question of the ground of individuation was superfluous. In existence (in reality) *only* the particular exists. Nature in general produces only individuals; only individual objects are truly things. Form is automatically always inwardly individual; it does not first become so by being taken up into matter. Indeed, on the contrary, one must ask what the ground of the universal is; at root this is ultimately only asking how we can designate in generic form things that always exist exclusively as individual objects! After all, the generic predicate cannot designate the single existing thing in its unity and indivisibility at all; obviously it cannot express that thing in its own inner specificity but only in an unspecific way. Hence the more we ascend in generality of knowledge, the more we distance ourselves from true knowledge. The universal does not possess the truth of existence but is merely a contrivance for labeling things. Petrus Aureoli argued in like manner. And just as William of Occam and then Johannes Gerson were also to do after him, he expressly reversed the concept of the realists with respect to divine knowledge: just as some realist extremists had denied that God had specific ideas of individuals, so now people were saying that God has *only* individual ideas and that God could produce only these ideas outside himself! It is only our human, confused knowledge in need of special assistance that uses universals.

William of Occam then began the actual victorious march of the new nominalism—or rather (from the metaphysical perspective) individualism. The fundamental principle of his conception of being was: *Omnis res positiva extra animam eo ipso est singularis* [Every positive thing apart from the soul is automatically singular]. Hence ideas also are primarily ideas of the individual, not of species. To be sure, God creates being in accordance with prototypical ideas, but in every model idea he thinks only something entirely individual, just as he can create only something individual in each creative act. To assume universal existence of genera and species is an idle hypothesis. But this movement did not attain the level of an individual system of being with its own special character; this was due not only to its involvement with other interests but above all to the difficulty of the matter itself. Duns Scotus was right: Whoever simply denied the reality of the universal and allowed only the individual's validity must ultimately give up knowledge in the larger sense altogether and will end up in one form or another in skepticism. We can never do without the universal as an essential moment of existence in the makeup of the individual itself.

Nicholas of Cusa took the second great stride toward positive valuation and conceptual representation of the individual. In very crucial respects he stood on the ground of realism and even of a hierarchical ordering tinged with pantheism. The Neoplatonist in him often breaks through entirely without reserve. But in a completely new way he now placed value on the special character of individual creatures. The conviction that sounded forth for the first time in Stoic pantheism—that there could not be two identical beings in the rich manifold of the world—now stood at the very heart of his thought. Everything outside of God, who is absolutely opposition-free and universally comprehensive unity, is differentiated. No object or change can be entirely like another object or change. Complete identity exists only in the abstract; coincidence exists only in God; actual objects however all differ from each other. Solely on the basis of the special space-time position every being in the world occupies, one must conclude to its qualitative particularity and difference from all other objects. That is why all our human knowledge deals with mere ''conjectures''; our thinking must always function with similarity

205

and measure, yet no two objects are ever identical, and measure can never "precisely" grasp what it is measuring. Universal concepts are not just names for Nicholas, but they always take us only a limited little piece of the way toward the true goal of knowledge: grasp of the concrete and individual. The real always remains incommensurable for our conceptualization; and the path of knowledge therefore necessarily goes on into infinity. But the fact that an individual differs from every other, indeed in every respect, is not mere shortcoming or lagging behind with respect to the universal (although such turns of phrase are also not lacking in Nicholas), but rather a special gift of the creator. "There is nothing in the universe that does not enjoy a certain unique being that cannot be found in any other." "Principles of individualization cannot occur in an individual in the same harmonious proportion as they do in another individual, hence every being is a unity unto itself and is perfect in its own way." "Every created being reposes in the perfection that it . . . has received, and it does not desire to be any other creature, as if that would make it more perfect; on the contrary, it prefers the being that God has given it as a divine gift that it wants to preserve from destruction and to perfect." Differentness down to the smallest detail is what ultimately makes the great harmony of the world. In its uniqueness every object is a member of the whole. What Platonists used to say about the mutual necessity of stages in connection with Plato's comparison of the world to a living thing, Nicholas emphatically extended to the individual. Every object in its uniqueness has a special and altogether necessary function in the structure of the world. The biblical passage about the talent imparted to each person to capitalize on was extended to all objects: "The gracious God has so created all things that every being, inasmuch as it strives to preserve its being as its divine vocation, accomplishes this in community with others." Thus all members of a living body mutually support each other so that each of them can be what it is in the best possible way. "The identity of the universe consists in its differentness, just as its unity does in its multiplicity." Every being has a most universal [universellste] agreement with and a most special [speziellste] differentness from every other being with which it cohabits the same world. "Most beautiful harmony consists precisely in greatest difference." Thus beings also do not come into existence one after another, as philosophers have otherwise taught; on the contrary, individuals are present simultaneously with the totality of the universe. Every single object is like a microcosm: belonging to the whole, the whole nevertheless also exists in its own completely special way in it. Because no being can be totality in general (in other words, God), the whole now exists in a particular contraction. This applies especially to man. Everything is somehow contained in him as crown of creation; in principle he can know all things in himself and from himself. Nevertheless he cannot know anything completely or with total precision: for each individual fashions the world only in his own individual way! People are like variously crumpled concave mirrors that reproduce the same object differently, except only that these mirrors are themselves living and are able to alter their crumpled surfaces themselves! No person is identical with another, no one thinks exactly as another does. "No one is like another in feeling, imagination, reason, in all activities, in writing, painting, and every kind of art, even if he tried to imitate another for a thousand years." Each person shares in the activity of divine reason; but each does that in his own way. Here, too, that is the way it should be; harmony of the whole rests on the manifold of individuals. Although in every kind of being, says Nicholas, for example, in human beings, one can always find some that are more perfect and more outstanding than others in some respect, nevertheless no one can say with certainty who is the most excellent: "God has arranged things in this way so that each person can be satisfied with himself even though he marvels at others . . . and in that way unity and peace prevail without jealousy."

From Nicholas the path leads to the monad theories of Bruno, Helmont, and Leibniz. That God with all his fullness and infinity exists not only in the greatest (in the world as a whole) but also in the smallest (in individual being) was a fundamental certitude both in Italian and in German philosophy of nature. It was not out of "esthetic individualism of the Renaissance" (as people are so prone to describe it) that this steady growth of the concept of the individual and its metaphysical importance ultimately grew. Bruno borrowed his main impulses from Nicholas and the end of Scholasticism. Once again the battle of Aristotelianism versus immortality of the soul flared up now in the Renaissance. Pietro Pompanazzi exposed the irreconcilability of the two theories—the heterogeneity of ancient philosophy and Christian faith—with a sharpness never known before. It is a prejudice for one to believe, on the basis of Aristotelianism, that God's providence and thought are primarily concerned only with the universal and have to do only indirectly with the individual—as if we needed a gradual transition from most perfect being to a lower world of individual creatures. Man needs tools for his work, but God works without such means: he creates the individual directly, and his providential wisdom relates immediately and everywhere to the individual. Renaissance Platonists still tried to hold fast to the unity of both traditions, philosophical-ancient and religious-Christian. Plato's doctrine of immortality provided support for that, and whereas [Renaissance Platonists] interpreted this side of Plato's system in the sense of Christian individual soul, they overlooked the fundamental difference between them for the most part. It was not until Giordano Bruno that matters again moved toward broad metaphysical unfolding of the idea of individuality. Cusa's doctrine of minutest being was given new wings by Bruno's deep religious enthusiasm for the world. The basic ideas were the same as they were for Nicholas. Every single object, not just man, is a special, unique mirror of the universe, indeed an essentially living one. Truly nondivisible being, within which we are to look for the basic element of world system, is not a static atom, a chunk of matter with absolute borders, but rather a monad, simple-imperishable individual life, an individual spontaneously functioning and existing form of God's universal life. Every individual being has its own incomparable task to fulfill in the totality of the life of nature. Individuality does not limit one to a single point of space or of matter, nor does it exclude one from everything else; on the contrary, the world lives in the individual function also. The seed of all objects exists in every individual object, but all objects do not experience the same unfolding and realization in every seed. Striving for development incessantly works in each, however; there is no monad without life. Individual ones encounter each other, group together in organisms, relate to a central unit of life that governs and guides them. These ultimate elements [*Minima*] are building blocks for all reality. Human souls with their immortality are merely a special higher type of these simple and imperishable units.

At the same time Cusa's ideas lived on in German philosophy of nature. Agrippa of Nettesheim, whose dependence on Cusa is very obvious, stressed independent life and self-enclosed uniqueness of individual beings so much that he viewed the connection between them and transmission of influence from one to the other as miraculous. From the purely material point of view the connection seems impossible; it is only in the concept of "sympathy"— that spontaneous resonance with one another that we know from the shared life of human individuals (who nevertheless abide entirely within themselves and are self-enclosed)—that organization of the individualized world makes sense. Paracelsus introduced a special principle for the particular life of the individual: *Archeus* [the source]. Every object contains an original individual seed that tends naturally to develop inwardly from its own resources; the system of objects is not so much governance of superindividual entities and forces, but rather universal self-stimulation of individuals to unfold inwardly. Valentin Weigel carried that further. The universal-communitarian element receded more and more behind spontaneous activity and the special character of the individual. Every object lives its true life only in itself; what lies outside it always provides merely an occasion but not power. All external influences merely stimulate the seed-forces. In this sense every being is free in itself; it is not coerced or driven by anything external. This is true for absolutely all objects; man merely demonstrates these features with greatest clarity; he is an inwardly complete being, an individual-spontaneous being

V. The Individual

whose very knowledge must in the last analysis always draw exclusively on
its own inner self. Both of the Helmonts further developed Paracelsus's doctrine of *Archeus*. Aristotle's entelechy was twisted into something individual
and became a "monad." All creatures were created from eternity in their
indivisible singularity, all process is self-development of these individuals,
and each one of them abides within itself. In the case of spiritual beings,
however, we observe the capacity they have to penetrate one another sym-
pathetically despite their singularity. For material being, singularity means
merely seclusion and isolated rigidity; for spiritual being, singularity also
means connection with all others.

Leibniz's theory of monads then provided the classical system of individualism. His entire life interest, from his first youthful work (*On the Principle of Individuation*) to his final legacy-writings, focused on the concept of
the essence, meaning, and value of individual being. Descartes, whose de-
duction began of course in Augustinian fashion with individual ego's self-
certitude, had defined soul-substances (which he now conceived as completely independent of all matter and any individualizing moments it might
contain) as absolutely individual in themselves, without bothering himself
much about the controversial issue of principle of individuation. On the basis
of religious life he was certain of the original and unshakable plurality of
individual souls (*res cogitantes* [thinking beings]). From this perspective his
organization of existence is purely pluralistic-individualistic. But the material
element, at any rate (which in his view was a totally different matter and did
not need to be affected by the soul-endowed individual at all), he regarded
as essentially indifferent generic being as opposed to any individual differentiation; as homogeneous space-matter or simply *the* bodily substance. Now,
whoever took Descartes as his point of departure and wished to overcome
dualism had to make a decision in favor of either individual substances or
of universal substance. It is very interesting to trace in Spinoza or the Occasionalists how newly strengthened consciousness in favor of the individual
made war against the pantheistic tendency to swallow up the individual—
whereby ancient valuation of the universal, of "idea" in the generic sense,
still continued to play an essential role throughout.

Leibniz now decisively transformed ontological concepts for the first
time to conform to the model of the self-given individual soul. His youthful
treatise was still linked to late medieval controversy, and his position was
close to nominalism, which had ultimately dissolved real universals and formal entities. The youthful Leibniz regarded the nominalists as the profoundest sect among the Scholastics and also as the starting point for all current
reforms in philosophy and the sciences. He played off Durandus, Petrus Aureoli, and William of Occam against ancient realism and attacked Duns Sco-

tus's conception of the reality of the universal as well. But like Duns, young Leibniz too searched for the *ratio individuationis formalis* [formal ground of individuation]! The particular cannot come about on the basis of more real generalities through negation; nor can the individual element in existence derive merely from some part (perhaps even a subsidiary one), for example, from matter or even from mere form. If Socrates is not Plato, there must be a positive ground for this in each of them, indeed in each of them as unity or totality! Hence the conclusion reads: "Every single individual is individuated through his total being." His later system then expressly appealed to individual soul and always issued forth essentially from it. It is through soul, our own self, that we learn what substance is and what the only thing is that we may call by that term. In Leibniz's view the absolutely opposite pole to true philosophy was Averroist "monopsychism," in which a single universal soul, like a soul-ocean, swallowed up individual souls. It is not only those who deny immortality of the human soul but also those who think living unity in an animal or a plant is transitory, who provide support for that false conception of being; it depreciates humanity and the entire world of living creatures. Spinoza and more recent Cartesians are on the same path. But only inner experience can convince us of the falsity of these doctrines; it shows us that we are something special in ourselves—something that thinks, is conscious, and wills—and that we differ from every other being that in fact thinks differently or wills differently. The I-he-you [*Das ego ille tu*] provides a distinct concept of substantial existence—not that idea of soul-ocean! Moreover, Leibniz adds, it is also demonstratively certain that substance is always an individual entity. In "analysis of substances" (in contrast with analysis of concepts) we always necessarily come to the point of demanding ultimate, indivisible, simple units as true basic substances, first and absolute principles of everything that exists. Substance as "independence" ["*Selbstand*"] and spontaneous activity is always necessarily a simple-individual thing, which accordingly cannot also be dissoluble-ephemeral, but must last forever. Everything that acts is specific substance! The truly indivisible unit, the monad, is necessarily individual. Through its pluralistic tendency the Atomists' material concept of being had an advantage in fact over Descartes's space-matter; but true elements cannot really consist in the material, in what is spatially bounded or located. Monads must not be passive and material but active and formal atoms: individual principles of form. . . . For Leibniz there is no general formal principle that is substantial-real and produces process and change. Thus he completely altered the meaning of ancient ontological concepts when he now called monads "entelechies" and "substantial forms." Substances are individual powers of development. Singularity and unique individuality is formal-essential for them, not accidental. Existing

210

V. The Individual

being does not differ from another only through a single characteristic and with a difference that is merely within the same species, but rather with its entire being. No part of it is completely identical with part of another, no matter what level it might occupy in the universe's framework of perfection. All substances are similar in their basic ontological structure (a point Descartes's dualism missed); but in the concrete every one of them differs totally from every other. *Principium individuationis idem est quod absolutae specifications [sic], qua res ita sit determinata, ut ab aliis omnibus distingui possit* [The principle of individuation is the same as that of absolute specification, whereby a thing is defined in such a way that it can be distinguished from all others]. If this *absolute* specification is lacking, then definition is also lacking, and we are then not in the realm of the real but of the abstract. Hence for Leibniz the conviction follows that in the entire world there absolutely cannot be two identical leaves or animals or objects (he then formulated his conviction as a fundamental principle in his *principium identitatis indiscernibilium* [principle of the identity of indiscernibles]), which obviously follows necessarily from the ontological principle of the ground. If there were two objects in nature that did not differ essentially from each other, we could assign no reason why they were two things instead of just one. This reason must instead reside in a difference inherent in the objects themselves and in their totality; it may not, say, be shunted off into so called *denominationes pure extrinsecas* [purely extrinsic denominations], into external and extrinsic moments (relative to the object), as people have liked to search for the difference "merely" in spatiotemporal arrangement, "only" in matter. Everything that exists must differ from and be distinguishable from everything else through an inner element, through something that necessarily belongs to the individual object. There are no contingent, unessential differences in this area. What belongs to an individual belongs to it essentially and substantially; not only its distinctive and very special inner activity but just as truly what opposes it and what it undergoes! Individual being is self-enclosed; nothing external-contingent is impressed on it or taken from it. The monad has "no windows" but lives its entire individual life within itself. Everything that happens to it and emanates from it is only self-unfolding according to inner functional law, the law of its activities that comprises its uniqueness. It is in this that the "autarchy" and "self-sufficiency" (Nicholas spoke similarly) of the monad reside, which always indicates a "certain perfection"! Just as man with his free will is the image of God, so also every creature exists in a certain way with its autarchy, with spontaneity of its individual "form" in which it fulfills itself in itself without needing any foreign power of external forms and powers. Every single individual being in the hierarchical ordering

211

of the entire world is what, according to Thomas, only the being of angels would end up as: unique in its own kind, formally unique being.

Thus only the concept of individual being is an actually fully "determined" or "complete" concept! All concepts of genus and species as such always remain "incomplete and abstract" and in a certain sense indeterminate. Only Duns Scotus's so-called *heccéité* designates something truly substantial; all merely universal concepts do not designate substances but only modifications of something existing. But the complete concept is then naturally something much more complicated and pregnant than customary concepts are; it must include in its conception every property or modification that ever appears in the individual to which it applies, everything one can truthfully say about it—even what is apparently merely external-contingent! Everything that ever happened to Caesar in his life belongs to the complete concept of this individual substance; if only one feature were missing (e.g., that Caesar crossed the Rubicon at a specific point in time), the concept would no longer be complete, not fully determined. In the concept of individual one must include not only predicates of the entire infinite time sequence in which the imperishable individual progresses eternally as well as predicates of spatial location in the universe (according to the real content of spatial relations)—all this as if contracted to a single point—but also everything that necessarily belongs to the essence of the most common individual being as people commonly represent it. *L'individualité enveloppe l'infini* [the individual embraces the infinite]; the number of characteristics or predicates thus included in every complex concept is actually infinite; one can never exhaust this concept through finite definition and discussion. Universal concept owes its lucidity and relative exhaustibility only to its relative emptiness and abstractness.

The world thus consists entirely of individual beings that spring forth immediately from God's creative hand (not first of all according to the higher pattern of ideas of genera and species, as merely diluted instances of universal form). Every monad is like an independently realized single reflection [*Einzel-Blick*] of divine essence itself, a unique mirror of infinite fullness of being. Thus individual being here is not, as it seemed to be in extreme forms of "realism," merely the instance generated through a system of limiting differences of a most universal category (God's One Being), but rather the result of a special act of creation by the divine person. Nothing more stands between God and individual objects. Now this does not mean, say, that universal being does not exist at all. Leibniz also recognized the realm of eternal truths and ideas in God's understanding; he too regarded these as constitutive moments in the structure of the concrete. But they do not have priority of reality and value before individual beings; on the contrary, their tendency is not fulfilled until they coalesce in the individual! All those eternal ideas, even though they are God's ideas, are not themselves realities but only "possibilities," *possibilités d'être* [possibilities of being]. Essentially they carry within them "tendency toward existence" or "striving for existence." Hence existing being lacks nothing of the purity and permanence of the universal, but conversely the universal always lacks something: complete existence! *Existentia est essentiae exigentia* [Essence demands existence]. Now it is precisely the principle of perfection, the "principle of the best," which brings mere possibilities together into existence. Not all possibilities are "compossible" with one another; not all of them, if they coalesce, can make up a real system. Only those essences become actual which in combination produce a maximum of harmony and perfection. *Ut possibilitas principium Essentiae, ita perfectio seu Essentiae gradus (per quem plurima sunt compossibilia) principium Existentiae* [As the possibility of the principles of essence is, so is perfection or degree of essence (through which a plurality of things is compossible) the principle of existence]. The actual is nothing other than selection and synthesis of the best from the range of possibilities. "Contingency," which since Antiquity characterized existences in contrast with eternal essence, now no longer expresses lack of substantiality and meaning, but on the contrary is the mark of ultimate and highest fulfillment: the creator's free and absolutely good will fuses together the eternal possibilities existing in the mind of God under the principle of "fittingness" or of the "best"! A highest principle of value thus transcends mere logical necessities and universal ideas; the one, concrete world is "the best of all possible worlds," the One maximum and optimum entity. "Contingency" is here only another expression for higher, "moral" necessity. In the single reality of the world, however, every member is a unique entity, an individual. That reality's perfection is its harmony: every single being is self-contained, self-sufficient, a world unto itself—yet all together they make up the great single system of the world. The world is not a functional unity in the customary sense (whereby the individual is after all always somehow absorbed by the universal or the whole and loses its autonomy), but rather is a system of meaning, preestablished harmony between individual beings, all of which preserve their independence, their total seclusion, and their unique existence. The system of the world is a conceptual one; and Leibniz is ready here also to compare it to mutual interpenetration in "sympathy." It is clear from the case of man's mind how beings are one and harmonious with each other without thereby losing anything of their independence and individuality. The most perfect of all individual beings are spiritual ones, the ones that "hinder each other the least," that is, that strictly exclude one another the least, as corporeal objects do for example. Perfection for spiritual beings lies in virtues, among which love is the most decisive: in it each one enjoys the happiness of the other! The "sympathy" of individual beings binds them together into a cosmic system of harmony.

All individuals on every level of the world system are related to each other with their entire undivided being. In its inner fullness and movement each one of them represents every other and therewith the totality. Inasmuch as each substance lives its life, it also lives the life of the others! The content of the world is identical in all of them, but it appears completely different in each of them—just as a single city presents itself in ever different perspectives to all individual onlookers situated at different locations around it. Every monad is absolutely unique and noninterchangeable, and every single moment of its existence differs from every other one; but at the same time all of them—in their utterly different perspectives and in their degrees of development of clarity and distinctness that differ at every single instant—describe one and the same thing. And it is not identity, the purity of a typical-universal entity, that is the goal of the development of life for the individuals here; nor is it fusion into an indifferent universe; instead it is full development of the unique innate character inherent in each of them in the law of the never-ceasing "series of its operations."

No later thinker has ever surpassed what Leibniz accomplished for metaphysics of the individual in this way; indeed no one has ever really appreciated and utilized it in its full meaning. To be sure, there have been other pluralistic systems besides Leibniz's, from the "realm of spirits" of his contemporary Berkeley (who in fact, as an extreme nominalist, belonged to an old individualistic tradition) on to the individualistic descendant of Schopenhauer's metaphysics of will and to Julius Bahnsen. But no one really broached the problem of the individual as such anew; people rather accepted than executed the dissolution of the universal. On the other hand, however, the subsequent period went beyond what Leibniz provided. Rather than developing the moral sense of life in individuality in his metaphysical system of monadalogy, Leibniz merely understood it as one element among others; it merely reverberated as a kind of background sound in its life. Leibniz left this task to another age, in which spiritual-moral life in general was more decisively at the core of metaphysical development than it was with him.

Individualistic initiatives of the theory of monads did indeed influence the eighteenth century in many ways, and then Shaftesbury also especially influenced it. Shaftesbury (whose metaphysical concept of individual being did not contain anything of serious importance) spoke with even more urgency than Leibniz about the life-goal of the entirely unique personality, about the moral obligation to develop its special character with all its inner richness, that is, the special capacities that each individual person possesses,

214

V. The Individual

and about the contribution that such development makes to the great harmony of the universe. But the generic ideal then went on to achieve actual primacy for the entire period of the Enlightenment. Men are indeed all individuals and we must regard each of them as such; but individuals are at root identical, and whatever characteristics distinguish them are quite extrinsic and random in character! The "natural" individual whom people wanted to make the foundation of law, morality, and religious doctrine was an abstraction, a generic norm. "Freedom and equality": People once emancipated from the sway of external ordinances and conventions were then also essentially identical to each other in all essential respects! It is an ideal goal of freedom to remove all inequalities from the world. Thus individuals once again became like atoms, atoms of society and of the "world of spirits." They were able to cooperate with each other in constructing a world because essentially they were entirely alike, and every one of them, as a natural-rational being, ultimately wants the same thing as every other. Hence the system of the world (as well as the social whole) is not harmony in the sense meant by Leibniz or Shaftesbury, who flatly claimed infinite differentness and even dissonant opposition between individuals; on the contrary, "the universal" is once again the foundation of the whole.

This Enlightenment concept of the individual also lived on effectively in Kant's practical metaphysics and theory of life. A pluralistically constructed "realm of spirits," of immortal individuals (of the kind in Berkeley's world or in Swedenborg's), is the tacit background of his rational faith. Accordingly, the idea of the absolute intrinsic value of every individual person and of his pure self-reliance in moral autonomy is the focal point of Kant's practical philosophy. The inner responsibility of every single person for his acts of will and mind pushes his unique being entirely into the foreground in contrast with all universal conditions of earlier doctrines that did not seek for the morally decisive element in the form of will but in goals and goods. And yet for Kant, too, every single individual in the inner privacy of his mental life (no one else can even peer in there!) is essentially only a "rational being in general." What distinguishes men from one another as special, unique, and individual is simply their sense "inclinations," their position in the world of the senses! Duty is one and the same for all of them, and this is so not merely with respect to what it identifies as a general imperative but also in the specifics of moral tasks. Variety of situations and conflicts in which individuals become involved (and perhaps must become involved, given their specific makeup) is not something essential; it all appears rather as the ephemeral and merely factual element in an individual, as something that he must ultimately overcome! That all individuals are supposed to preserve their singular structure and perspectival uniqueness throughout the entirety of eternal evolution—as Leibniz held—is an idea totally foreign to Kant. Every interpretation of the categorical imperative (which commands me always to behave in such a way that the maxim of my will could serve as the principle of *universal* law) in an individualistic sense changes its meaning and essentially misinterprets Kant's intent. For Kant, too, everything comes down to a community of rational beings, which is made possible by the fact that all of them will essentially the same thing and that in the spiritual-rational core of their being they are totally alike. Only "empirical" self is individual in the sense of something unique; the special character of individuals is merely a fact; it is not itself something of importance and value.

In opposition to this primacy of the generic-universal in Kant and the Enlightenment as a whole were the leaders of new intellectual movements—Storm and Stress, Neohumanism itself, and then above all Romanticism. In all of them, elements of Leibniz's world picture and Shaftesbury's theory of personality broke through in a new guise. Hamann and Herder, Goethe and [Wilhelm von] Humboldt, Schleiermacher and Friedrich Schlegel fought for the unique dimension of the individual in nature and humanity. The proper locus for the problem of the individual was now history, with its unique and specific interpretation of the meaning of the evolution of all the figures that emerge in history. With the decisive importance of leading geniuses for all human development, the higher existence of the individual in comparison with the merely generic universal-human now became particularly clear. The ideal of equality fell apart. A single passage in the Kantian system had anticipated this new valuation: his assessment of the artistic genius whose esthetic lawfulness was fundamentally free of every universal rule. Everyone now linked up with this point. The demand grew loud to expand the idea, extend it to the moral meaning of life also, and to introduce it into the idea of the spiritual cosmos in general.

Our task here is to deal with themes of metaphysics, not those of philosophical reflection and mental life in general. Following F. H. Jacobi's significant precedent (which did not mature into a theory however), Fichte then achieved the greatest metaphysical formulation of the idea of individuality (indeed, precisely oriented toward moral-spiritual and historical meaning in the life of the individual). F. H. Jacobi was the first to call attention again to the importance of Leibniz's idea of individuality and emphatically stressed how the concept of the individual constituted the beginning and end in the system of monadology. Then he personally turned his energetic attention against the tendency to overvalue the universal (a tendency one finds in all philosophy of mere understanding) to which the age of Enlightenment had so unconditionally surrendered. Understanding, in isolation, is essentially hostile to individuality; it tends to dissolve all particularities into the universal

216

element still comprehensible to it through concepts! Concepts of understanding always fail in the face of the individual, and a fully comprehended individual is as unthinkable as wooden iron. Kant's moral law is in fact the triumph of rational reflection in the ethical sphere: there the highest thing in reality is something universal, an identical law for everyone. But Jacobi posited life in opposition to mere knowledge. Life is never something universal; it is always individual. All of reality is articulated into *individua* [individuals], particular living beings who differ essentially from one another in their inner independence. And the heart of existence is *personal* life—development of specific-unique, sensual-spiritual beings. Actuality unfolds in a living chain of personal carriers of existence, all of whom are incomparable-individual in their essential core. If understanding or "knowledge" wants nothing to do with that, then the deeper power of knowledge must step in: instinct. For instinct does not aim at generality and law but at living will, the moral impulse of the individual; it aims at personal existence! Instinct itself is always individualized in us, because the existential drive that expresses itself in it is absolutely identical with the essence of the individual; thus it lacks the abstractness of understanding. And it is not true that instinct belongs to the "physical" and as such would belong to individual life in any case, from which one could separate the spiritual-rational as something foreign to individuality, something to be overcome; this Kantian separation of man into natural and rational being is in fact annulled. "The instinct of material-rational natures is concerned with preserving and elevating personal existence; accordingly it is constantly oriented toward whatever advances this." "The absolute drive of the individual is to preserve and elevate its special nature." Whereas the senses, as the Enlightenment and Kant emphasized, signify an individualizing principle, Jacobi thought that for that very reason they border closely on the spiritual meaning of existence and are themselves affirmed thereby. And all "higher" spiritual powers then become means that instinct generates precisely in order to develop the materially given special character of individual being in a positive way to the absolute uniqueness of spiritual personality, to "elevation" of singularity! The sequence of sensibility, understanding, and reason does not indicate that the individual is fading away more and more, but rather that he is being intensified and deepened.

With respect to assessing correctly the spiritual value of knowledge, this means for Jacobi a new valuation of language, of all "opinion" (which is individual, and always rooted deeply in a particular persons's feeling of self), and finally of "presentiment" [*Ahnung*]—in contrast with the presumptuous claim to absoluteness of understanding and the conceptual-universal. For moral life, however, the result is a demand for "self-determination" in the sense of the personal character that develops its own life on the basis of its own special nature. Individualizing instinct defines itself here entirely in the direction of personhood, of incomparable-unrepeatable "personality," and ultimately of moral genius. Hence for the moral life of people here, it is not universal concept or moral law (identical for all) that is the decisive instance, but guiding, exemplary personality! All moral laws are themselves already abstractions from the individual form of life of the religious or moral genius; it is genius that first supplies "rule" and universal element to laws. Thus at bottom the universal does not rank above the individual. All moral value shines forth in the heroic deed of the great, unrepeatable, and unique person who asserts his new values in the face of opposition from a crowd that hangs on the universal element of tradition (which itself in turn came into being once through an individual act)! In the governance of history it is always the individual element only, never the conceptual-universal, that sets the example and leads. It is through heroes that moral life is reborn time and again; it is from their individual ethos that every general norm of average "morality" derives. Just as the conceptual-universal can never be the ultimate norm for living individuality—the incomparable variety of figures in art, for example—but instead all generality here is but a fossilized abstraction of something exemplary-unique, the same holds true for morality. And every individual should believe in the inner originality of his own nature or his own moral genius and always act as though his vocation was to reach the highest goal of the original-personal element in him. This elaboration of the personal-individual element is a fundamental goal of all moral development. "The history of humanity is the history of progressive individuation through the advance of personal values in individuals." God himself—as the highest, eternally living person, absolutely distinct from all objects and creatures, not some universal law—is the only absolute norm, the highest standard of morality. And this norm can express itself and appear only in the individual instinct and genius of particular and always unique persons, in whom the rays of living being are refracted. God's will in revealing himself is the instinct of moral individuation.

With Jacobi all of this still lay in a very disorganized state and had not matured into systematic form. This philosophy of individuality still owed an explanation to the inescapable claims of the universal, nor did it clearly and distinctly define the relationship of particular-individual to the whole and to the harmony of beings. Fichte, on the other hand, in fact now fitted the new demands (although here, too, in no way completely reconciled with the others) into the framework of a great metaphysical system.

How one divine life splits up into the "system of egos or individuals," which (with their ideas of the world) make up the *real* world as a world of individuals is a question, the comprehension of which is really the principal

V. The Individual

task of *The Theory of Science*. Individuality is "the absolute locus of facticity." Our task is to "deduce" the system of egos and their worldview that we actually observe and to comprehend the sense and importance of that split of the One into the many, the manifold. Just as for Leibniz monads came into existence immediately, as it were, from creative acts of God's vision of the world, without intermediate stages and mediations by more real generalities, so now for Fichte also the *"actus individuationis primarius"* ["primary act of individuation"] was an immediate contraction and, as it were, self-distribution of the One life to individuals. This act of concentration or contraction is "absolute creation"; One life becomes here the generator of infinite and at the same time specific plurality. The "split" is first of all the condition of all consciousness and self-consciousness; only mediately, in the form and concentration of individual egos, can divine life become conscious of itself or possess real consciousness. But then above all: the split is the condition of all action and behavior, of the exercise and intensification of freedom! If life is supposed to act and present itself as practical power; if it is not to develop its power just in general but for something definite and defining, then it must transform itself creatively into the forms of the individual and steer itself toward individual activity. "There is no action except in individual form . . . only in individual form is life a practical principle."

A single freedom is thus split up into a world of free (hence also conscious) individuals. Although the worldview of all these individuals (traced in their interindividual agreement to universal harmony by Leibniz) is essentially the same in all areas, related to a single external nature, and all this because after all at bottom One ego is active in all individual egos; and although the external "view of nature" thus does not really proceed from the individual but from the One super- or pre-individual ego; nevertheless the "inner view" of moral consciousness—the sphere of willing, choosing, deciding—is essentially an affair of personal consciousness, an affair of the individual. "It is freedom that is divided up!" "Division" is only an imperfect image here because it is borrowed from the perspective of the spatial-external. Just as Christian doctrine sees God's image in the individual person above all, to the extent that the person's will, despite all creaturely dependence and finitude, has been created perfectly free, so does the One freedom exist *in its entirety* in every individual. "Every single one of these individuals divides the One determinate ego through its own proper form, and it necessarily bears this latter form; it is . . . free and independent." Individual self is created in the primordial act of individuation as "willing and free being" with the "power to create a will for itself and a law for its will." The true core of individuality lies in the will however. Freedom is always at the same time demand, challenge, positing of moral purpose! The rise of individuals signifies above all the appearance of special and thoroughly specific moral "decrees." The One free life first expresses itself fully "through its decrees to individuals." "Every individual comes into being through and for the sake of an ultimate moral purpose"; the individual is a contraction "to a point of unity of obligation and linkage of successive obligation from this point of unity." Ultimate purpose splits up, so to speak, "into several particular tasks . . . and every individual has his own specific task through his mere existence in the sphere of universal life. Each person should do what absolutely only he should do and can do . . . only he and absolutely no one else." Thus each individual has his own altogether special "vocation"; beyond physical individuality given us by nature (which, according to Fichte, it is our task to overcome and to annihilate in its isolated egoism) arises ideal spiritual individuality, which represents the special moral decree, the specific vocation of a particular being. "Natural instinct, specific moral task, and absolute freedom as the mediating link between the first two are the three components that constitute the essence of the individual." Indeed freedom also is not a given, finished reality, but something that constantly seeks to be elevated out of possibility into actuality, something that one is supposed to preserve, enliven and intensify through one's own personal decision. "The individual creates himself anew at every moment with absolute freedom; through his earlier existence (now deposited in the sphere of facts) he defines the execution of a purpose, to be sure, but not at all the purpose itself; on the contrary, he posits this himself with absolute freedom."

Every individual's life task is unique, therefore, and entirely distinct from that of all others. Everyone without exception has his own exclusive share in supersensible being, one that does not belong to absolutely any other individual apart from him therefore; and this share develops in him for all eternity, appearing as continued activity in a way that it can develop in absolutely no other." Divine life appears in each person in a different form, one unique to him alone." "No one can contrive for himself the special share he has in supersensible being, nor . . . can he make himself known to another person, inasmuch as another individual simply cannot know this share, but he has to find it immediately within himself instead." Here, then, every sort of talking "in general" fails! Every new individual being that comes to be (for they come to be in the creative flow of divine life and are not given once and for all, as Leibniz thought) represents the meaning of life anew, differently, and incomparably—hence only this individual being understands it completely and the meaning of life opens itself up only to his own living good will. "I . . . this determinate and expressly specific person, am here and have come into being so that in me God's eternal decree concerning the world should be conceived in time from another hitherto completely hidden aspect, should achieve clarity and should intervene in the world . . . ; only this one aspect of the divine decree that is linked with my personality is the truly existing element in me.'' Every single individual is ''something conceived and decreed in the eternal idea of the Godhead itself, something conceived expressly for himself and in relation to himself.'' Every being and action should therefore ''leave behind an imperishable and eternal result in the world of spirits, and the life of each particular individual a special result that belongs to and is demanded from him alone.'' Every individual is a unique ''thought of the Godhead.'' And just as according to Nicholas the goods in the rich world of God are distributed in so many ways that everyone is satisfied with himself even as he marvels at others, so that no creature desires to be another one but wishes only to preserve and perfect God's gift within itself, so now according to Fichte ''the striving to want to be something other than what one is destined to be, regardless of how noble and great this other might seem to be, is the summit of immorality!'' Virtue that is generated through perfect freedom, on the other hand, ''is the summit of originality; it is the immediate working of genius, that is, of that figure that has assumed divine being in our individuality.'' The moral law here does not, as in Kant, demand consistently universal lawfulness from the individual, but rather integrity of being within himself in his unique vocation.

And this uniqueness of every individual—which is not at all chance and whimsy but is grounded in the ''moral world order'' and the meaningful-lawful distribution of God's life—is what first brings the overarching unity of all existence to completion. Because every individual accordingly is and should be an altogether specific entity, it complements all others and along with them constitutes a ''closed system'' of selves as an eternal ''community of spirits.'' Individuals are not ''exactly so many separate worlds,'' but rather mutually complementary expressions of One divine life. This unity of life is ''an organic unity on the basis of commands given to all individuals; hence these commands cannot contradict each other or give rise to dispute. The command given to one is not given to another and vice-versa. . . . If each one now does only what he is commanded, then the freedom of all meshes together as one!'' The living world order does not allow any individual (i.e., any task) to appear twice in the same form; a person can simply never do or be exactly the same as another person! The formation of his freedom leads every person inescapably to his own innermost being. But the more deeply he enters into this innermost being, the more he at the same time precisely fulfills the meaning and plan of the whole and influences the whole toward the One realm of individuals. Only as members of a whole and in its ordering are individuals ''something in themselves''; only as such do they also have a common sphere of activity that expresses itself externally in their world-

view. "Particular being cannot live in itself and for itself but instead everything lives in the whole." "The individual exists only in the whole and has
meaning only in reference to this whole." "That is why whatever one person
does no other can do . . . because the one in fact does not act as one but as
representative of all." Thus Fichte's demand also leads to the view that "all
individuals without exception know the images of all others" and learn "to
comprehend them along with their own in organic unity" and that they do
not, say, steep themselves only in immediate consciousness of themselves
and development of their own freedom, but rather are supposed to "represent" their tasks and to be creative in deed and work—thus showing others
what is special to them and in turn receiving what others have to offer. In
actuality, even individual personal consciousness in fact arises only in immediate reciprocity with the Thou. What a person is and should do is something he experiences through the tacit challenge of others he encounters in
life; it is on the basis of what they have done and in turn what they have not
yet done, what they have begun or have left alone, that the occasion and
incentive to his own acts first surface for him. One cannot conceive a particular individual apart from the social totality of which he is a part. The existence of others restricts his freedom, to be sure; in their freedom he experiences boundaries to what he may or should do, but at the same time his
freedom thereby first acquires specific content; the special character and peculiar obligation of his own life first develop through this conceptual resistance!

Thus what the individual does in pursuit of his own path of freedom
influences the whole, and the more profound and free the development is,
the more it corresponds to his uniquely special character. In all its results
moral activity has an effect on the One life whose members we all are, on
the common worldview of everyone, on the so-called material world, and on
the stream of moral tasks. The "product of freedom" goes beyond individual
self-consciousness into world-consciousness and has consequences for the
entire spiritual world. It is a "treatment of the entire community from the
perspective of an individual point in it." This is the meaning we are to take
when Fichte always talks about the fact that every individual with his goals
and activity should vanish in the "race" [*Gattung*]. The race is the whole,
which itself essentially consists of and functions in individuals! "Agreement" of individuals means here not so much being-similar as rather com-
plementing that works harmoniously in oppositeness and reciprocity! Humanity means here "a varied race of men" ["*ein Menschengeschlecht von
Mehreren*"], a "community" extending through all temporal development,
but not a uniform type to which all individuals would have to assimilate
themselves! Hence [Fichte] also regards individuals as imperishable in their

V. The Individual

free activity. No individual who has actually come into being by dividing [the whole] and who pursues his vocation can ever perish; a man who has once fully matured into his own freedom and his own gifts continues to develop throughout all endless ages and through all successions of worlds. Individuals are not simply examples of "genus" nor merely ephemeral appearances of the One life, but rather are its essential unfolding. But [Fichte] demands "annihilation" of the individual only in the sense of overcoming the sensible-egoistical for the sake of the higher spiritual "vocation"—which is itself in fact a uniquely individual one.

The place that Fichte's philosophy of history (in the final phase of his philosophizing) conceded to great individuals or geniuses in the progress of the development of mankind is of a piece with this. "It has always been the law of the supersensible world that the latter has broken forth in history originally only among the few, the elect, indeed those destined by the counsel of the deity; the great majority of the rest was intended to be formed . . . first by the few. This is how it has always been and how it will be." "In the world of spirits every being is noble to the degree that it is rare; and it is ignobler to the degree that it is present in greater numbers. One can name individual people in world history who outweigh the value of millions of others. God expresses himself immediately through extremely few people; they are the ones in whom and for the sake of whom the world really exists. The many exist to serve them as their instruments."

Finally, if these last formulations of Fichte, so reminiscent of the individualism of Nietzsche in their bluntness, seem to deviate from his usual basic attitude and threaten to burst the system of meaning in the "world of individuals," it is nevertheless an essential part of Fichte's metaphysics of moral life that the "class" ["*Gattung*"] expresses itself and attains its own reality and fullness only in individuals who develop extremely rigorously, who surpass any sort of average type, and who ascend to the level of heroic genius. The human race is destined, in the context of absolute freedom in every individual, to make itself all that it should be; it should raise itself to pure spirituality across its entire range—through singular and individual forces. But to do that there is also need of (and the many individuals above all have need of) great individuals who are leaders; once there was need of seers and prophets, now and in the future there is need of great learned men and of those who lead with their knowledge. The entire meaning and value of life depends on individuals.

VI.
Understanding and Will

In conjunction with developments that occurred in the last three themes discussed, we have already hinted at change in the value-emphasis of the soul's functions. Although one could still interpret thought with reference to objectivity, greater emphasis on the life of will and soul brought the core of subjectivity to the foreground. Whereas thought adapted itself to demand for immobile and static being, the primordial life of the soul drove forward from its source in the will. And in knowledge and metaphysical evaluation of individuality also, reference to the position of will and the tasks of individual persons' wills had a decisive role to play; this contrasted with universality of knowledge, which seemed to lie beyond all individual subjects and was always oriented toward the existence of a superindividual soul. The issues broached on all sides were worked out in peculiar fashion in centuries-long discussions about cooperation and order of priority between intellect and will—discussions that problems about how one should live and what the purpose of life is urgently raised over and over again.

As has often been observed and discussed, the unconditional preponderance of insight and intellect over any energies of will and soul constituted a conspicuous fundamental feature of the Greek conception of life—at least to the extent that the decisions of philosophers expressed that conception. Socrates was the first to declare it with full rigor: Whatever the will aims at, it can only be something that perception and knowledge represent to it; the primary function of the theoretical faculty entirely determines its choice. Hence all willing and acting depends entirely and totally on knowing as the most original and profound element in the life of the mind. Good and bad

224

acts are the result of true and false insight. All willing in general, like all desire, is necessarily directed toward an object that presents itself as "good" (as having worth); thus all people in fact really will the good in some way—to the extent they have recognized it. People err only because they mistake or are ignorant of true greatest good, which can provide genuine and lasting satisfaction. Disturbance and distortion of insight through urgent desires is the decisive cause of evil. The heart of theory of life is therefore: Clarify insight and arouse insights! Virtue is insight into causes, it is knowledge; all wickedness stems from ignorance. Opposition between good and evil does not lie in the will itself; on the contrary, dualism between sensual-dull desire and spiritual-intellectual clarity produces it. Even the path of purification is not so much a battle of will against inner perversity and intractability as a struggle that first arises between sensual desire and incipient or clearly developed knowledge about a clear goal. Correct willing and acting follows of itself with objective necessity from correct knowledge. No one really errs willingly; instead, evil always arises only from lack of insight—and this then became a fundamental principle for Aristotle, too. Only the person who acts properly really knows what he is doing! It is the knowledge with which he sets out that totally determines the direction and form of his willing. Thus degrees of knowledge also distinguish degrees of appetitive life: desire follows from sensation; willing in general from opinion; rational-moral willing from clear insight into principles. The content presented in a known object attracts desire or will or sets it in motion; it is as a secondary consequence that [desire or will] then also moves the body. Original motive force is always knowledge or the object as presented in knowledge.

Pregiven insight determines acts of will. Hence if the problem of freedom of will surfaces, it is immediately turned into a question of freedom of judgment and knowledge. Freedom of choice, as discussed first by Plato and then especially by Aristotle, is essentially a mutual weighing of clarified ideas—whereby the will automatically abides by the outcome. Reflection, as a higher form of knowledge, is really the deciding moment in freedom of will. To decide is a theoretical decision, so to speak, a kind of inferring: it is a specific act of will only to a lesser degree. Activity is actually inference even in the case of animals, although the premises here do not stem from reason and are not deliberate: the desired value, the object represented, posit the major premise; possibility and need for acting posit the minor premise; and from them the conclusion follows: the action itself. Hence in the case of the human being, willing first presents itself entirely as an act of reflective understanding alone. Finally, with Plotinus even true "freedom" itself is not freedom of willing but freedom from willing: disinterested intuition and thought exalted above desires and actions of will and no longer discharging into them.

In general, then, as far as final valuation of understanding and will is concerned, one always exalted knowledge far above anything that will can offer. It is not as if, on the one hand, will and action depend completely on previous knowledge but, on the other hand, they use it as a basis for higher activity or new creation; no, will and action always remain something subsidiary and provisional in comparison with true knowledge. In the Greek thinkers' feeling for life there was always something unresolved and lacking in willing, indeed, as is quite obvious in the case of desiring. Acting is always merely a transition from lack to acquisition; but knowledge is calm, complete possession. The gods are exalted above activity and even above all virtues of will; they live in pure possession of knowledge. Knowledge is not only presupposition and positively determinant cause for everything else but also ultimate goal, highest good! Not only is virtue founded on knowledge, but the highest of all virtues are themselves virtues of knowledge, the dianoetic virtues that Aristotle's *Ethics* contrasts with merely ethical ones.

According to the metaphysics of the classical systems, it is only in knowledge that the soul is linked to ultimate, true reality. For Plato *logistikon* [reasoning faculty] is that element of the soul that preexists its earthly existence. All feeling is of a lower and secondary nature compared with it and borders on the bodily-sensate. Eros itself is but transition, after all, a child of poverty that finds the repose it seeks only in vision. Willing and acting are not the highest goal: what would there be to transform or to shape in a being whose entire reality lies in unchanging, pregiven forms and whose material influence is entirely without importance to those forms! All the meaning of life and all true, insightful striving is oriented essentially toward serene possession of spiritual knowledge of being; that possession also elevates the soul for the first time above change that smacks of the transitory in material agency—change which is after all always involved in all the soul's willing and desiring. The contemplative person is taken beyond the world of activity. Thus Aristotle's God is pure self-thinking, elevated above everything related to will and activity. He is thinking in the strict sense (not as later, e.g., Descartes understood *cogitatio* [reasoning] as consciousness in general or as Kant's "reason"-concept embraced not only the theoretical principle but also the practical principle, hence pure will itself); and if one also speaks of "energy," this does not refer in any way to anything caused by will or even to the mind's referring to self or actively applying itself! Aristotle's "active reason" is pure knowledge and contemplation. In contrast with all other functions of soul or spirit, knowledge and pure thought alone are completely independent of what lies outside them; they have their object and their purpose within themselves! Hence there is no higher happiness or profounder blessedness for a person than to possess the eternal forms in

226

purely rational knowing. Delight in contemplating far surpasses any delight in creating; true and perfect eudaemonism of the intellect soars above happiness of will.

This went even further in the late period of ancient thought. Plotinus's glorification of pure contemplation left little of value remaining for the voluntary element of human life. ''Political'' virtues stood on the lowest level of morality. Just as everything derives from the nous, so everything yearns and strives for pure intuition. Even irrational nature longs for knowledge and only for that. As for people, it is only their awareness of the impurity and opaqueness of the material world that must protect them from giving themselves over to that world in their behavior. [Plotinus] demanded that one avoid the external sphere of action and dedicate oneself inwardly to the eternal—and that dedication flows exclusively into knowledge. All action makes sense only as preparation for *theoria* [theory]! Happiness and perfect purity exist only in theory. At bottom the will itself is after all only an appendage of thinking, and acting is but a feeble substitute for *theorein* [theorizing], just ''weakness of reflection'' or a consequence unimportant in itself. All real life of the spirit is ultimately knowledge; the soul's essential core manifests itself only in passively contemplating eternal riches.

Christian feeling for existence presented a totally different ordering of spiritual functions. The intellectual optimism which said no one is bad by choice and no one is wicked except through ignorance of true good has no place here. The depth of the experience of sin points to the contrary: people are bad only through free choice! Matter and murky sensuality are not the real sources of evil; instead, it was the original will-act (itself not conditioned in turn by something else) of turning from God and his commandments. Sinful man acts even when he knows better; indeed, that is precisely what makes moral conflict most acute! That we see the good and would even like to do it—but do not will it with our whole soul and see it through with all our strength—is precisely what first tears open the great chasm between ''spirit'' and ''flesh'' in us; this is a completely different chasm than ancient dualism of matter and idea, of body and soul. Hence the will is now the fundamental principle of the moral world and of the spiritual world in general. For the first time freedom of will now becomes the really decisive, self-grounded (not essentially referred back to previous knowledge) principle. The good is not an object of knowing; philosophy of life does not proceed from represented and known ''highest good''; on the contrary, contents of moral consciousness appear as commands of God, as demands of the highest will on the will of each individual. That each person seeks goods and desires happiness is still in no way decisive for the path of virtue; instead, everything depends on whether he strives for his welfare in God and with God or apart

227

from God and against God! The important thing is to assimilate commands of God's will into one's own will, to affirm and fulfill them. Sin is disobedience, not ignorance. In this matter the only role knowledge plays is that of mediator between command and the will's reply to it. One assumes knowledge of commands; and when it is lacking, one looks even here for a cause in the will! In moral life everything is will and action. Conversion of will or turning the will to God is now the most profound and decisive event. And on that basis, action and intervention into reality are demanded. The important thing is to build up the kingdom of God, not simply to grasp an existing realm of ideas! The world in the ultimate sense of the eternal-real is no static, immobile existence in which there would be nothing to change, but rather a kingdom of living persons who are to fulfill the destiny of their souls and who always face an ultimate decision. Thus everyone must will and work in himself and do the same for others; each in his own place is responsible for developing the kingdom of God. Spiritual-moral life is edifying activity by spontaneous voluntary beings; it is not mere *theorein* [theorizing].

God himself is will and deed. Whereas the pure "energy" of Aristotle's noetic God spent itself in the act and being of self-contemplation, the Christian creator and preserver of all things is energy in the full sense of act and deed! His knowledge comes into play more as a means of guiding creatures to their will's goal (the purpose that divine will itself has set down for them) than as an end in itself. God does not abide in calm stillness of immobile contemplation; instead, he is always involved in busy activity—willing and guiding, commanding and revealing, loving and imparting his grace—in relation to the changing world of creatures. God is almighty and all-powerful lord of the world, not just its static model and distant self-composed idea. Thus in God and man alike, it is not *logistikon* [reasoning faculty] that is center and core; the spiritual person lives instead as a being of will, demonstrating his higher life in acts of spontaneous feeling, of attraction and aversion, not in receiving or carrying about static ideas inside him.

Godlike willing now no longer carries that dimension of dearth in it that always provided ancient philosophers a reason for degrading the life of will below the self-sufficiency of intellect. "Love" in the Christian feeling of life is something other than the Eros of Antiquity. It is not a child of poverty either, nor desire for something still unattained, but rather wells up exclusively out of inner power and fullness! God can love also; he is love itself, will oriented toward all good! Hence the fulfillment of all human existence is not participating in eternal forms through knowledge, but living in love that arises unceasingly from itself, in the purity of will and heart of God's kingdom. It is the locus of all true happiness. Union with God is union of

VI. Understanding and Will

will, not a question of his merely touching us by way of knowledge we receive.

And whereas the Greeks took it for granted that all willing builds first of all on previous knowledge, now the relationship is exactly reversed: only that person can see and understand God who is pure of heart and whose will carries him in the right direction! Faith, hope, and love do not align themselves with reference to preceding insight; on the contrary, they (which are the fruits of Godlike willing and loving, even will-related activity of the soul) are the basis for first opening one's eye toward the kingdom of truth. Complete and correct knowledge of the eternal-true grows only on the foundation of good will and as its consequence.

The doctrines of the Fathers of the Church of course expressed many of the new motives and expanded the view of inner life by putting new emphasis on will and freedom of will; but on essential points most of them stayed with the ancient priority; and again, those who did so most unconditionally were of course those trained in the Greek tradition. In this area as well Augustine was the first to bring about fundamental change.

The goal of *gnosis* [knowledge] dominated the early period, well beyond the actual Gnostics themselves. For all that, the idea still became prominent that the pure light of eternity and knowledge has been darkened for us by sin and life in the flesh—whereby [the Fathers] (especially from Tertullian on) more and more distinctly stressed that evil does not reside in matter and the physical itself, but in the act of the will that turns away from God. The importance of free will for man's entire life—for the image of God in him as well as for all danger of sin and guilt—was now illuminated by philosophical reflection with a sharpness of emphasis never known before. Correspondingly, the apologetes—from Justin Martyr and Theophilus [of Antioch] on—now viewed moral will and acting as purification from error and a path to pure insight. Overcoming sin, improving ourselves and recovering purity of heart are what first make us worthy to know God; it is not until we are thus like him that we can hope also to understand him. The pure heart alone is the stainless mirror that is able to grasp God; knowledge of God first blossoms forth from obeying and from freely turning oneself over to higher governance. Faith itself (this is something that Clement of Alexandria, linking up with Stoical motifs, stressed especially) is free anticipation and assent, spontaneous self-giving. Piety is the path to wisdom, not the other way around. We know God first and foremost in his will and his commands; and at bottom only that person grasps the will of God who, in fear of God and love of God, obeys and carries out in himself the divine will itself.

But the real goal in all this is still knowledge of God, or gnosis. And often it seems that this is the only essential issue! With Clement of Alex-

229

andria, nevertheless, the contrary motive is also at work. In the stages that his theory of life defines, faith leads to knowledge, to be sure, but this in turn leads to love, at which point the legacy and possession of the divine first properly begins. And an important point here is that—in contrast with development from faith to knowledge that transpires only in the individual soul—with love the real kingdom of God begins: community. (From the standpoint of the ancient overvaluation of purely cognitive life there was virtually no access to the intrinsic value of the community and its central spiritual importance: for in knowledge every individual exists alone with the ideas he sees, and he needs to know nothing about others who might see the same in similar fashion.) But this inheritance and participation in the fullness of God is then once again extended to vision in which the soul attains the ultimate bliss of contemplation. Thus for Origen in particular everything ends with the vision of God, which appears to leave behind it anything relating to will and *praxis* [action]. Admittedly, in his system the will advances with incomparably greater force into the foreground than it did in the Greek theories in which he was schooled. For him both generation of the Son and creation of the world arose from the Father's free act of will (which therefore exists before the Logos!); and what exists now has its genuine core in interaction between free created beings and God's uncreated will. The external world exists only as arena and occasion for free acts of will; the human being stands between angels and demons (who themselves have freely turned away from God) and now has a choice. What distinguishes him from everything merely natural and from all objective existence of things is precisely his freedom of will. But this freedom of will is then determined in the ancient sense after all; reason is what selects and weighs, and its judgment is the determining factor in deciding. Thus reason's insight is also the highest goal. It is not restoration and resolution in God's will or the blessedness of unity of will and community of will in love that stands at the end of all things for Origen, but rather contemplation of eternal ideas in God. Knowledge and vision of God is the only "action" that remains. Happiness is happiness of knowledge, not of will.

But still another important motif comes into play in these matters in speculations about the Trinity. Confrontation between understanding and will was also at work in the battle concerning God's "essence" or "energy." In the spirit of ancient valuation of understanding and static ideas and above all in the spirit of Plotinian emanation, Eunomius sought to understand God's energy (which is active in creating the world and in all acts of world-governance and grace) only as something secondary and situated below "essence." In opposition to that, Gregory of Nyssa and Gregory of Nazianzus emphasized the original unity of energy and essence and the fact that God's essence reveals itself and allows itself to be grasped in the effects of energy, of his will directed toward the world and expressing itself in reality. Especially in the case of man, it is the living influence of God's grace-giving will that matures him toward good and toward knowledge of salvation itself. Man's goodwill stands out from the living element in nature; but in that will God's will, hence God's very essence, resonates. The important thing for man is not a correct grasp of propositions of faith but piety of life and disposition. We come to know God in works of human piety: that is where spirit, the will of God, works in us. It is the power of the spiritual God that effects sanctification of will in us when we demonstrate that we are freely turned toward the good; the energy of the Holy Spirit governs the goodwill of each person. Only the will of God working within us can truly unite us with God, bring us closer to him, reveal his very self to us. Insofar as it is possible at all, we can know the hidden God, or God's essence, from the energy of God that he exercises within our inner selves. Only the pure can share in the pure one. Thus in the progression from essence of God (which one was still supposed to interpret in the ancient way) to God's energy and efficacy of will in the Son and the Holy Spirit and in the progression from eternal and hidden primordial principle to creation, world-governance and action of grace, the will moved more forcefully into the foreground than the doctrines of Antiquity would ever have allowed.

Augustine stood, then, on entirely new ground and found new expression for the changed attitude toward life. People have often described how [Augustine's] powerful will-life now used his own personal experiences as material for creating a new order and how in the process a psychology and metaphysics of will emerged that went far beyond the ancient world picture. The question of the origin of evil was now pushed to the very beginning and with it the new answer that emerged: it does not derive from special "substances" (as Augustine expressly said) or from lower levels of being or nonbeing, but from estrangement, alienation, perversity of will! Now, too, Augustine grasped in its full seriousness the idea of freedom of will that is ultimately subject to no external or even internal compulsion. Nothing is so completely within our power as our will; it is that element in life that belongs especially to us and derives purely from us. Insofar as we are independent individuals, we are precisely wills. Above all, everything that towers above the merely natural dimension of our existence and into our higher calling, everything that refers to our final supernatural destiny, stems from the will.

It depends on will, not on insight, whether a person is and becomes good or bad, whether he tears himself loose from true being or gives himself over to it. It is not sensual desire that is the first beginning of obfuscation of the true, luminous goal; on the contrary, when one becomes enmeshed and coerced by the habit of lust, this is itself a consequence of perverted will and of freely given surrender to lust! It is not different pieces of knowledge, confused and rational, that originally struggle for supremacy in the human soul; instead, the battle fought there is a battle between two wills, as it were: without being decisively swayed by any ideas, human will turns toward good or evil. The hallmark of the will is that it is entirely within our power and is prior to any coercion through ideas themselves. The Platonic–Aristotelian image of the scales proves to be unsatisfactory: even if there is perfect equilibrium between goal-positing representations, the will can still decide; even if two men were exactly identical in nature and in the contents of their consciousness at this moment, one of them can still choose differently than the other. Will stands above all particular motives; in principle it precedes all given content of the life of the soul. Hence the entire weight of responsibility rests on it. It is because it is essentially free with respect to anything given or emergent and because it determines itself completely by itself, that eternal reward and eternal punishment can result from its actions and consequences. It is not the fate of insight, but the free act of will that determines human weal or woe.

The will lies not only before and above everything that the soul otherwise contains and accomplishes but is also interwoven into all this; indeed, it is the really spiritually active element in it! For Augustine all ego-activity and spontaneity is at bottom the work of will: everything we may in the proper sense attribute and ascribe to ourselves. Activity of will is present in all powers of the soul: *voluntas est quippe in omnibus, immo omnes nihil aliud quam voluntates sunt* [indeed, will exists in all people, all people are always nothing other than wills]. The dynamic of will lives in our emotions, and even knowledge itself depends on will at every level. The ordering has reversed itself. To be sure, in an act of will we also always refer to something known and given, but our will's influence on directing and selecting knowledge is more decisive in developing our life. Just as gravity determines all movement and direction of bodies, so does will in its own way determine direction and changes of spiritual processes—not only with regard to good and evil but in general in all formation and further development of even the simplest knowledge. A person does not love what he has come to know correctly, but rather he tries to know whatever he inwardly inclines toward. It is through acts of will that the given first becomes cognitive property, a conscious asset of the soul. Thus spontaneity of will functions even in sense activity: of course external touching of sense organs by objects of perception precedes the will, but that touching does not also by itself produce real comprehension in the act of perception. On the contrary, something else is still needed: attention, which raises impressions into conscious ideas and even influences the direction and movement of organs. And even the reflexive relation between conscious image and its object is a result of inner spontaneity, that is, of will. Deception, for example, is false reference of an impression to an external object; it is ultimately the responsibility of the will that executes this reference. Perception would never deliberately refer to objective things unless this attentive and combining function of the will were operative throughout. Will brings it about that we actually receive images of objects into our inner being and that we grasp and interpret them in our souls beyond their purely physical influence.

The same holds true in very similar fashion for higher types and levels of knowledge. Activity of the will conditions all knowledge and first brings it into being. The activity of mind and its direction always essentially determine all inner elaborating of ideas, calling things to memory, and combining things imaginatively or logically. Judging and concluding, every process of knowledge in a specific direction presupposes striving and willing in this direction. Discovering grows out of searching, searching is a will-to-find. All progress from the unknown to the known always assumes that one is striving for a specific something for knowledge to possess.

Thus darkening of intellect, which prevents a person from seeing and understanding the good and the Godlike clearly, flows from perversion of will that has directed intellect toward the worthless and thereby also to merely sensual-physical knowledge; but lack of goodwill is not merely a consequence of faulty knowledge! The path of salvation must therefore begin with and rest on a change of will; revelation is given first to faith, which is an act of goodwill, an act of inner conversion and assent prior to all real understanding—it is affirmation without intellectual compulsion by what is already known. We must first will and love the eternal before we can possess it in knowledge. It is not metaphysical contemplation, new knowledge of truth, that allows redemption to mature and leads us to life and blessedness, but rather converted will. And this will is "inspired" by the Holy Spirit, the eternal divine principle of will and love that unites all beings with one another and with God in a community of the kingdom of God. As creator and especially also in his action through grace, God himself is all-powerful love and all-good will. Through love dedicated to God, human striving becomes one with and united to the providential will of God; one wins eternal life, for which every restless heart yearns, only in this way.

But even here in the case of Augustine, the ultimate crowning reaches back to the ancient ideal of pure vision after all! Augustine's eschatology reaches beyond happiness through union of will and fulfillment in eternal love toward quiet absorption in the eternally true and beautiful. This knowledge also (which is contemplation of the ideas in the mind of God) depends, to be sure, as a work of grace on the life of will and on how worthy of God the free person is; but it establishes itself on that basis as ultimate fulfillment and genuine happiness! The receptivity of the *visio beatissima* [most blessed vision] once again subordinates all spontaneity of the will's energy and union in love after all. On this ultimate question of life Plato and Plotinus, the Greeks generally, still have the last word for Augustine.

Of course Augustine's new ideas permeated Scholastic discussions everywhere and exercised their influence, but the ancient preponderance of intellect then asserted itself over and over again. Whether principles of Aristotelianism or those of Neoplatonism affected the systems more, in either case nous was preponderant and was itself the ultimate goal. No longer entirely in its ancient form and rigor, to be sure: will no longer disappeared from the concept of God, even though occasionally one placed it, as belonging to the person of the Holy Spirit, after wisdom and self-knowledge in the Father and the Son, and one seemed to link it only with creatures. Nor did people forget again Augustine's new idea of activity of will in knowledge itself. But none of that was sufficiently serious to establish the new valuation of will in the face of firmly established layers of systematic motives that people had once taken over from the ancient world.

Scotus Erigena, Anselm [of Canterbury], Abelard: all of them—after they had expressly recognized the independence and spontaneously active power of free will and the importance of faith (as assent conditioned by purity of will and heart)—nevertheless once again demanded pure intellectual vision (in which the energies of will are silent) for knowledge itself. To be sure, Anselm's *Credo ut intelligam* [I believe so that I might understand] put the basis for all ultimate knowledge in forces of the soul and moral will; but the goal itself is still pure knowledge. The blessed, he says, will have joys in proportion to how much they love; and they will love in proportion to how much they know. Happiness of love is merely an added consequence of highest knowledge. It is just that the path in that direction at its beginning calls for purification of heart and love of good, which alone enables one to ascend out of the world of mere sense knowledge to knowledge of higher things. Faith, with which a person must be satisfied in many ultimate questions, nevertheless means here only a preamble to knowledge. Augustinian echoes are also present in Abelard. But his interpretation of the motif of will and of freedom of will still follows entirely in the spirit of Antiquity; he describes even purpose or intention—which are supremely important in moral life, more than all execution and action—as a moment of intellect or inner reflection. Hence freedom of choice for the will means for him, as it did for Aristotle, deliberation or free formation of judgment in the sphere of reason. And people always sought for happiness in pure vision from the time

VI. Understanding and Will

of Scotus Erigena on, who in spite of his breaking free from Neoplatonism by setting divine power of will above the nous (which went so far as the thesis that God's will can actually make objects that violate the eternal causes and laws of nature), nevertheless sought the ultimate goal of life exclusively in contemplative union with God.

On this question only the Victorines truly looked for a new path, even beyond Augustine. As in so many other issues, they were the appointed developers of the new motif in the problem of the will also. Bernard of Clairvaux had already linked the stages of knowledge taken over from Neoplatonism to stages of the soul, of humility and love. Hugh of St. Victor now carried this forward. In all knowledge, will and understanding work together; and true knowledge always stems from the good life of the soul, as lucidity flows from love, blindness and error from sin. But previously given insight does not determine the will itself; will can do evil even in the face of better insight from reason. Will surpasses understanding; love is more fundamental than knowledge. Hence ultimate happiness also is pure willing elevated above everything earthly, boundless loving that transcends all the inadequacy of mere knowledge. In the hierarchy of heavenly beings (according to Kahl) the choir of angels closest to God is designated by love, and it is only the next one that is designated by wisdom. We experience inwardness of union, "enjoyment" of God, in love. But here, too, interpretation in the direction of knowledge is not lacking: this ultimate union of soul and will with God is in fact also ultimate vision or contemplation.

Then ancient valuation of understanding celebrated a complete victory once again: in the High Scholaticism of Albert and Thomas, determined once again in entirely new fashion by Aristotle. Whereas Albert the Great preferred to mediate in this area, Thomas set himself squarely on the foundation of Aristotelianism. The question that had now become a major problem and center of interest in Scholastic discussions—Which power of the soul ranked higher, understanding or will?—Thomas decided unequivocally and definitely in favor of understanding. For him only understanding really ranks as a principle of higher spiritual life that rises above the merely temporal! Will is only a special kind of natural desire, always related to material realities of our existence with their spatiotemporal particularity. It is only intellect that can first impress the spiritual character of free and higher striving and commitment on will itself. Will is intellectual appetite! The notion of an independent willing—already determined spiritually within itself—recedes entirely, even though according to Thomas God not only knows himself in the Son but also wills himself in the Holy Spirit and presents himself as an end that desires itself! For Thomas, too, the decisively determinant element even for all life of will is the knowledge it presupposes. Thus he puts the moment of comprehension of good and evil inherent in affect, as a feature of knowledge, in the foreground; but, following the ancients, he essentially crams freedom of will into deliberative reflection, into free judgment of reason. Intellect is the true *ratio libertatis* [cause of liberty]; and nothing essential is changed by the insight that arises out of the new attitude about life, that the act of choice itself as such is not something judgmental but something voluntary, an appetitive potency.

Intellect determines will; we can will only something that we first see as attainable and worth striving for, something that presents itself to us as good. Hence will is spontaneous power only in a restricted sense; ultimately intellect, the *bonum intellectum* [known good], is what moves it. "Intellect is what first and through itself moves the will." Thus the most important thing is to arouse proper insight that can provide the will with the true goal. Intellect impresses the final end on all willing (divine as well as human), and a person even selects intermediate links differently, depending on how elevated his insight is! The value-priority of intellect is thereby already given. *Intellectus altior et prior voluntate* [intellect is higher than and prior to will]. Intellect moves will with respect to final cause (*respectu finis*); the *objectum intellectum* [known object] is the true *causa movens volitionis* [motive cause of volition]. Conversely, will also ([Thomas] now acknowledges this in the new tradition) exercises influence on intellect; but this is determination only by way of efficient cause (*per modum agentis*) and has only intermediate value; the end is always more valuable than the agent. Understanding therefore moves will in higher measure and sense than, conversely, will moves intellect; intellect is the higher mover. Thus in itself the true also ranks higher than the good, which is something good only by participating in the true. And whereas in the case of knowledge the absolute can be a direct and self-given, present object for intellect, it is always merely an intermediate object for will: will must let itself receive intellect's offering. The end of all spiritual efforts—as spiritual, that is, "reasonable"—is therefore originally possession through knowing. Only understanding also actually presents the highest being as pure supertemporal good.

Hence there is also no doubt about the fact that ultimate happiness lies beyond the sphere of will! Of course Thomas does recognize the determinative power of will in the act of faith (as assent without necessitating proof); but faith is in fact a stage we are to overcome. Likewise, the vision of God is supposed to experience "completion" through the love of God necessarily consequent upon it, inasmuch as a person can then find complete repose through his will also in what he possesses through understanding. But these formulations express more of a conciliatory tendency than a genuine systematic attitude. The latter is rather aimed purely at knowing. According to

VI. Understanding and Will

Thomas, happiness "does not rest on an act of will"; will cannot be our end because in itself it always strives for the thing willed, and every being finds peace only in its end. Only intellect offers the final end and the happiness of perfect possession. *Ultima hominis salus est ut secundum intellectivam partem perficiatur contemplatione virtutis purae* [Man's ultimate salvation is that he be perfected with respect to his intellective part by the contemplation of pure virtue]. Wisdom takes us beyond love (this habit of the will); in contemplation the very presence of the thing thought of exists in human understanding, identity of thought with its object, ultimate happiness of innermost union. Even in earthly life the highest happiness one can attain is that of speculative knowledge in the science of ultimate causes and highest ends; the dianoetic goes beyond the practical here also. Happiness in the beyond lies completely in pure contemplation of truth, in the *visio divinae essentiae* [vision of divine essence], in which even the "theological virtues" (still permeated with will) are transcended by a wide margin.

The sharp contradiction which the Aristotelianism of Thomas Aquinas evoked in this question as well as in others then led also to a new valuation of will which went beyond what Augustine and what the Victorines, following his lead, taught. The Franciscans—whose religious quest, from the founder of their order on, always set out to open up the living soul's sources of faith and of love anew in opposition to ossifying dogmatism and intellectual knowledge—were the chief carriers of the new tendencies in this sphere also. Even in the older Franciscan school there was a spirit of mystical-affective life, in which the Victorines strove to rise above the sphere of theory and its delights. Bonaventure inclined clearly enough toward valuating will higher than understanding. For Bonaventure, the higher one ascends in the scale of spiritual life—as the Middle Ages, building on Neoplatonism, taught that scale—the more preponderance of the knowledge-moment vanishes in favor of powers of soul and of faith. He saw theology as *scientia affectiva* [affective science]: content and end lie beyond the sphere of mere knowledge. And no matter how many elements of pure understanding entered into his concept of happiness, no matter how much even his going beyond understanding (which in its highest perfection itself cannot grasp God fully) contained a tendency toward another, higher form of knowing, he nevertheless regarded will (will in its highest form, as love) as the decisive force in uniting with God and in ecstatic rapture as the force that elevates man above himself. In his concept of synteresis, however, Bonaventure strove for a special spiritual lawfulness of the will: what guides feeling and will in their striving for good is not some sort of knowledge introduced about the good but an immanent power. Just as intellect has its own light to guide it, so does the life of will have its inner stimulus to good. Reference to value in willing goes parallel with power of judgment and inclination toward truth in thought. Orientation toward the good is not a habit of intellect that intellect then impresses on will; on the contrary, it is an original, autonomous power of the life of will itself.

What began here was fulfilled in the work of Duns Scotus. A great new phase in understanding the life of the soul began with him; what people were able to teach in subsequent centuries in treatises and essays of the Renaissance and beyond about emotions and the power of the will stands under the influence of the great master of the "period of decay."

The first opponents of Thomism prepared his way. In Henry of Ghent Augustine's idea of will achieved new force and extension. Now (in contrast with the ancient Aristotelian doctrine of active intellect) [Henry] stressed the essential moment of passivity in all knowledge purely as such so that knowledge could be spontaneously active only with respect to something previously given, something deriving from the object. True spontaneity really resides in the will. The will's power is absolutely *simpliciter activa* [simply active]; here starting point and ending point of motion are not the object but the willing person himself. And so only the active will is really free; not the understanding, which after all ultimately depends on the object. Understanding is forced to recognize what exists and is presented to it. But will remains free in its decision, even with respect to the givenness of the good. Thus judgment of understanding does not absolutely determine will; knowledge provides it merely with possible directions for its activity and makes choice possible for it; but it does not firmly impose any one of these directions on it. Will always takes its decisive impulse from itself! Understanding is not the cause, either total or partial, of movements of will (which, indeed, apart from being a sensitive appetite, is itself a spiritual activity of soul), but a *conditio sine qua non* that itself, in its own turn, can be directed by will! Like a servant, intellect carries a torch in front of will: without it the master could not see and walk; but the master (the will) determines the choice of paths and directions that are to be illuminated and scouted. Free will, as *primus motor in regno animae* [prime mover in the realm of soul], can sooner be the cause of delusion and error, of faulty research and illumination, than knowledge and ignorance can be the cause of good or bad will. Thus all virtue is a habit of will, but not originally determined by the relationship of knowledge to passions. And what leads up (through virtuous being and living) to perfect union with God can once again not be knowledge. Knowledge merely picks up its object, mediated by an image, from the outside; but will penetrates the beloved object and is transformed, as far as this is possible, into that object. Union is deeper and more inward here! And so enjoyment in knowledge is always tied to being and action provided from the outside;

238

but enjoyment of will lies in transition toward and even entry into the object. We experience God more immediately, more perfectly, and more happily in willing, therefore, than we do in understanding. The true is after all just a specific good, but the goal of will is absolute good. Hence the object of will is greater than the object of intellect. "We always grasp God more through love than through knowledge, because in fact the will is more closely united to its goal through love than the intellect is through knowledge."

William of Ware and Richard of Middletown (still in the old Franciscan school) struggled toward similar ideas. As the latter said, will is the noblest power in the soul because it is truly free and spontaneous. No knowledge can really bind it; knowledge can create a disposition, but not dependence. The image of the ancillary torch was decisive in Richard's view also. The power to change the soul, to turn inwardly into oneself and also to force another is after all an original property of will, which is purely self-dependent activity, and in fact is activity first and foremost. It is will that chooses paths and walks them—hence the final end of all life is a goal of will, not of intellect; goodness ranks higher than truth! Not only is faith the ground of all higher knowledge, but love transcends knowledge. Since God is pure act or living activity, so happiness cannot consist only in the static condition of mere present-possession but must itself bear the character of action. A human being becomes most like his creator through a "good act" of will, ultimately of love. More than in knowledge of God (as truth), happiness lies in Godlike acts of will whose goal and content are absolute goodness.

All of this finds its strongest expression and its broadest development in Duns Scotus. His doctrine of absolute primacy of will—his system of will, one could actually say—attained, within the Scholastic tradition, the most extremely opposite position to the intellectualism of Antiquity. The Christian world's attitude toward life thus achieved its own proper conceptual expression as purely and independently as never before, not even with Augustine. The break from Plotinus and all Platonism was just as completely and clearly accomplished in this area as that from Aristotle, whose subsequent influence in Thomism Duns Scotus particularly opposed.

Duns refuted in detail the view that previously given knowledge of the object of willing determines the act of will—whereby the known object then really becomes the cause of willing, whereas the latter itself only partially conditions activity. Will is in no way originally and necessarily oriented to the general end of "the good," which we are then merely supposed to discover rightly. No matter how much, in the case of particular influence on actual objects, knowledge of them is a *causa sine qua non* [indispensable cause] of activity, nevertheless knowledge in no way determines the operative principle, the will. On the contrary, will determines itself entirely by itself

239

and is the *movens per se* [mover in itself] in every activity, the unique and total cause of its volitions, the *causa sufficiens omnis actus sui* [sufficient cause of every one of its acts]. Further question about the cause of will is meaningless: here we have something absolutely ultimate. Active-free willing (which he sharply distinguishes from passive stimulations of the appetitive faculty) is essentially free, even with respect to the determining causes of understanding. Decision is always a pure act of will; it is not actualized because knowledge forced it! Nor does the state of knowledge in any way firmly determine what the act of will decides. In fact the will always possesses the *possibiltas ad utrumque* [possibility (of choosing) either thing]; it can decide this way or that, turn to good or to evil, to something it recognizes as the higher thing or to what it knows is lesser! Indeed, the will can not only withstand enticements of the senses but likewise goods presented by understanding; will often decides against better insight of reason. Regardless how much a natural inclination toward good and toward happiness exists, will nevertheless always remains free to reject highest goods, even when it recognizes them as such. With respect to one and the same object and without any change in knowledge taking place in the matter, the free power of the will can behave positively in one instance and negatively in another. The will as such is always *causa indeterminata ad alterutrum oppositorum* [an indeterminate cause with respect to either of (two) opposites]. Immediate internal evidence demonstrates that such a will, as the principle of "contingency" and even as an itself-undetermined total cause of contingent behavior, exists; but it is at the same time also a necessary assumption of our consciousness of moral responsibility. We do not rebuke the understanding in moral judgment, but rather the will; we do not feel that the former is the cause of sinful behavior; no, we attribute decision to the latter alone and in itself. If the known object or if knowledge of the object determined the act of will, then this structural necessity would be decisive: the natural process of the influence of object on subject would always univocally determine the will; thus it would never be possible for contradictory possibilities for decision to exist, which, however, constitute the foundation for every concept of responsibility.

Certainly there is no such thing as totally blind willing that would not have to link up with object-consciousness at all. But it is precisely here that the figure of intellect as torchbearer for will applies. Will is the real "mover in the entire realm of soul." Intellect is only the *causa subserviens voluntati* [cause serving the will], not the determinative ground for action by the will; on the contrary, it is "will that commands intellect and is the higher cause with respect to its act." This becomes very clear in the distinction between two phases in all knowledge about the object of will: between *cogitatio prima*

VI. Understanding and Will

[first reasoning] and *cogitatio secunda* [second reasoning] there exists, as the actually decisive element even for the status of knowledge itself—activity of will! "First thinking" actually precedes willing and first provides an occasion and a rough selection. Willing has no influence here. But for the very reason that only a naturally given and involuntary connection is at issue here, there can also be no question of sin and accountability at this point. Sense impression or sudden idea as such still stands prior to good and evil. But now the issue is what attitude the will adopts with regard to what is given it and is stimulating it (but in no way determining it): whether it now reacts with devotion or repulsion, with love or hate! And this special attitude it adopts then becomes decisive also for the known object itself and for its disposition in the phase of "second thinking"! For, depending on the will's command, will now actually takes hold of the object indeliberately offered to it, looks it over, and reflects on it, or it neglects it and exchanges it for something else. In the process this is the totally decisive point: that just as with the sense organ of the eye, so also in every look by the soul, there is not merely a single self-isolating object presented, but there is always also—accumulated around the actually fixed object in a wide circle—something indistinctly grasped that is present as well. And just as the eye that involuntarily catches a glimpse of a flower can then deliberately and selectively turn its attention to something from among the many things surrounding it (something already given in the first look, though less specifically), so it is in general the act of will that, following "first thinking," then determines on its part to apply the cognitive organ to individual objects in the vicinity of its momentary horizon. Thus "second thinking," which then cooperates so significantly in the voluntary choice and the reflection that result in action, is itself already the result of voluntary choice; the original tendency of will already essentially determines the lights and accents of knowledge here. Will can take something that is scarcely cosensed and raise it to something that irradiates everything; it can also take something that is absolutely pressing on it with all clarity and by casting a glance toward something else remove it so far away that it finally disappears from consciousness altogether. Merit and guilt already exist in the very direction of reflection, in knowledge-seeking; knowledge of "second thinking" underlies attribution or moral judgment. Thus knowledge does not determine the good and evil of will; on the contrary, the latter is the basis for developing knowledge. Understanding does not determine will but the reverse: *voluntas imperat intellectui* [will commands intellect]. Sinful direction of will is the cause of delusion; pride, for example, leads to misreading values foreign to us, affects our aversion from good that we could know. And vice versa as well: it is good will that

241

opens up the soul to knowledge of attainable true goods and of paths that lead to them.

Duns Scotus continually emphasized that knowledge itself falls under action [*praxis*] in a certain sense, that in its formation and cultivation it always bears the work of will within it. His view is not that the act of knowledge itself is volitional or that its cause is in the will; nor should one take primacy of will to mean that knowledge absolutely depends on it or is only executing its intention! He maintains the special character of the cognitive relationship between subject and object throughout. But the direction in which knowledge develops or focuses its attention simply does depend essentially on will. Of the two powers of the soul—each of them fully independent and original—it is in fact will that is the dominant and higher power. Insofar as *cogitatio* [reasoning] occurs at all (which is not itself subject to will: will has no immediate effect on knowledge), mediate or indirect (but nevertheless most important for any development of insight and for all progress toward further and broader knowledge) influence of the will comes into play at once. Through such influence on knowledge, my knowledge first really becomes *my own* knowledge, in my power; it is not merely the impact of given objects on my soul. No matter how essential the subject's receptivity is for the act of knowing, nevertheless self-activity must also always accompany it; indeed impressions are activities of the self, occasioned by the stimulus of the object. And the further one ascends the levels of knowledge, the more important this moment of spontaneous activity becomes; with memory a modifying and even generative power of the soul already comes into play, and at the same time the influence of will's direction also becomes manifest. Acts of will permeate all our higher cognitive life—when we fully assent to, or dissent from, acts of thinking and researching, judging, and concluding.

Hence, Duns could not consider knowledge the purpose of our life. Truth is one of life's goods, but it is not the good itself, the ultimate end. There is a passive and an active element in man, just as there is in every living thing. Now, the active element—the living-busy element—is always the higher. But knowledge is still essentially passive. It functions with the necessity of a natural power: here it is object that totally determines subject. All knowledge is objectively conditioned and depends on external objects. Purely in itself, intellect must, whether it "wants to" or not, give in to the stronger idea and the compulsion of objective facts. *Intellectus cadit sub natura* [intellect falls under nature]: knowing is still a kind of natural process in which a thing forces itself "with natural necessity" on another, the subject. According to Duns Scotus the human being first elevates itself above nature through will (which *nunquam necessitur ab objecto* [is never necessitated by the object] but always remains free with respect to objects). The assessment

242

VI. Understanding and Will

of Antiquity is now entirely reversed. Then will (scarcely distinguished from desire in itself) was considered a mere natural force and movement in nature; in addition, it also entailed the shortcoming of having to strive outside of itself toward what it desired, toward an object not yet attained or made into a possession. Intellect on the other hand came "from the outside," from a higher region into the otherwise naturally determined soul; it is thus at rest in itself, in contemplating an object that is present and self-given. Now it is the other way around: intellect naturally depends on something externally given; it is harnessed into the system of nature and always refers to another; it is thus never self-sufficient. Will, on the other hand, rises above the system of nature and necessity: it is active and free; it is the core of pure subjectivity and of its special life; it is also the center especially of the independent-spontaneous individual, the counterpart to divine spontaneity and freedom! Will is not oriented toward the other and the external, nor is it determined by them. Whereas in knowledge objects influence the subject, in will, for its part, subjectivity gains authority and influence over objects. In goodwill, however, and its highest form, the love of God, will then really rests purely in itself and desires nothing other than to live in a Godlike manner. The principle of contingency ranks higher than that of necessity. God has placed human beings above and beyond nature as free subjects who function contingently and purely spontaneously. And so, not only did [Scotus] reject the ancient opinion that held that will first attained a spiritual dimension through understanding, and not only did he constantly stress that will itself already bears "intellectual" character within it; but now matters occasionally appear in reverse order (with special reference to Aristotle): higher capacity and elevation of self above nature arise, even for intellect, only through union with the free will that guides it and steers it to ultimate ends. Theology is practical science: here knowledge is a means for the goal of purity of will, not an end in itself for the reflective faculty. The important thing is to create ultimate willing that is self-sufficient; knowledge of highest things also serves this end. The purpose of existence and the best that man can attain is not knowledge but the activity of good and pure will, ultimately the inexhaustible life of supernatural love; but these goods arise solely out of self-determination of the will.

Thus one now also no longer sought for happiness in the vision of God and of divine ideas. The philosopher's highest happiness might lie there, says Duns Scotus, but the philosopher as such is still attached to the world. Faith leads man higher than knowledge does; and faith is commitment of will. The life of the Christian and the instruction of practical theology take us beyond the happiness of dianoetic virtues. We experience happiness through will. It is not concept or intuitive knowledge that effects real union with God, as

243

Thomas thought; no, it lies above all in willing and in love: love lays hold of the highest good within itself and completely. This is the advantage the good has over the true: it imparts something of its own essence to one who desires it purely! The true does not do this. Thus whereas the ancients and with them Thomas sought full possession, self-givenness of the eternal, in knowledge, Duns now emphasized the distance-dimension that always still remains in knowledge; he held that only the willing person who wills and loves the good is truly united for the first time with the one willed! We become united with God in the most immediate and most perfect way through love; regardless of how greatly knowledge is also elevated to highest being in the final perfection of the soul, it is love that effects real union with and enjoyment of God.

And now we draw the consequences of this for God's essence also. Hitherto people had usually sought for essential causes of the world and all existence in God's understanding and his eternal ideas. Even though apart from that there was some appreciation for the dimension of will in the act of creation and in God's work of conservation and grace, nevertheless the real force of law remained—entirely in the spirit of Antiquity—with understanding and its contents. As Thomas himself taught, God's will is absolutely bound by the *regula sapientiae* [rule of wisdom], the law of intellect. He creates what understanding recognizes as good; for God as well as for men it is insight that determines the act of will. Essential relationships of ideas (as ideas in the mind of God) still ultimately determine the structure of reality here also. Duns Scotus denied such dependence of God's will on God's understanding, of the contingent on the necessary. God's will is the first cause of all existence. To be sure, his choice is bound to possibilities allowed by logical laws: God cannot will something that is self-contradictory. But within these bounds of possibility God's will is entirely untrammeled and is itself the only cause of his willing. The order of nature is good because God has willed it; but God did not create it because his understanding presented it to him as good in itself! Hence divine will—alone and by itself—is also the ultimate ground of moral world order (with the exception only of natural law expressed in the first two commandments of the Decalogue) and of the order of salvation. Everything other than God is good only because God has willed it; God did not will it because it was already good in itself and he recognized it as good. Not the rule of wisdom but God's will itself is the "first rule." Goodness is not in fact the object of thinking but the original (allowing no further grounding) form of will. Will itself is the unique and ultimate "cause" of the good. To ask questions beyond it would be senseless.

The influence of this theory of will reached far beyond the late period of Scholasticism, although it is not easy to trace the connecting threads. The

VI. Understanding and Will

history of Scotism in the Renaissance and Modern Period still remains to be written. It is well known how William of Occam, following his master, emphasized independence and superiority of will over understanding with great bluntness and magnified the idea of the legislative power of God's will to the point of paradox. He put such heavy stress on freedom of God's decisions that the great new meaning of special lawfulness of volition, not derived from understanding, was often hidden behind an image of absolute arbitrariness. Even with respect to human action he cut off the will from thinking in a manner harsher than Duns Scotus intended. Skepticism against all natural knowledge—especially against natural morality and natural theology—that arose in connection with nominalistic theory of knowledge, because of the extreme bitterness of its attitude did severe damage to the new idea of will. The aim of arriving at a "natural system" of mind and values—which was so essential to the incipient Modern Period—had to turn aside again from Occamism in spite of common opposition to the realism of Scholastic concepts, and this also caused the thread of primacy of will to be broken again during long stretches of later development.

The great attack by Scotism also did not finish off the ancient tradition of intellectualism at all. In addition to [Scotism's] continuation (through Durandus de Saint Pourçain especially and Petrus Aureoli, and then through Pierre d'Ailly and the Occamists in general) and the renewed spread of Thomism, there were also efforts at mediation (e.g., by Gerson). Many thinkers wavered undecidedly between the two conceptions of spiritual life. The hesitation was most noteworthy in Meister Eckehart. In innumerable passages he expressed his views on the issue of the time: which power of the soul was nobler and which one led to blessedness; but he made as many statements in favor of will as he did in favor of understanding. If, on the one hand, understanding related more purely to simple "being," whereas will seemed to grasp God only in the "garment" of goodness, so that reason was supposed to possess the real key to the essence [*Grund*] of God and only then could it express what it had grasped to "its playmate the will," we read just as often, on the other hand (and people usually overlook this in descriptions of Eckehart's doctrine): Only will—as "husband of the soul," not reason as wife of the soul, the receptive "contemplater" who is never as free as will—can produce the final "change" [*"Überschlag"*] of soul in its union with God. "The highest power is love; it guides the soul with its knowledge and all its powers to God." "If the soul, in receiving God, uses its inwardness in memory and its reason in intuition, so love brings the soul into the heart of God." "The other power is will. It is nobler and by nature throws itself into the mystery [*Unwissenheit*] that is God." Even in passages in which he is trying to mediate, the transition to ultimate union itself is will-like in nature: "The

245

powers have a simple nature in common, which effects a change [*Über-schlag*] in the will.''

Like Eckehart, Nicholas of Cusa also vacillated between primacy of will and primacy of understanding. And so did the entire chain of conceptual structures that developed out of German mysticism. As often as the motif of will recedes in it, it nevertheless always reasserts itself. Sebastian Franck, for example, was altogether emphatic in viewing man as essentially a being of will; Agrippa of Nettesheim sought for the bond of the human with everything higher, and ultimately with God, exclusively in holiness of will, in purely voluntary acts of faith and of works; Jacob Böhme tried to grasp the world-process as proceeding from the force of God's will in giving birth to himself and ''as eternally desirous will'' [*als den "begehrenden Willen der Ewigkeit"*]. Nicholas Taurellus, whom Leibniz held in such esteem, emphatically argued on the basis of his position on will against Aristotle: Human happiness does not consist in knowing the eternal, but in loving and willing God; God's own happiness, after all, does not consist in self-absorbed knowledge but in self-generating will. In the philosophy of the Renaissance as well we encounter traces of will on all sides: Augustinian and Scotist motives reverberated, for example, in Pico or Pompanazzi or Lorenzo Valla; and Aristotle was consistently the enemy.

But interest in the matter now abated more and more. Problems about structure of the world and system of nature determined philosophical directions for centuries to come. And if people did reflect on the subject and his powers of soul, the entire focus of interest was on the knowing subject. Life of the soul—willing and loving—faded away altogether. Other influences of the period helped to push cognitive reason entirely into the foreground and to evoke the age of Enlightenment, which wanted nothing more to do with will's arbitrary meaning. Once again ancient intellectualism advanced victoriously at many points during this period, most emphatically in the case of the thinker whom we have seen several times working in opposition to the new metaphysical tendencies: Spinoza. Once again he regarded will merely as desiring, something stemming from deficiency and searching for fulfillment. Spinoza tried to mediate in the old controversy about primacy. But when he declared that understanding and will were one and the same thing, he was in fact adopting his image of this identity (the image of the mental) essentially from the standpoint of knowledge and its ''ideas.'' In opposition to Descartes's stress on the preponderance of essentially infinite free will over the finite limits of any created understanding, he labored to demonstrate that, on the contrary, knowledge determined every act of will; and whereas Descartes (to whom we shall come shortly) tried to discover a volitional moment of affirmation and denial in judgment itself, Spinoza then regarded this merely as an opportunity to define will in general as affirmation of ideas—affirmation which was ultimately "involved" in [ideas] themselves! The act of knowledge already includes the act of will within itself; and just as consequences of ideas and idea-relationships are in the conclusion, so also willing is only a necessary self-linking of ideas; there is no free, original will. "In the mind there is no willing, no affirming and denying, except insofar as what the idea already contains as idea." Thus the spiritual life of divine substance is also not active willing then, nor purposeful acting, but rather unfolding in eternally necessary sequences of ideas; the spiritual attribute of deity is pure *cogitatio* in the strict sense. But our life is good and virtuous insofar as insight determines it: this is what distinguishes higher man from the merely desirous creature. Reason and clear, distinct knowledge should condition—and necessarily determine—our striving. But this is once again our ultimate goal, it is the highest good! "Spirit's highest good is knowledge of God, and spirit's highest virtue is to know God." All of this takes us back entirely to the ancient valuation; and although *Amor Dei intellectualis* [intellectual love of God] is its final word, nevertheless [Spinoza's] definition of love in general and his description of God's love in particular leaves no doubt that this affect of the soul is nothing but a consequence and flowering of knowledge itself; that is why it is called *intellectual* love and its happiness is the happiness of vision alone.

Yet even in these centuries of rationalism and Enlightenment the motif of will by no means disappeared. It still resounded most strongly in Descartes—and all the more perceptibly in this case because one can never properly succeed in really assimilating it into a rationalistic framework. Descartes himself vacillated to and fro on this question; completely opposite declarations face each other unreconciled, and one looks in vain for a definitive formulation of his conviction. But the issue on which he stands altogether solidly and univocally in the camp of Scotists, even of Occamists (moreover, as far as we can see, without being aware of the historical context) is the question about the relationship of divine will to "eternal truths." Although the *Meditations* (in using the ontological proof for God's existence) conceives of God himself as an essence united to his existence by rational necessity, nevertheless the real core of divine being for Descartes absolutely does not lie in the permanently given essence of a structure that is intrinsically determined and therefore also rationally comprehensible in principle—but rather in creative activity that is prior to all knowledge and all cognitive necessity! In the face of all reproaches from respondents he insists on this point: God is *causa sui* [cause of himself] in a positive sense; he is in relation to himself what efficient cause is in relation to its effect.

What champions of will had described as its profoundest characteristic is said here of God in general. Thus for Descartes perfection of divine being rests above all on absolute freedom of almighty will. Infinity of God is, above all, unlimited power to will and to create. He expressly designates this infinity as indetermination, as absolute indifference of will. In the light of that, Descartes could view it only as diminution of God's perfection—indeed it seems to him virtually blasphemy—to think of God's activity as bound by eternal laws, by ideas and truths whose structure and validity would no longer be subject to his will! That would mean, he says, that fate and inexorable necessity would hover over God, just as they did over Jupiter or Saturn in Antiquity! And Descartes is not at all satisfied if one shifts eternal ideas into God's understanding and eternal essence itself; for him the crucial thing is precisely the highest predicate of absolutely unlimited and indeterminate universal power, primordial power of creative will that transcends and precedes all determinations and laws. He absolutely refuses to think of essences of objects as emanating from God like rays of sunlight. Instead, for him the only image that is accurate here is that of a king issuing laws! Absolutely free primordial will that itself first creates and lays down laws and necessities has stepped in here in place of eternal nous and its immanent necessities. Not only are existences created by God and dependent on his absolute will, but even essences themselves—mathematical and logical and all eternal laws! "For God, order, law, and ground of the good and true" do not precede will's decision; it is will that first establishes them. Divine will is their "active and total cause," just as truly as it is for objects. Even "grounds" therefore have a further cause (whereas with Spinoza there is a tendency to reduce all causes and even the *causa sui* to consequences of eternal ideas and essences). *"Je sais que Dieu est auteur de toutes choses, et que ces vérités sont quelque chose, et par conséquent qu'il en est auteur!"* ["I know that God is author of all things, and that these truths are something, and that therefore he is their author!"] If we are accustomed to use the word create [*creare*] only with respect to existing things, nevertheless the objective fact remains that God as *efficiens et totalis causa* [efficient and total cause] of these truths *disposuit et fecit* [has disposed and made] them! Descartes does not shrink from drawing this conclusion even for the principle of contradiction. For us human beings, at any rate, who are subject to laws ordained by God, something self-contradictory is absolutely impossible; hence it seems to us that even God could not create it. But just as every *ratio boni* [essence of good] depends totally on God's law, so does *ratio veri* [essence of truth]; I can never say that God could not bring it about that two and one do not make three but only that God has so ordered my understanding that such a thing is unthinkable for it. Contradiction is a boundary for our understanding, but not a boundary for God's omnipotence. For God every truth is just as contingent

248

VI. Understanding and Will

and just as fundamentally an act of will as any reality is. Even the laws of *ratio* [logic] are products of will, ordinances, commands, as it were. And it is only because God's will does not, like a human sovereign's, vacillate or more or less decide [*umbeschließt*], but rather (itself unchanging and eternal) issues its decrees given once and for all to stand forever, that those truths that make up the content of our rational knowledge are "eternal" and "metaphysical" truths, elevated above all change or temporal contingency. They are absolutely valid for us; we are bound by their unshakable necessity in knowing and in willing. But for the will of God, which is prior to all binding and necessity, they are contingent: "necessary truths" are really fortuitous! Regarded from this standpoint, therefore, human knowledge grasps only expressions of will. The "innate idea" is not, like the content of Platonic anamnesis, an original object of knowledge rooted in its own necessity but a law imposed on finite beings by an almighty-free will! No understanding can ever attain to the last "ground" of eternal truths; ultimate causes that intellect can still understand do not have still another cause, but proceed instead from the *causa efficiens* [efficient cause] of the absolutely groundless will of God, which accordingly surpasses all understanding. Although Descartes then says, in mediating fashion, that understanding and will are one in God and there is no sort of advantage and priority between them, the sequence of his expressions nevertheless shows that he regards the power of will as the more profound: "*Je dis que ex hoc quod illas* (namely, eternal truths) *ab aeterno esse voluerit et intellexerit, illas creavit . . . car c'est en Dieu une même chose de vouloir, d'entrendre, et de créer. Ex hoc ipso quod aliquid velit, ideo cognoscit, et ideo tantum talis res est vera.*" ["I say that from the · fact that he willed and knew them (namely, eternal truths) from eternity, he created them . . . because in God to will, to understand, and to create are the same thing. From the very fact that he wills something, he therefore knows it, and for that reason alone such a thing is true."] The existence of infinite, omnipotent freedom of God, independent of all possibilities and impossibilities, is so to speak the "most eternal" of all truths; it is from it that other "eternal truths" grasped by our understanding first issue forth from his free act. Whatever God wills is for that reason "good" and—"true"!

Free will is the ultimate and profoundest element in human beings too. Despite how much the intellect stood in the foreground of Descartes's essentially epistemologically oriented interests, nevertheless he viewed understanding—just as he did emotions in their own way—as an essentially passive movement and determination of soul; only will is active in the true sense! Human understanding is also always narrowly confined: it always relates only to the little bit that presents itself to it in the course of things. But we can call will, even in finite beings, truly infinite: for there is absolutely nothing to which it could not extend itself in principle with its Yes or No. In this single respect man is equal to God himself. Concerning everything else within me I can imagine greater and more perfect features, but my will or mere freedom of choice is something I experience as so great and so absolute that I can think of nothing greater in this regard! In my free will I am the image of God in an immediate sense. No matter how much God's will must be greater than mine with respect to his relation to the sphere of knowledge (which is limited in me of course, whereas in God it is identical with the decrees of his will) or with respect to power of execution or generally anything at all that touches on the object of will, nevertheless—looked at purely in itself and only in its form of freedom—it is not greater; even finite man's freedom of will is absolute in itself! Thus highest perfection in us is free will, which stretches in all directions infinitely beyond intellect, which is always limited and determined by its object. It is well known how Descartes tried to answer the question concerning the origin of error (which is so essential for his metaphysics of knowledge) on the basis of his theory of will. According to that theory it is will that leads to judgment and, in instances where we have insufficient knowledge available to enable us really to decide, it enmeshes us in error. Thus all our mistakes are our own fault, the fault of our will! Whereas the ancients regarded even freedom of will as really freedom of judgment and understanding, now Descartes holds the reverse as true: freedom of judgment is freedom of will. Imperfection involved in erring is codetermined by the gift of God's image in free will, a gift in itself incomparably greater in worth than all error can ever be in worthlessness. But it is an affair of will also to free oneself from the sin of error and to restrict the use of freedom so that it does not go beyond the realm of attained certitude.

But this demand and rule for the will then leads directly to dependence—of knowledge-oriented will as well as of true will to act—on clear and distinct vision of understanding. Descartes reverts altogether to old paths, even to corroborating the old axiom (which signifies the extreme opposite number to his doctrine of error as will's fault): *omnis peccans est ignorans* [every sinner is ignorant]! Here, too (without Descartes's properly recognizing its contradiction with his voluntaristic theory of God and in general its discrepancy with his own theory of will), he sees indifference of will as the lowest form of human freedom of will: true freedom first comes into being when will allows itself to be determined by clear and distinct insights of understanding. For Descartes, too, man's will has a ''natural'' disposition toward the good; thus when evident insight presents him with the good, he can do nothing else but strive for what is offered! According to this line of reflection, therefore, will is in control only over unclear ideas; but it must infallibly pursue what it knows clearly and distinctly. Thus

250

VI. Understanding and Will

Descartes's theory of moral behavior, too, is ultimately just an echo and development of Socratic and Stoic ethics; hegemony of reason and of will determined by insight of understanding over physical, inherently murky drives and passions is the ultimate demand. Intellectualistic ethics ultimately takes its place next to voluntaristic theory of error and judgment! As far as human understanding and will are concerned, Descartes never escaped from his vacillation between the two poles of primacy of will and superiority of intellect. At any rate, to the extent that laws seen clearly and distinctly by understanding are in turn in their origin decrees of the creator, to that extent will holds the upper hand. But Descartes did not draw the conclusion from it (which would have suggested itself to every immediate follower of Duns Scotus, e.g.) that therefore only Godlike, God-coordinated will can also guide finite understanding to knowledge of the good and the true. Instead matters remained here with self-sufficiency of innate ideas implanted in our intellect.

Primacy of will remained a permanent motif of French philosophy in the subsequent period also. As with other issues, so here also, Malebranche brought to light the inner linkage that connected ideas of his master with Augustine and all Augustinian tendencies of the Middle Ages. He stressed anew the influence of attention and of will in general on all development of human knowledge and with it the dependence of error on the fault of will, and he vigorously championed independent freedom of divine (as well as human) will. Here, too, God is above all the totally incomprehensible (in its ultimate being) volitional cause of everything that exists and has value. Malebranche's occasionalism ultimately interpreted everything that happens in general as the immediate effect of the continuously active power of the will of God, who is action in his very inmost being. Whenever we perceive movement or know anything at all about the organization of the world, it is at bottom God's will that we sense. As is generally true otherwise in the metaphysics of the Modern Period, whenever one stresses process in contrast with static and fixed being, the will also comes more to the fore, with regard to God and man. In certain features and despite contrary tendencies, the motif of primacy of will lives on in Pascal's appeal to the heart and its own "reasons" that reach farther and deeper than the knowledge of understanding. Here, too, only one who opens himself up in love to highest being can come to know that being. In carrying forward this line of thought, Pierre Bayle's skepticism already possessed the Kantian orientation in full: to negate knowledge in order to make room for faith; to emancipate personal autonomy and certitude in moral will and action from domination by theologico-dogmatic knowledge as well as from the otherwise demanded rational insight of metaphysics and "natural religion." Theoretical illumi-

251

nation became less important for our existence and life than self-assurance of moral conscience and disposition of will in one's mind. From this point Voltaire and Rousseau built a bridge to Kant's system of primacy of the practical. Long stretches of French metaphysics of the nineteenth century also still drew life from the conviction of will's supremacy and of freedom's absolute power, which is prior to all lawfulness grasped through knowledge—from Maine de Biran on to Ravaisson's and Secrétan's voluntarism and to Lachelier's, Boutroux's, and Bergson's metaphysics of freedom. Among the leaders of this development one can trace connections everywhere with underlying religious ideas and with the influence of ancient tradition.

Moreover, despite how much the intellect gained the upper hand in the period between Descartes and Kant, nevertheless even here will attained much more importance for the ultimate existence of objects and of persons than ancient intellectualism had ever admitted. Leibniz attacked indifference: what Descartes had said concerning human will only—that true moral freedom is rationally determined—Leibniz, appealing to classical Scholastic systems, now demanded for God's will as well. But he also placed very great value on coordinating God's will as a proper and inherently spiritual power with understanding, keeping it independent (in accord with its root and principle) vis-à-vis the function and eternal laws of intellect, the eternal truths. It is true not only that every will and every desire has a "natural tendency" toward good; but that the *volonté décrétoire* [decree-making will] (clearly separable from all physical nature) of the creator has its own law of goodness. Besides the principle of contradiction, as the principle of intellect, a primordial law of pure and perfect will enters the picture here: *lex optimi* [law of the best] or principle of appropriateness [*Konvenienz*]! Alongside the logical absurdity of something self-contradictory, there now appears (as something special, not provided by the form of understanding)—"moral absurdity"; alongside logico-metaphysical necessity appears moral necessity (which from a purely theoretical standpoint is just contingency); alongside *ratio* [logic] of intellect appears a special kind of reason, the will's own special meaning of law. And this will-ground is the first *ratio sufficiens* [sufficient reason] for the created world! All laws of intellect or of theoretical reason remain in the realm of pure possibilities; the meaning of will, the special form of law of God's creative activity is what first compresses possibilities into a single reality, the best of all worlds. For human beings also (despite how much the idea of enlightenment and the representative function of the soul stood in the foreground for Leibniz) Leibniz views the will as the genuinely motive and living principle of the life of the soul in general: unceasing spontaneity of the soul (in which its proper substantiality consists after all

252

and which also constitutes its likeness to God) is a matter of the will-like element in it, not of representation and knowledge. The substance of soul is action, but this means: uninterrupted passage from one idea to another. It is the will and its incipient form, desire, that accomplish this transition and continual forward thrust. Development and clarification of knowledge itself is the work of this innermost driving force of the monad. "Idea" always signifies only the momentary state of the soul, but will always signifies orientation toward higher development! And if the goal of impulse [*des Treibens*] is knowledge or enlightenment, then the basic idea of infinite progress demotes the ultimate denouement and end of activity of will to mere contemplation. As striving and inner spontaneous activity of soul, will is eternal, just as creative will of God is in another way. Hence a special emphasis is put on will here after all; and this remained in force even during the intellectualism of the pre-Kantian eighteenth century (especially with Crusius).

The new stress on will was not lacking in English philosophy either. Berkeley's spiritualism in particular had a decidedly voluntaristic character. "Spirits" are active natures, and to the extent that they are active in producing or influencing ideas, they are called beings of will. It is this moment of activity that elevates them above mere passivity of ideas and makes them genuine substances! As such they then also exist beyond all knowledge and they are (like God himself) ultimately incomprehensible—because after all knowledge through ideas can grasp only what is passive. Spiritual power-substances are of course also receptive, as all perception of outer objects and all knowledge demonstrate; but this receiving is at root nothing other than accepting a word that God's will speaks to us.

That our ideas of external world are not an arbitrary matter but instead escape the influence of our will does not indicate to Berkeley that they might be products of a real world of objects; on the contrary, in his theory it points directly to the fact that another "will or spirit" exists that produces [those ideas] and impresses them on us! According to Berkeley the cause of appearances in us can be only an original will; and it is from the will of God that these sequences of images possess their marvelous regularity and order, which we experience and investigate in "nature"; these "natural laws," like the ideas themselves, are the immediate expression of the goodness and stability of divine will. If God "instructs" us through the figurative language he speaks, this is not instructing us about existing being as object of knowledge but rather conducting us directly to his own will-being. Just as facial features directly express a person's character and intent, so also in those images of an external world we do not perceive dead objects but the living will of God.

Hence the motif of will reverberates perceptibly in this period in the same measure as existence of nature and the problem of knowledge of nature posed by it take second place behind the life of spirit. And so the great turn away from naturalistic interests and tendencies that Kant's philosophy achieved toward the end of the eighteenth century also led to a new great peak in the chain of voluntaristic systems. Kant's and Fichte's voluntarism carried forward the work of Augustine and Duns Scotus. Kant's conceptual language speaks continually of practical "knowledge," indeed precisely at the core of his theory of will itself, and defines will, as opposed to desire, as the faculty "rational" being has of determining its activity through the "idea" of rules or of acting "in accord with principles of thinking" (so that Kant designates will simply as "power of desire grounded in reason" or "capacity for choosing only what reason acknowledges as practically necessary, that is, as good"). These pervasive intellectualistic formulations cannot deceive one who tries to probe more deeply into the meaning of Kant's concept of "practical reason" about the fact that here will signifies the real root of spiritual reality. To be sure Kant also recognizes determination of will through what understanding provides it by way of ideas and knowledge. And it may seem at first as though only the higher lawfulness of intellect were building up the will in the direction of a "higher" faculty of desire, as opposed to lower drives of sensual desire. But as soon as Kant raises the question of freedom of will and its moral importance, there is no more room for doubt: such *appetitus intellectivus* [intellective appetite] always remains desire after all and is unfree; it is not will in the proper sense. "Reason" that is involved in this context—precisely because it is theoretical knowledge and only secondarily carries over into the sphere of activity also—never gets beyond the "hypothetical" function of providing advice regarding ways and means toward preconceived goals of desire. Where the view that was the point of departure for Socrates (and all who follow him) obtains, namely, that cognitive reason points out the way for "natural" basic inclination of our life of desire, there Kant can see only absolute lack of freedom, hence absence of genuine, moral will! For here is where Kant (and this was really interwoven into Socrates', Aristotle's, and then even Thomas's view) held that we ultimately desire happiness; but "rational," reason-directed desire is just as interested in and bound to a pregiven goal of striving as any blind,

VI. Understanding and Will

sensual desire is; it is therefore at bottom unfree and causally determined, just as all "natural" events in general are. The core of will as a true spontaneous agent that is inwardly independent of external attraction and the true meaning of freedom can, on the contrary, lie only in a special higher lawfulness of will itself. Mere arbitrariness does not lead beyond natural appetitive determination, determination which for all its supposed indifference nevertheless covertly has the last word. But insofar as a person subjects himself to pure law of will—which in contrast with all theoretical knowledge signifies a new and different law of the spirit, an a priori not of theoretical knowledge but of action itself—his higher faculty of desire really becomes "pure will" that is independent of any external givenness and therefore also of all knowledge of being. Pure volitional meaning of moral law reveals itself in the fact that it appears as an imperative and expressly rejects any question of a being lurking behind obligation, a thing-in-itself behind the absoluteness of command. Here good does not appear as object (which could be known), but as immediate demand which one must take absolutely as such. The categorical imperative, to which every will feels itself inwardly bound, is not an object of evidence or proof or inference or any other kind of knowledge one can think of, but rather an original fact of the spirit itself in its voluntaristic core; it is an "intelligible" fact in the sense of the spiritual and a priori (to that extent, of "reason"), but in no way in the sense of something given to intellect and comprehensible by it. Theoretical reason (as Kant expressly says) can comprehend only the incomprehensibility of this priority of duty and willing! Hence freedom and free will (which are given at the same time as the command to duty) exist essentially beyond the realm of all possible knowledge; they are an absolutely irrational entity, even though practical "reason" supports them or is identical with them. Moral law reveals itself clearly to our consciousness in the feeling of awe, but Kant does not regard this feeling as a kind of knowledge at all, as some kind of grasp which feeling has of contents of duty or meaning of duty; on the contrary, preceding contact of will with the will-a priori simply "produces" the feeling itself. Awareness of duty is an affair of will alone; it has absolutely nothing to do with knowledge. As with Descartes, so here too in an altogether altered context: what belongs to will exists beyond anything that touches intellect; nor does knowledge in turn experience the triumph of understanding the will and thereby surpassing it!

Thus true will, of itself, is just as sharply distinct from all types of desire (sensual-blind as well as rational-reflective) as cognitive reason is from all empirical sense data. The law of the will is not "natural" attraction toward good (which desire would have in common with willing), but a principle of *practical* reason that exists above the natural and even beyond the theoretical

255

and all the objective connections necessarily inherent in it, an autonomy of will that stands in opposition and hostility to all merely desirous behavior. At the same time, through his theory of the purely formal and completely object-independent structure of moral-autonomous will, Kant made an extremely sharp distinction and separation from everything intellectual. Accordingly, because volitional goals do not originally define good and evil in will and action, so neither can knowledge of such volitional goals have any importance for freedom and lack of freedom, goodness or badness of behavior! Desire, to be sure, depends on its object and relates in its whole makeup to the quality of that object; but according to Kant it is not the good object (recognizable as good beforehand) which sanctifies the will that is directed toward it; instead, we should think of the quality and form of goodwill (which is sharply distinct from all desire for objects) as set apart from any content of activity. Freedom is freedom from the content [*Materie*] of willing; it is at bottom a will-to-[conform-to]-the-law-of-willing itself. The meaning of the life of will lies purely within itself, not in objects and knowledge of such. Thus the all-important thing for man is to elevate himself to what is unconditionally demanded and to create within himself a will that moral law itself determines. For Kant, too, will in this sense is *causa sui*, absolutely creative principle; it is autonomy, that is, not merely following its own law, but above all self-legislating, an act of will that dictates its own law unto itself and thereby first defines itself as genuine, pure will. Freedom is not indifference, nor is it allowing oneself to be determined in desire through cognitive and reflective reason; it is instead self-determination of will, subordination of self to commands coming from one's own will-ground. Will becomes "rational" law unto itself; it does not borrow [a law] known from elsewhere! Hence will, precisely as free will, is essentially independent of all evidence from understanding; and neither it nor its freedom are ever an object of knowledge but purely and simply content and action of practical consciousness itself, of inner determination of our spiritual life through command and obligation; it is then an entirely secondary matter when it also presents itself as knowledge about obligation and as moral "knowledge."

For its part knowledge ultimately points to will. Not that Kant made knowledge in general depend on will in its execution or its laws and truths; theoretical reason is competent and self-sufficient by itself for its rigorously demarcated tasks. But Kant nevertheless pursues a direction hitherto always connected with will—to look for spontaneity also in knowledge itself. In his theory of formative functions of understanding and of pure sensibility, he carried this further than anyone else had. However minimally this action of knowing is itself volitional creation, nevertheless for Kant all spiritual spontaneity refers back to one, unconditioned act of spirit, untrammeled by any sort of receptivity, an act of will—as though to the root, as it were, and the archetype even of formation in knowledge also. Theoretical reason, with its finished-given purity and lawfulness, appears already as a faded version of the absolute, self-legislating spontaneity demanded and won by practical reason. The One reason and primordial lawfulness of pure spirit reveals itself more profoundly in pure will than it does in intellect. Intellect after all always has an Other, from which it must receive what it is to form, and it is always restricted to given materials and to the physical; but will frees itself from everything material and lives in absolute spontaneity purely within itself under its self-given form, in an act of autonomy. Opposition to the intellectualism of Thomas Aquinas is now complete: *there* intellect ranked higher because it lived in present possession of the known object, whereas will seemed never to be at rest in itself but was always striving to go beyond itself. *Here* it is precisely will—which according to its moral meaning is not determined by its relationship to object and ends but solely through its own "constitution" and form of law—that lives and works entirely within itself (independent of, unrestricted by, and unproduced by anything external) like no other spiritual behavior apart from it!

According to Kant all knowledge always remains limited to "appearances"; it does not advance to the absolute. What lies beyond the senses is unknowable. And, as is well known, this does not signify resigned skepticism on his part, but is simply something that must and should be so! Throughout the entire development of Kantian thought from the [seventeen] sixties on into his last works, this fundamental motif is pervasive: We must limit knowledge and keep it so, in order not to endanger the purity of moral will. His entire battle against proofs for God has this voluntaristic-ethical meaning. Kant regarded activity on behalf of an order recognized in advance as ultimate being and in service of a God proven by intellectual compulsion as entirely incompatible with inner independence and spontaneous freedom of morally good will. Every preknown goal of will destroys the purity of autonomy, determines the will in a causal sense, and turns it into desire-for-happiness. Hence it was necessary to reject reason's "pretensions" in favor of pure volitional value. One may not elevate knowledge above primordial spontaneity of goodwill, but must instead assign it a lower, more restricted place. No matter how important knowledge might be in itself, its value is less than that of morality, which is a matter of will. Dogmatic metaphysics is not just a useless endeavor, but above all an offense against the simplicity and incorruptibility of pure will. The imperative and will (which alone is appropriate to it) must maintain higher rank before all knowledge of world and objects. The order of the supersensible which we are to create must be and remain unknowable; given-known being would only stand in the way of autonomous spontaneity of will, indeed even destroy it. Knowledge is also always only an issue and preoccupation for the few, whereas volitional good is everyone's affair; "dianoetic virtues" could not be decisive when the issue at stake is the meaning of human life in general or the "worth" of every human person.

In reality, knowledge also remains bound to series of conditions which we shall never be able to review with complete synoptic vision. Only the will grasps the absolute, the truly infinite! In our entire rational faculty it is only the practical, pure act of will that helps us beyond the physical world! Autonomous will carries the unconditional within it, compared with which cognitive reason only longs in vain for the "thing" in itself! Beyond the realm of nature and prior to its existence lies the realm of ends, which is a realm of freedom. This is not an established order of given objects, but rather an order of persons which we must always first build up through acts of will. Above and beyond representation and object, idea and knowledge of existence, there exists always, as the heart of everything, that kingdom whose form and laws are relationships of will: command and obedience, harmony and mutual respect; a kingdom that exists in action alone, never in mere being. "Will" is a person's "true self"; it is not "I think" but "I will" (will what I should) that truly leads to the metaphysical content of my existence and of all existence. Whatever is more than phenomenon in us—"the intelligible" (though definitely not really comprehensible by intellect and not part of it)—is our willing; "rational" beings in general are beings of will. It is in their will alone that they can encounter highest and absolute good, never in knowledge or in an object.

Through their autonomous action (which is creative in itself, fashioning "pure" will) volitional beings create an order in which knowledge can have no part: original community! Every knower remains isolated from another who also knows; only the fact that they are related to the same object also unites them, in roundabout fashion. In contrast with ancient solitude and isolated self-sufficiency of the merely cognitive, this had always been a fundamental motif of the Christian conceptual world from the patristic period forward: will and love build up togetherness, community, the kingdom of God; they unite man with God and with all spiritual beings. Now the same thing is a final meaning of the categorical imperative with the special double meaning of its concept of universality: universality of law (to which the maxim of will should raise itself) is condition and foundation for the "community of rational beings"; to will the universal and necessary means to will community, indeed, to build community in this willing! The reverence each person has for autonomous power of will in others and their common agreement in subordination under universal law binding on everyone create a kingdom of ends which, as a kingdom of freedom, also means to signify inner connectedness of all to all. Thus even for Kant, however little he outlined a metaphysics of a religious Beyond, the life of rational beings in the supersensible realm is an act of will, not knowledge; indeed, the kingdom of ends exists only insofar as volitional beings elevate themselves to it and assume their place in universal self-created order. For Kant, in fact, freedom is not a result of supersensible being (which one could know), but it first establishes such being itself. Accordingly, happiness also (which in [Kant's] theory of postulates provides complement and completion of the quality of will in the "highest good") is happiness of pure (hence worthy of happiness) will, and there is absolutely no more talk here of happiness of possessive knowledge; the latter could come into question only to the extent that knowledge too is always a goal of willing (among other goals), and to attain knowledge (as a good alongside many others) is to fulfill a striving.

It is well known how the postulates rest on the theory of autonomous will, how "faith" finds its place here, on behalf of which the *Critique* had restricted "knowledge" to mere appearances and the physical. Again it is the moment of will that determines the concept of faith in its special character: assent without the compulsion of proofs, assent that is possible only to the extent that moral, self-legislating will prevails, which maintains its absoluteness and originality against everything else, especially against all knowledge. Here "primacy of practical reason," in the narrower sense of the word, encroaches on the theoretical itself; ultimate interests of theoretical reason in fact gain more from the interest of moral will than they do from theoretical reason itself. Will and intellect unite under the chairmanship of the former in a kind of knowledge—which, however, can claim importance and validity only for the realm of behavior and is also supposed to orient itself only to the life of will. The old idea that at the end intellect's highest knowledge and vision was supposed to effect fulfillment of what faith always strove toward has no more place here. God, freedom, and immortality—as postulates of reason and even as "knowledge"—are supposed to remain a matter of will also, hence a matter of "faith"! Will is the only organ that allows us to take possession of the "intelligible" realm; will's assent to the law of pure willing in general leads us into the midst of the absolute meaning and ground of existence. But intellect can "comprehend only the incomprehensibility" of this entire order and lawfulness of the supersensible.

In the concept of moral freedom as autonomy of will Kant found the "keystone" of his critical edifice. Fichte's absolute idealism began its deductions at that point; he wanted his entire edifice to be nothing more than a single great development of the concept of freedom. Primacy of the practical was promoted to metaphysical origin; "practical reason is the root of all reason." "Freedom is the standpoint of all philosophy," theoretical as well as practical. Fichte discovered the metaphysical system of the two worlds (to which man simultaneously belongs, according to Kant, but without demonstrating the unity of the two) precisely in the concept of *praxis*, of behavior and tasks of will itself. As essential meaning and purpose of our being, action is also the root of our existence and of all knowledge! Whereas Kant had stressed that at bottom all "interest" is practical in nature, now Fichte tried to derive the interest of knowledge itself, indeed of its existence and its objects in general, from the sphere of practical reason: the realm of volitional beings.

It was especially the first formulation of Fichte's system that brought the voluntaristic motif to its strongest expression—in steady growth and self-clarification of the idea, from his *Review of Aenesidemus* and his first *Theory of Science* to his writings and lectures at the end of the [seventeen]nineties and to *The Vocation of Man* with its fundamental principle of eternal, infinite will. Fichte's later development then saw other tendencies come forth as well, which for a time seemed to hide its origin in will—more in manner of expression and in arrangement of questions in any case than in ultimate systematic meaning. Exact analysis of Fichte's second system (which we cannot provide here of course) would be able to discover the underlying voluntaristic sense everywhere there also. Although from the very start Fichte sought in the absolute for a principle underlying all duality of knowledge and will and their relative independence with respect to each other, he held that the absolute he sought expressed itself originally and most immediately in the life of will. And although on the other hand, it is obvious that thought also—namely thought of a goal—belongs to every specific act of will, [Fichte] now completely separated "knowledge" of this sort in its origin from any grasp of objects or being; it even takes on the character of will, so to speak, and becomes a freely active "sketch" of an archetype, in contrast with any affiliation of otherwise imitative knowledge to previously given being. There are no longer any original "Ideas" in Plato's sense here, that is, as static being and object of nonvolitional contemplation of what knowledge possesses; on the contrary they are only tasks and projects for creative spirit as living will itself! This is precisely the ultimate reason for Fichte's hostility to all "dogmatism": according to this world conception, preexisting being—via the path of knowledge—will always restrict free will and cripple its active force. Not only *The Vocation of Man* but also lectures of his last years developed this idea: If the realm of created objects stands finished and complete (which was of course the view of Antiquity especially), as something with which the knowledge of subjects must harmonize in its mirroring function, then there can be no practical activity or complete freedom of will! In that sense, knowledge conditioned and determined activity, but it depended in turn on the condition and influence of objects. To assume freedom there is to leave oneself open to a palpable vicious circle. For Fichte the demand for freedom of will in the further sense of actual acting and forming entails rejecting every remnant of "dogmatism," including especially the Kantian thing-in-itself. In his view absolute idealism in the theoretical sense follows immediately from the character of absoluteness that freedom of will essentially bears. If knowing conditions all specific willing and acting with respect to their intended goal, then—if freedom is really supposed to exist in us— this knowledge must in fact be essentially independent of all previously given being, hence it must spring forth originally from inner activity and freedom. All knowledge, even of objects, must itself, together with those objects, first be the product of creative freedom that life of will manifests. Spontaneity that breaks through in the free act of will is itself the ground of knowledge. Whereas all other systems make knowledge the principle of life, says Fichte, "our philosophy conversely makes life the highest thing and always leaves only a witnessing role to knowledge!" This "life," however, expresses itself only in free voluntary activity of spiritual beings. Infinite will, "will that works purely and simply as will . . . that is absolutely through itself at once both act and product ("deed"!) ["*Tathandlung*"!], is the deity according to *The Vocation of Man* (which, however, strongly simplifies Fichte's basic ideas); and everything that truly lives and exists in it results from inner division and expressions of this eternal will that holds and bears every finite thing in its sphere. "Action" ["*Tathandlung*"] in this sense stands prior to all being and knowledge of being. In itself this will—as absolute *causa sui* and this self-positing that is creation out of nothing in the strict sense—is absolutely incomprehensible being, prior to all knowledge and consciousness, just as every act of free willing in us presents something absolutely incomprehensible: to wish to understand it is to deny it! Consciousness and understanding first come into being with the absolute (hence incomprehensible "according to laws of nature and thought") act of "division" in which the One, infinite will contracts itself, so to speak, into particular will-individuals. It is through this creative act of the One will that specific willing first comes into being, that is, willing in time and with respect to specific ends, and with these ends the contemplation and knowledge of objects first comes about. Individuals (the "rational beings" whose plurality Kant simply assumed, without inquiring into the volitional meaning behind that) are thus in their core and origin not centers of ideas and not results of divine "glances" at the system of phenomena; they are not contractions of God's view of the world, as it were, such as Leibniz's monads, but contractions of God's original will, products of this active "moral world order," "decrees" of moral law! "The true law of reason in itself is only practical law, law of the supersensible world, or that sublime will." "The genuine essence of humankind consists in *acting*, and the genuine root of self is not at all thinking and representing but willing." "Practical self is the self of original self-consciousness," will-to-act, "innermost root of self." "A rational being is directly aware of himself only in willing and would not be aware of himself and, accordingly, of the world, if he were not a practical being." "My true being is determination of will." Thus individuality, self-awareness, and view of the world are first of all result and expression of volitional relationships. "It is my relationship in the series of other moral beings alone that to my physical eye . . . transforms itself into corporeal world. There is no certainty except moral certainty; and everything certain is so only insofar as our moral relationship indicates it." The self is knower only because he acts, knower only because he wills! Visible world is only the phenomenal expression of the invisible world, which is a system of individuals, that is, a "system of individual wills," a union of and immediate mutual interaction between many autonomous and independent wills. "All reality comes to us only out of volitional intuition linked with thought." The physical world is the "result of eternal will in us"; divine will is "creator of the world," indeed creator of a view of world or worldview in finite volitional beings: "only in our souls does he create a world, at least that out of which and through which we develop it—the call of duty." Duty is "the intelligible in-itself that transforms itself into physical world through laws of physical representation." Every object of knowledge is—according to the meaning of its origin—the resistance of will and determination of will for specific tasks, expression of obligations of will. "Awareness of actual world derives from need to act, not conversely, that need to act derives from awareness of world. . . . We do not act because we know, but we know because we are called to act." Every "Must" of knowledge stems from an "Ought" of willing; every determination of idea or object from "vocation" of will. Even our conviction about the reality of the external world is faith in the full meaning of will: on the basis of the moral determination of our life of will we are obliged in practice to accept this phenomenal world—which is really the expression and condition of our willing and acting, "material for our fulfillment of duty—as real (although regarded theoretically and only as contents of knowledge, it is not real at all)! Even our own body is only "the physical representation of our pure will." Knowledge and certainty of knowing exist for a human being only insofar as he is a moral being, insofar as he is volitional being. Ultimately intelligence is always merely self-awareness of behavior and of behavioral obligations. Fichte regards even consciousness of the unity and harmony of the phenemenal world for me and for all other rational beings

VI. Understanding and Will

(which according to Leibniz derives from pure order of knowledge and existence of preestablished harmony) as at bottom only an expression and result of unity of will within which we all live together. It is an expression of the eternal order of will which (in the ''split'') allots specific tasks to each individual, but always within the single great sphere of the One final end. The apparent sphere of unity of duty-fulfilling matter corresponds to the real systematic unity of moral tasks. All knowledge of objects expresses therefore first of all consciousness of willing and of obligation; it expresses a specific determination of duty in the system of volitional beings. Hence, also, the first original knowledge each individual has is not directed so much to the world of objects as it is to other free beings; and this ''knowledge'' (which for its part is in fact a condition for the individual's self-awareness in general and thereby especially for his world picture) is itself conditioned by will's original relationship to those free beings: by demand for freedom and specific activity that resounds altogether immediately and inescapably toward each individual from the free will and activity of others. Because he is implicated in the chain of volitional tasks and volitional deeds in which each individual finds himself a member, whenever he begins to will something and thus to exist, his action and existence are limited for him at the very outset. It is not that we are conditioned by goods and objects presented to us conceptually (whereby idea and knowledge extrinsically determine desire and will), but rather it is free will-agents, with whom we live in an order of will and obligation, who challenge us and thereby give our individual being its specificity, precisely because it is our ''vocation.'' In this way freedom is not (as it is via the path of understanding) destroyed by being incorporated into the world system, but is rather bound and limited purely within itself, that is, it is contracted into individual tasks. All knowledge of being and cognitive restriction is a consequence first and foremost of such self-determination of will. Hence according to Fichte the object and goal of our pure moral willing and acting are not really the world of knowledge or existence of objects and goods, but the spiritual world of volitional beings. The morally willing agent ''never directly wills objective being but only the will of another . . . the object of a human being is always a human being.'' ''The moral person wills the morality of all, as a closed system.'' Every will wants to influence wills; and all knowledge and grasp of objects is only means or expression of such will-activity. Creation of absolutely good will in the entire human race is the only and all-determining final goal of spiritual life.

Thus for Fichte individual immortality is not based on cognitive participation in eternal being as it was for Plato. Here the soul is not imperishable in its own right as a supersensible knowing substance. On the contrary, will's free activity and will's own pure inner formation are what first achieve im-

263

mortality for man! For Kant it was will's self-elevation into a higher order where the idea of immortality was conceived of as necessary, and not mere givenness of being for "rational" beings. Fichte then removed all doubt about the original volitional nature of personal immortality in his later doctrine, which said that not all persons who ever existed survive corporeal death but only those who have actually fulfilled their vocation in this (first) life, that is, those who "have generated will within themselves"! It is not because they know the eternal but because they will in accordance with eternal law that they survive perishing worlds, which in fact are themselves only "spheres of visibility for individual wills." Just as Goethe concluded from the pathos of activity of Leibniz's monads that "we are not all immortal in the same way" but that through incessant striving we must first make ourselves into a true "entelechy" and thereby elevate ourselves to activity-filled eternity, so for Fichte immortality is a matter of active struggle through moral will that determines itself to freedom for freedom's sake, to activity for activity's sake, and to eternal life. "No individual is morally generated; each has to do that for himself; the arena for this moralization of life is the present world: it is the locus of will-formation for all future worlds." The personal achievement of surrendering ourselves to law is what first guarantees us "eternity and infinity of self and will." Whoever does not raise himself to true freedom and morality of will—perishes; a different, new individual replaces him and assumes the tasks he left unfulfilled. It is not mere existence of soul and its innate cognitive link to ideas that makes it immortal but only its own act of will and development of will.

"Blessedness" of spiritual life does not mean (as it formerly did) being filled with eternal vision; on the contrary, living activity of moral willing itself constitutes the happiness of human will that is truly united with God and fused together with infinite will itself! "Will to be what you should be, what you can be and for that reason want to be"—that is "the fundamental law of higher morality as well as of happy life." No matter how much Fichte's *Instruction for the Blessed Life* is reminiscent of ancient doctrines of contemplating God in its manner of expression, in the end it leaves no doubt about the volitional nature and purely volitional origin of this life in "love"! Knowledge, even that of immediate self-awareness, always remains merely penultimate: it still contains duality. But happiness arises solely from the "impulse to be united and to fuse together with the imperishable," the impulse that is "the innermost root of all finite being." But we can attain this happiness of being truly absorbed in another (which knowledge never attains) through a highest act of freedom; through that act the self devolves "into pure divine being, and strictly speaking one cannot say that the affect, love, and will of this divine being would be his, inasmuch as two beings simply no longer exist but only one being; no longer two wills but absolutely only one, and that one will is all in all." Love is not only the origin of that "division" of One will into volitional individuals—the split that first makes self-consciousness and knowledge possible at all—but also that which most intimately reunites what has been divided! Hence happiness is no longer merely, as it was with Kant, something that added to the act of will and to worthiness to be happy (which is the predicate of good will itself); instead it is the life and quality of pure willing in eternal love itself. But Fichte ranks this love (as volitional life) "higher than all reason and it is itself source of reason and root of reality." Creative activity of will is the origin, goal and complete ultimate happiness of existence; intellect first arises out of this activity, looks at it, and has to forge instruments for it. Thus the "happiness" of this religious metaphysics is also no longer something hostile to activity, estranged from willing and acting in reality, as all happiness through contemplating ideas and God ultimately was. More strongly than any previous ethics and even much more strongly than Kant, Fichte emphasized the moral necessity of activity in reality, of transforming and building. Living the life of God means here: incessant working, willing, and acting in the direction and manner of creative will itself! God is not an inert object and possession of contemplation, but he is "that which those seized by him do"! Life in love necessarily appears as tireless willing and working, acting and building. True religiosity and higher morality is necessarily active; "the most unlikely manual labor" can (as Fichte expressly emphasized, in sharpest contrast on this point, too, with the assessment of Antiquity) be filled with ultimate happiness and fullness of life—more than mere reflective, contemplative banishment to "purely static and passive vision" can ever be.

Love is, however, "not only the source of truth and certainty in general but also the source of perfect truth in actually existing man and his life." Ultimate and complete knowledge of truth, reflection of the highest science of the absolute, itself proceeeds from pure love of this absolute! Fichte turned Spinoza's *Amor Dei intellectualis* [intellectual love of God] into something voluntaristic: as he sees it, highest love does not issue from the wise person's knowledge, but rather even knowledge of the divine-absolute issues from the moral-religious person's will. Fichte was the only philosopher in the entire history of Christian thought to draw the consequence for philosophy and for his own system out of the motif that says that true knowledge arises only from correct will. According to Fichte, primacy of practical reason, inaccessibility and inexplicability of freedom as the absolute, has no theoretical but only a practical "rational ground": the "decision" of moral-religious will! The system of true idealism (with all its theoretical deductions and proofs) proceeds from this first positing as from a "first article of faith," that is,

from free assent of will and voluntary choice, but not from original determination and boundedness of knowledge. "All my conviction is only faith,
and it comes from feeling [*Gesinnung*], not from understanding." Fichte's
famous proposition that everyone has the philosophy that corresponds to his
makeup [*Sein*], as is well known, has precisely this meaning: The kind of
person someone "*is*" means here: what a person *wills* to be, what—as a
living, willing, spontaneous being—he freely decides in favor of: material
dependence and bondage to objects and knowledge of objects, or absolute
spontaneous activity in the direction of eternal spiritual will. "Whoever has
my disposition, an honest good will, he will also uphold my conviction: but
without the former there is no way to produce the latter. Once I know this,
I know whence all formation of self and others must flow: from will, not
from understanding. If will is steadily and honestly directed toward the good,
then understanding will automatically grasp the true." "Only improvement
of the heart leads to true wisdom." "Intellectual intuition"—the highest act
of spiritual elevation, which Fichte says is the source of all metaphysical
knowledge—thus presents itself as a volitional process. It is moral decision
and act of inner rebirth that first generates new free thought and knowledge.
What Fichte demands from the philosopher is that he install a new eye by
developing a new will.

No metaphysics of will since then has known how to defend the absoluteness of primacy of will so well against claims to sovereignty of understanding passed down by the ancients as Fichte's ethical idealism, based on
Kant's moral philosophy, has been able to do. (Even in Jacobi's philosophy
of faith the primacy of will indicated so often nevertheless always bends once
again toward the theoretical element of a feeling knowledge.) But the motif
continued to live on and was influential in the philosophy of the nineteenth
century. Schelling carried it forward most profoundly. For him—not only in
the period when he depended on Fichte but precisely in later periods of his
thought—absolute, divine being was at bottom "immanent, only self-moving
will." With Jacob Böhme he sought among the dark drives and strivings of
primordial will for the first beginning of existence, of its tensions and oppositions; for him it was in the self-begetting [*Selbstgebären*] of this noncognitive will that all reality and actuality first arose, and understanding was
initially really born from it as well. All being stems from potential being,
everything actual from potency. But only will directly shows us this relationship and divergent flux [*Auseinander-Fließen*] of potency and act. Will
in itself is potency *kat' exokhen* [par excellence], willing is act *kat' exokhen*."
According to its original metaphysical sense every capacity is "really only
will at rest; transition from potency to act is willing." Hence "in the ultimate
and highest instance, there is no other being except willing. Willing is original

266

VI. Understanding and Will

being and all predicates apply to that being alone: groundlessness, eternity, independence in time, self-affirmation. All philosophy strives only to find this highest expression." It is, again, the question of the *causa sui* or self-positing, which points to the creative potency of will as ultimate metaphysical reality. And whereas Spinoza included individual objects as modes of one absolute being-substance, Schelling's system describes reality "as individual wills comprised in primordial will."

Schopenhauer's well-known metaphysics of will, which wielded such widespread influence in the nineteenth century and up to the present, and which made voluntarism so popular, arose initially then from directions from Kant, Fichte, and Schelling; but to the same degree as moral-religious meaning (in which this entire metaphysical thought current indeed arose) now receded and perished with him, and to the same degree that morally determined will now tended to coincide entirely with desire in general again, intellect once more gained the upper hand and claimed the ultimate highest word for itself! Despite how penetratingly Schopenhauer described irrational and itself-blind, noncognitive will as the metaphysical origin of all things, including understanding itself (in this point still totally at odds with the nous principle of the ancients!), nevertheless the pessimism of this idea of sense-lessly and blindly raging will directed anyone searching for salvation beyond the entire province of will toward emancipation through intellect. The latter is of course not original; it is only the light that will has enkindled for itself, a late and merely "physical" product and "secondary phenomenon" of metaphysical will to power, a phenomenon that remains at the service of will in all life and activity. But inasmuch as this product of will then soars to illuminating insight regarding the futility and unhappiness of all willing and even points the way toward self-destruction of suffering will, this intellect outgrows its own origin, wins the upper hand, and itself becomes the more profoundly operative and final instance that produces the ultimate metaphysical turning point of life! Intellectual intuition points out the path of redemption and negative happiness that comes through silencing the will; freeing itself from will's frenzy, peering into the meaninglessness of all existence, it forces recalcitrant will itself to self-destruction. Even where in Schopenhauer—in a manner analogous to "love" in earlier systems—"sympathy" appears as a path to eternal death, it is not so much the act of real union of wills that he praises as it is the insight clothed in this feeling that forces itself on us in the process: insight into the metaphysical unity of all beings and the senselessness of any pleasure purchased through the suffering of another. Thus in the end, intellect that leads us to eternal rest is victorious after all over will, which is once again understood as desire and as something dissatisfied in itself and pointing toward fulfillment elsewhere. The nonvoluntary intuition of Platonic Ideas, which once constituted the final end and highest form of the blessed life, still constitutes here (in esthetic contemplation) the great and decisive preparatory step to redemption. In the midst of the most unqualified system of will, intellect has elevated itself once again to the level of victor and ultimate metaphysical instance.

It was a fundamental motif of Nietzsche's theory of life and metaphysics to posit unconditional affirmation (undiluted by or surpassed by any other instance) of living and creative will as ultimate ground of being and life in direct opposition to his teacher's pessimism about, and hostility to, will. His principle of "will-to-power" also has precisely this thrust: to make meaning and happiness of volitional tension independent of good and evil and from worth or worthlessness of ends and objects mediated to will by intellect as an external entity that imposes obligation on will. Will seeks to maximize itself and to assert its own life and fullness of power—that is its meaning and its greatness. Everything cognitive is in its service and is product and means of its activity. And once again, although totally otherwise than in Fichte and deviating far from the original meaning of doctrines of will, it is willing for the sake of willing and of the tension of willing—far from any happiness of serene contemplation—in which ultimate happiness and the entire meaning of existence is supposed to lie.

Index of Names

Index of Names

Homer, *112*
Hugh of St. Victor, *14, 20, 124f., 133, 135, 199, 202, 235, 237*
Humboldt, Wilhelm von, *216*
Hume, David, *16, 33, 144*
Huygens, Christiaan, *72*

Irenaeus, Saint, *52, 64, 120, 163*

Jacobi, Friedrich Heinrich, *216ff., 266*
Jesus Christ, *196*
Joachim of Flora, *165ff., 180*
John, Saint [the Evangelist], *184*
John Damascene, Saint. *See* Damascene, Saint John
Justin Martyr, Saint *229*

Kahl, *235*
Kant, Immanuel, *9, 11, 12, 16, 19, 30, 33, 44, 53, 69ff., 72, 73, 74f., 77f., 99, 100, 105, 106ff., 109, 134, 135, 136, 138, 178ff., 185, 192, 215f., 217, 221, 226, 251, 252, 253, 254ff., 260, 261, 264, 265, 266, 267*
Kepler, Johannes, *31, 54, 58, 72, 73, 74, 99f., 131, 132, 170, 172*
Knittermeyer, Hinrich, *20*

Lachelier, Jules, *252*
Laplace, Pierre Simon, *69*
Leibniz, Gottfried Wilhelm, *9, 14, 16, 19, 25f., 27, 28, 29f., 30, 33, 36f., 53, 54, 59, 61f., 73, 74, 75, 77, 95f., 99, 101ff., 106, 113f., 133, 135, 136ff., 138, 141ff., 144, 145, 147, 150, 163, 167, 170, 175ff., 180, 181, 182, 183, 186, 190, 191, 207, 209ff., 215, 216, 219, 220, 246, 252f., 261, 263, 264*
Leonardo da Vinci, *31, 53*
Lessing, Gotthold Ephraim, *61, 180, 185*
Leucippus, *70, 85*
Liebrucks, Bruno, *19*
Locke, John, *25, 33, 132, 138, 144*
Lucretius, *70*
Lully, Raymond, *33*
Luther, Martin, *55, 58, 59*

Mahnke, Dietrich, *15, 20, 21*
Maimonides, Salomon, *134*
Maine de Biran, *252*
Malebranche, Nicolas de, *33, 95, 96, 100, 135, 136, 137, 138, 141, 142, 144, 174, 175, 177, 251*
Melancthon, Philipp [Schwarzerd, Philipp], *25*
Melissus, *87*
Methodius, *64*
Montaigne, Michel de, *25, 28, 133*

Nemesius, *119, 162*
Newton, Sir Isaac, *53, 69, 71, 72, 99, 100*
Nicholas of Autrecourt, *140, 144*
Nicholas of Cusa, *14, 16, 20, 26, 27, 30, 31, 55ff., 58, 59ff., 61ff., 65, 66, 73, 90, 96ff., 99, 101, 102, 105, 106, 141, 171ff., 175, 176, 179, 192, 205ff., 208, 211, 221, 246*
Nicholas of Oresme, *171*
Nicolin, Friedhelm, *19*
Nietzsche, Friedrich Wilhelm, *9, 16, 17, 75, 78, 80ff., 188, 191f., 223, 268*
Norris, John, *144*

Occam, William of, *14, 31, 32, 55, 93f., 130, 133, 135, 138f., 170, 171, 198, 205, 209, 245, 247*
Origen, *46, 64, 89, 91, 105, 120, 140, 162, 163f., 230*

Paracelsus, Theophrastus, *20, 26, 27f., 30, 54, 58, 175, 208, 209*
Parmenides, *40, 41, 43, 83f., 86, 100, 117, 140, 154ff., 159, 181, 189, 193*
Pascal, Blaise, *96, 251*
Patrizzi, Francesco, *96*
Paul, Saint, *52, 61*
Petrus Aureoli, *205, 209, 245*
Philo, *87, 115, 120, 201*
Pico della Mirandola, *36, 58, 246*
Pierre d'Ailly. *See* Ailly, Pierre d'
Plato, *10, 18, 21, 25, 26, 36f., 40, 41, 42, 44f., 62, 64, 68, 69, 76, 84, 85, 86, 87, 88, 90, 91, 95, 97, 105, 111ff., 114, 115, 116, 117, 118, 123, 134, 135,*